A MAN AND A PRAM

A MAN AND A PRAM

MARK CUNDY

APEX PUBLISHING LTD

First published in 2008 by

Apex Publishing Ltd

PO Box 7086, Clacton on Sea, Essex, CO15 5WN

www.apexpublishing.co.uk

Copyright © 2008 by Mark Cundy
The author has asserted his moral rights

British Library Cataloguing-in-Publication Data
A catalogue record for this book
is available from the British Library

ISBN 1-906358-04-4   978-1-906358-04-4

All rights reserved. This book is sold subject to the condition, that no part of this book is to be reproduced, in any shape or form. Or by way of trade, stored in a retrieval system or transmitted in any form or by any means, electronic, mechanical, photocopying, recording, be lent, re-sold, hired out or otherwise circulated in any form of binding or cover other than that in which it is published and without a similar condition, including this condition being imposed on the subsequent purchaser, without prior permission of the copyright holder.

Typeset in 10pt Times New Roman

Production Manager: Chris Cowlin

Cover Design: Siobhan Smith   ESSEX COUNTY LIBRARY

Printed and bound in Great Britain

Author, Mark Cundy has his own website: **www.markcundy.net**

This book is dedicated to my Mum & Dad,
without whom so much in my life would not have been possible.

Foreword
by Chris Tarrant OBE

When, a few years ago, a complete stranger called Mark wrote to me staying he was walking round the world, and would I help him with some funding, I thought "yeah, right, walking round the world? Of course you are!" But it was a good cause and I thought he might get as far as Belgium so I sent him a few quid, wished him bon voyage and thought no more about it. A long time later I was watching the local news in some small town in Australia and they carried a brief report about some lunatic pom pushing a baby stroller round the world. "My God" I thought – "it's him!"

A long time later, I was chatting on my mobile to a mate of mine who was working on a radio station somewhere in deepest Hicksville, USA, and he said "There's an English nutter on the news here, pushing a pram around the world". "My God" I thought – "it's him again … and he's still going!"

This book is the story of one remarkable man's devotion to his private Boy's Own adventure. This is not the tale of a pampered rich boy's gap year; this is a working class Essex lad's day by day account of the realisation of a dream.

It started in the planning stage on his dining room table in Southend and never, ever really wandered off course for the 400+ days this epic trip took. He writes candidly of the highs and lows of his amazing journey: deep depression in Poland; bitter cold and infuriating bureaucracy in Russia, the loneliness of New Year's Eve somewhere in Eastern Europe in a tiny, cheap room shaking his own hand at midnight while singing Auld Lang Syne to himself; of the joy of finally getting to Australia and being able to speak in English again; of the Southern states of the USA; of the joy of arriving in New York, knowing he was almost home; of somehow persuading his 77-year-old dad to join him on the last 'little hop' from Salisbury to Buckingham Palace.

It's an incredible story but this is not a Hollywood script, this is not Forrest Gump, this is an extraordinary tale of a young guy who didn't just 'talk the talk' he really did walk the ultimate walk.

Acknowledgements

I'd like to express my everlasting gratitude to the following individuals and organisations, without whom the walk truly could not have been completed:

Thanks for a bed for the night to:
Amy, Welling, UK
Woodstock Guest House, Sittingbourne, UK
Eric Broos, Brugge, Belgium
Rosemarjim & Matthieu, Gent, Belgium
Olivier & Linda, Antwerp, Belgium
Oostemalle Monastery, Oostemalle, Belgium
Gerrit & family, Glandorf, Germany
Harald, Berlin, Germany
Dom Nad Rzeka Hotel, Skwierzyna, Poland
Hotel Fugo, Konin
Wojiech, Warsaw, Poland
Tor & Mary, Moscow, Russia
Greg Klemm, Moscow, Russia
Fiona, Melbourne, Australia
F1 Motel, Brunswick, Austrlia
Seven Creek Hotel, Euroa, Australia
John & Val, Wagga Wagga, Australia
Shirley Hotel, Bethungra, Australia
Wendy & Lew, Cootamundra, Australia
Carrington Hotel, Harden, Australia
Helen, Rowan & Caroline, Goulburn, Australia
Terminus Hotel, Marulan, Australia
Jeremy Moss Hotel, Moss Vale, Australia
Millagong Motel, Millagong, Australia
Belgo Motel, Belgo, Australia
F1 Motel, Liverpool, Australia
Lynne & Kevin Sullivan, Sydney, Australia
Andrew Plog, Santa Monica, USA
Aira, Los Angeles, USA
Mary McFry, Fontana, USA

Jack, Palms Springs, USA
Marjorie, Quartzsite, USA
St Michael Hotel, Prescott, USA
The View Motel, Cottonwood, USA
Moestlywood Guest House, Sedona, USA
Weatherford Hotel, Flagstaff, USA
Monte Vista Hotel, Flagstaff, USA
Fred, Winona, USA
Travelodge, Winslow, USA
Travelodge, Grants, USA
Jeremy, Ken & friends, Albuquerque, USA
Holiday Inn, Tucumcari, USA
Kenneth, Amarillo, USA
Econo Lodge, Shamrock, USA
Travelodge, Elk City, USA
Days Inn, Clinton, USA
Days Inn, Claremore, USA
Super 8 Motel, Cuba, USA
Days Inn, Eureka, USA
Kristin & Tom, St Louis, USA
Super 8 Motel, Greenville, USA
Steve & Jeannie, Columbus, USA
Cliff & Erika for Buckeye Lake, USA
Wade & Janet for Cambridge, USA
Inn on the Georgian, Somerset, USA
Paula & Al, West Chester, USA
Bill & Linda for Newtown Square, USA
Clare & Farrell, Philadelphia, USA
Amy & Bill, Princeton, USA
TJ for New Brunswick, USA
Redruth Guest House, Redruth, UK
Nebula Hotel, Liskeard, UK
Kathy's Guest House, Yeovil, UK

Thanks for various acts of kindness to:
Chris Tarrant
Lord (Jeffrey) Archer
Go Travel Insurance, Basildon, UK
Harvey Rose & Sons Opticians, Westcliff, UK

Hoageyweb, Southend, UK
Gaye Boyman
David Billany
Paul & Lisa Schofield
Ian & Cheryl Reynolds
Hoverspeed Ferries, UK
Frau Beckmann, Vinzelburg, Germany
Maria & Pawel, Elk, Poland
Anya, Vladivostok, Russia
Quartzsite Chamber of Commerce
Quartzsite Veteran of Foreign Wars Association
Tiny & Cecil, Quartzsite, USA
Roger, Prescott
Prescott Chamber of Commerce
Roger & Carol, Sedona, USA
Tina, Flagstaff
PJ, Arkansas (for help in New Mexico)
Tucumcari Chamber of Commerce
Hayes (for help at Glenrio, Texas)
Lelita, Mid-Point Café, Adrian, USA
Vega Chamber of Commerce, USA
Elk City Chamber of Commerce, USA
Clinton Chamber of Commerce, USA
Chandler Chamber of Commerce, USA
Sapulpa Chamber of Commerce, USA
Ocology Centre, Maryville, USA
Greenville Chamber of Commerce, USA
Else, Columbus, USA
Mayor Ryan, Brownsville, USA
Somerset Chamber of Commerce, USA
St Stephen's Catholic Church, McConnellsville, USA
AACR, Philadelphia, USA
Ruth & Ron, Brunswick, USA
Graham & Carol-Ann Payne, Watford, UK

Special thanks to:
Mum & Dad
Margaret
Tom King, Echo Newspapers, UK

Radoslaw & family, Swalzedz, Poland
Hotel Rondo, Kutno, Poland
Natasha, Ludza, Latvia
Highway Patrol Officers/State Troopers of California, Arizona, New Mexico,
Texas, Oklahoma & Missouri
Milly & Earl, Salome, USA
Deb & Rachel Misra, Gallup, USA
Tommy, Amarillo, USA
Nancy & Jon for Oklahoma City, USA
Newcastle Medical Centre, nr Newcastle, USA
Mary & Jimmy, Tulsa, USA
Becky & Dick for Zanesville, USA
Pat Spirano, Brooklyn, USA

~ 1 ~
Breaking Out

I steered the car out of the business park and headed along the familiar route back home after another long day at the office. The 14th of June 2004 was a bright, sunny day and I drove with my jacket off, window slightly open to admit a breeze and let the rest of Watford share my musical tastes from the stereo.

Although I hadn't had the satisfaction of handing my letter of resignation in to the elusive head honcho himself, I still felt that mixture of the joy of cutting myself free together with the usual anxieties about whether I'd done the right thing. This time, however, things were a little different. No modest sidestep into another office; instead I was giving it all up to go walking around the world.

I'd mostly enjoyed my role as Training & Development Manager, but after the latest takeover (the fifth in seven years) we were all feeling the strain. Our new American owners were very keen that we should ditch what we'd been doing to date and start doing it their way. All I knew was that I yearned to be free from the tedious routine: out of the office, out of the 'normal' lifestyle, with no approval needed except my own.

The start of the year had seen pretty much the original Directorate still in place, but by the time I left only one remained. Familiar faces had jumped or been pushed and the company felt less and less like the kind of place I belonged. The idea that by using a different font size on my documents from my colleagues in Hungary I would bring about the fall of the empire was of course amusing, but not in public. The corporate culture was becoming a corporate cult and the business nous of the original team that built the firm was being smothered by layers of uniform 'quality' initiatives. Naturally this wasn't the only reason I decided to go off walking around the world, but the changes that accelerated my departure were well-timed to coincide with plans I'd been quietly making in the background.

I continued driving through the familiar Watford roads and finally parked up. Jacket slung over my shoulder, I walked up the stairs to the rented flat I had called home for the past five years. Although Friday night was drinking night, I reached for the leftover vodka to kick off my Monday night contemplations. With that single-page resignation letter I had just started the clock ticking down towards my last day of work, towards the few short weeks of prep time and the date of departure on my world walking odyssey. As the alcohol hit the spot, I began to relax away from the troubling practicalities as the dream of the global stroll bubbled to the surface. And whilst the evening was spent mostly in reverie of the journey to come, my mind also wandered back along the road that had brought me thus far.

~ 2 ~
Baby Boomer

I was born into a working-class family in Essex in the swinging sixties. My Dad was the local bobby on the beat, whilst Mum gave up work when my sister arrived in 1963. I followed in April 1966. From an early age, like many boys, I took on an eye for detail in things that interested me that bordered on the pedantic. Doing something at 6:00 did not mean doing it at 6:10 and the Vulcan in Star Trek was called Mr Spock, not Dr Spock.

What an irritating little turd I must have been.

I passed through the school years without drawing too much attention to myself, with English and music my preferred subjects. My lack of athletic prowess and ball skills meant that playing football for England was unlikely; my spotty, bespectacled face didn't reflect a rock star in the making either. In truth, as for so many others, there was no burning desire in me to head in any particular direction. When the time came at 16 to choose further education or join the nation's workforce I did both. I applied for jobs in the Southend area, whilst starting 'A' level studies in English and Geography. Three months into the courses, I was offered a position working for the local credit card company and I took it. I would have to wait another 20 years to get my degree.

First jobs are a rite of passage - with a hangover of adolescent angst about whether you will be liked, whether you will 'fit in' and whether to achieve these aims you'll be labelled a troublemaker. For many the twin aims of trying to prove your competence whilst trying to be personally popular can be mutually exclusive. I've known colleagues in their forties and fifties who have still not yet resolved this dichotomy.

I settled for playing the long game - a gradual rise through the ranks and an affected nonchalance for joining the 'in-crowd'. Of course, I wanted to be liked and invited to parties as much as the next person, but I knew that my teenage self was not built to be the centre of anyone's attention. By the time I left Access Credit Cards, my Mick Jagger impressions had made me a minor

3

staple at parties whilst my skills in the job had guaranteed a good reference.

For those living in Southend and the surrounding areas, sooner or later there comes a pull towards London. Just 40 minutes down the train line lay astronomical career prospects and the exciting lifestyle that only the capital can offer. Just short of my 21st birthday I answered the call.

The spring of 1987 found me unpacking cardboard boxes in my first home away from home, a shared flat in Acton, West London. The area was ethnically diverse, ten minutes from my new workplace and, frankly, a dump. But I loved it. I was now making my own way, making all the personal decisions and mistakes necessary to grow up. I took singing lessons, did amateur dramatics, went to football matches, house parties, theatres, clubs and bars. I enjoyed my time in London, although with no real career beckoning at Citibank the job became a means to the end of paying bills and having fun.

Despite the diversions of London life, I still wanted to carve out some kind of personal, individual achievement. For a few years I'd been writing songs and decided the time had come to go into a recording studio to see how they turned out. Some of them were bloody awful, others bearable, a few pretty good. Throughout the '90s I invested a stack of money and much time and effort into writing and recording. I enjoyed it, but, in the face of critical and public indifference, I finally accepted that I was not going to be the British Springsteen. I left the stage for the last time, happy with my efforts, but knowing that I was out of time.

* * *

There were two common threads during the eight years that I spent in these two 'normal' jobs: an indifference to material accumulation and hostility towards the trappings of settling down. The 1980s, we are frequently reminded, were the 'me' decade, where those of us working in London and the south-east were ferociously updating our must-have shopping lists. Filofaxes, cars, clothes - your every purchase was a statement of identity.

I never fell into this narcissistic groove, with the result that I was probably the worst-dressed member of the pack. I didn't care then and I still don't.

More pertinently, the 'settling down' trappings were anathema to me. I knew that my time in the London job was limited, but my feelings ran deeper than that. I have always regarded whichever situation I find myself in as being more likely than not, transient. I have never considered the place I am living, the job I am doing or any possessions to be permanent. This is an excellent state of mind for those wishing to be flexible in all aspects of life, but not good for asset accumulation or stable relationships. So you can have all the fun and adventure you want, but the price you pay is few possessions and strained or non-existent relationships. I can - and do - live with that. Being the youngest in the family for so many years meant I had no younger sibling to take the mantle of indulgence from me. I never had to surrender gracefully my wildest dreams in deference to the new kid.

Four years after relocating to London, my next move put into practice all I had preached. At 25 I quit the job, took my meagre savings out of the bank and went to live and work in America in the summer of 1991 - at Walt Disney World in Florida to be precise. The EPCOT Centre is Disney's second theme park on site and features the 'World Showcase' with pavilions representing France, Germany, Canada, China, the UK and several other countries around the world. My job title was Cultural Representative for the United Kingdom. My actual job was to sell Paddington Bear, Peter Rabbit and other prime British merchandise to the predominantly American visitors and charm them with my accent. I could do that! As a foreign adventure it was fairly tame, as Disney flew me out, gave me accommodation and shuttled me back and forth to work. Best of all was the apartment complex called Vista Way, which provided a home for 2,500 under-thirties from all around the world. If anybody didn't have fun at Vista Way - it was their own fault!

Romance, friendships and fun bloomed and died during my 12 months of living and working in the artificial world of Disney. I loved the international flavour of the life we lived and mixed freely with new friends from around the world. However, it soon came to an end and, signing off from my year in the Florida sunshine, I headed home to England in the summer of 1992.

Penniless and jobless, I was brought crashing down to earth by the first employment agency I visited back in London. "We'll just ignore what you've been doing for the last year and concentrate on getting you back into finance." The age of valuing different life experiences had not yet dawned.

I managed to stay in England for the next six months (working as a mortgage account manager), but once I had saved enough to get away again I was off. There was a whole world out there, so I bought a round-the-world ticket, which took me back to America for six weeks of shoestring travel, followed by cheap stopovers in Hawaii and Australia, before landing in Bangkok, Thailand, for a one-year stint as an English teacher. I had spent three months earning a diploma as a Teacher of English as a Foreign Language (TEFL) whilst in London and wasn't going to leave it gathering dust.

After playtime in America and Australia, I stepped off the plane in Bangkok and into a taxi, which drove me past a huge Buddhist temple on the side of the road on the way into town. All the road signs, menus and information boards were in the curious Thai script. This was a very different prospect to the cushioned landing and support during my year at Disney and I had to hit the streets to try to find a job and make it work myself from day one. I ended up working at the British-American language school, teaching individuals and small groups for the first few weeks, before branching out to teach in banks and other large companies.

Several students who became my friends took me around the markets, temples and river taxis and generally made sure I got the full Thai experience. I played snooker, had dinner with my student friends' families and, of course, visited the steamy bars of Pat Pong (it has to be done).

Every three months I left the country to renew my tourist visa (the school was not too scrupulous about paperwork) and I took trips to Malaysia, Japan and Taiwan. It was during my visa visit to Taiwan that I fulfilled all my rock star dreams, on invitation from a Chinese millionaire to perform at the annual Toucheng festival. I had been recommended by the Great Abdullah, a magician friend of mine who lived around the corner from my apartment block. Every night of the week in Taiwan, I got on stage to sing in front of an audience of more than 60,000 people attending the festival from the surrounding towns. Each time I stood on the side of the stage before going on, I was waiting for someone to put their hand on my shoulder and expose me as an impostor, but I got away with it every time as the 'British rock singer'. I'm pretty sure the sweeping valleys of Toucheng have not echoed to the strains of 'Honky Tonk Women' since!

Counting my Thai bahts from time to time, they appeared to shrivel every time I converted them back into pounds and, as the year progressed, I knew that I didn't want to grow old in the Far East. So I said my goodbyes and hopped on a plane back to England, arriving home on Christmas Eve 1993.

And there I came to rest. It seemed to all and sundry that I had had my fun and now was the time to start getting serious about a career, settling down and finally buying a property.

Luckily, I got my old job back with the mortgage company, which was then almost instantaneously taken over and the whole operation moved up to Watford. I passed my driving test (at the age of 34) and after four years' study I became the proud owner of a business degree in Human Resource Management. Life was good for many years and I wore my thirties very comfortably around my shoulders, free of the need to be 'cool' whilst apparently becoming so with my relaxed style of training delivery, according to the new generation of twenty-somethings.

And yet ... and yet ... the holidays I was taking were somehow unsatisfying. Interesting, certainly, with the European capitals offering much to the city-hopper, but in 2002 I ditched the idea of another city break or beach week for a much more demanding leisure break. So as not to be suffering alone, I enlisted my dad (74 years young at the time) to join me on a two-week walk along the West Coastal Path in Cornwall.

This was by contrast a joy. We ached, suffered indigestion and blisters, got rained on and generally collapsed at the end of each walking day, but it was terrific not only to spend time with my dad, but also to reach the end of a two-week break and feel that something had been achieved. That set me thinking.

Back home, I turned up a website dedicated to Dave Kunst, the legendary American adventurer who had walked around the world between 1970 and 1974. I sat and marvelled at the story and reflected on how quickly my body had adapted to the demands that I had made on it during the two-week break. Could I? Was it feasible? How would I pay for accommodation and food? Where would I stay? How would I be able to communicate due to the language barrier? Stop! Concentrate too early on the details of any fledgling dream and it will wither under the weight of logic. These were vital questions that needed to be answered, but I didn't have to find all the answers immediately. The first thing to do was to see if it really would be possible for me to walk for 20-plus miles every single day over a sustained period.

The summer of 2003 found me walking from London to Amsterdam. With great ceremony I announced to friends, family and colleagues that I would be walking 250 miles over two weeks in support of Cancer Research UK. After losing two family members to the disease, I was committed as much to doing some good as to having a great adventure. Starting from Buckingham Palace, I walked on average 18 miles per day along the A2 in Kent and then caught the ferry from Dover across to Calais. It was a disaster. My feet were bleeding by Dover and the blisters were not healing in time for the daily slogs. Eating at lunchtime gave me awful indigestion or severely slowed me for the afternoon's efforts. And my backpack was way too overloaded.

By the time I reached Holland I was quite depressed, taking the train from The Hague into Amsterdam and spending my three days in the Dutch capital mostly in my room with my feet in the air. I was really anguished that, after conceding my musical aspirations, this dream also appeared to be slipping away. Not anguished enough to spend the night in an Amsterdam coffee shop, but quite disconsolate and wondering what to do next.

I cheered up a little back in England as those same friends, family and colleagues congratulated me on my efforts and said not to worry about the last stage as they couldn't imagine walking further than the end of their street. With all sponsorship pledges honoured, I sent off a cheque for £1,500 to Cancer Research UK. This also made me feel a good deal better.

I resolved to use this experience as part of a learning process and started planning the next escapade. One colleague in Watford gave me the single most important piece of advice I received in my whole walking 'career': every morning, before walking, slap a generous amount of Vaseline on your feet; it may feel a little squelchy after putting on socks and shoes, but it eliminates any trace of blisters. And it works!

April 2004 was the do-or-die walk, which would finally tell me if the world walk was going to be feasible. If I broke down during this one, I would have to shelve the dream and think of something else to commemorate my early mid-life crisis. Bruges to London was the chosen route, just 150 miles this time, but ample to assess whether I had learned the lessons. This time it went like a dream: the Vaseline saved my feet every day; I did not eat at lunchtime, instead making do with breakfast and supper each day; and my much reduced backpack rested easier on my shoulders. I'd cracked it! And another £1,000 winged its way to my favourite charity.

The first vital question had been answered. I could walk all day long over a sustained period - okay, only two weeks, but with careful planning and a little flexibility I was confident that I could do it for 14 grinding months. Now to start addressing those other pesky logistical details ...

~ 3 ~
A Man with a Plan

With my resignation delivered and friends and family in the picture, I could now follow up the practice walks with detailed planning without having to keep everything hush-hush.

In terms of the contents of my backpack, I eliminated anything that did not have a life-saving or public decency merit attached to it. I carried five t-shirts, five pairs of boxer shorts, two pairs of socks, a toiletries bag, one current map, a logbook, a compass, a camera, plus route and travel documents. As a result, my stuff fitted nicely into the smallest backpack available. My trousers, jacket, boots, pullovers and hats were worn, not carried, and were replaced when they were falling apart or as the weather dictated.

After careful consideration and with all the usual enthusiasm and diligence that Brits apply to learning foreign languages, I decided not to bother. I still had some French from school and a smattering of German and made the effort to learn 'please' and 'thank you' in each language. As for the rest, I would get by using charades, noises and pointing. I admit I was not exactly diving into the diverse cultural waters, but after walking 20 miles and arriving in a town all I would really want would be to find a hotel, have a shower and get something to eat.

I exchanged a few messages with my new hero, Dave Kunst, who was quite happy to e-mail me personally about his own walk back in the 1970s. The most important thing he told me was not to kill myself in terms of physical preparation, but simply spend a few weeks getting used to walking long distances and then just go - starting low and building up from there.

I took his advice and spent six weeks walking between 10 and 20 miles a day around Southend, making sure that for the first week or so I did no more than 15 to 18 miles each day.

One of the biggest advantages I had over Dave was the technological advances since he completed his walk. Back in the '70s he would not have had the benefit of the Internet, e-mail and mobile telephones. I designed a website (www.worldwalker.co.uk); I felt it was important to have a reference point for media, supporters and anyone who was interested in more information. I also felt the need to spend even more money painting myself into a corner, so there was definitely no backing out.

I hammered three websites where kind souls place a page about themselves offering free accommodation in their homes to travellers. Through these sites I obtained free lodging in the homes of new friends in Belgium, Germany, Poland, Russia, Australia and the USA. I stopped hammering when I found myself sending messages to people asking if it would be possible to stay with them for one night in ten months' time.

Next - how the hell was I going to pay for all this? I had a modest level of savings that I had been squirrelling away for a few years, with a vague idea of buying my own place. Philosophically I was ready to sacrifice all, but if I could avoid watching all my hard-earned funds disappearing I'd be much happier. To help out with the finances, I wrote more than 300 letters, faxes and e-mails to companies, individuals, TV stars, movie stars and music stars asking for a contribution of just £50 from each to help towards my expenses.

Many did not even reply. Those that did sent back standard letters about how they had already donated to various charities. I still shudder to think that I almost snatched a whole £50 out of the coffers of the FTSE 100 companies - how would they have coped with such a loss? In the end I received only two positive replies. Lord (Jeffrey) Archer and Chris Tarrant both sent back cheques for £50, bless them. So that was it - I would rely almost exclusively on my savings to pay for food, accommodation and other living expenses along the way.

I did manage to secure help with two of the most crucial requirements: travel insurance and contact lenses. A local firm agreed to give me free travel insurance for the whole trip. Being as blind as a bat, I also needed contact lenses to see where I was going, and my childhood opticians agreed to supply me with free lenses for the entire period.

The biggest part of the preparation was planning the route I would take. The walk was divided up into four sections:

London to Moscow (1,800 miles)
Melbourne to Sydney (550 miles)
Los Angeles to New York (2,800 miles)
Land's End to London (350 miles)

The route to France was clearly following in my own footsteps along the A2 road to Dover and then a ferry to Calais. From there, the most direct route to

Moscow was through France, Belgium, Holland, Germany, Poland, Belarus and into Russia. However, a number of new cyber friends were unanimous that I should avoid Belarus for reasons of personal safety and lingering Soviet-style red tape. Heading north in Poland and crossing through Lithuania and Latvia would mean that I could go straight into Russia without troubling the Belarusian border guards. It also meant that I would still be in the European Union with no visa requirements until actually setting foot in Russia.

Melbourne to Sydney provided just a 'slice' of Australia, covering 550 miles. This was forced on me by ticket restrictions. With no financial backing, I had to take an all-in-one round-the-world ticket with several restrictions on timing. Something had to give, so I settled on Melbourne to Sydney as a respectable stretch through the island continent.

The biggest chunk of all would be walking across the whole of the United States from LA to New York. I knew that at some stage during the walk I would be frozen and at another stage I would be fried, so I decided to take my chances on a stroll through the western states in the summer.

I also decided from the beginning that I would plan exactly where I wanted to be on any given day from start to finish. This may have seemed wildly optimistic, but I preferred to have a definite planned route with fixed timings rather than saying, "Okay, let's try to finish Lithuania in 10 days." Armed with an AA Road Atlas for Europe, I sat down at the dining room table in my parents' house to map out the route. More than once I wondered, sitting in the cosy confines of the family home, what the reality would prove to be once I was out on the road. Jabbing my finger along the roads of Poland with tiny towns identified as targets, I just made a tick and prayed that there would be somewhere for me to sleep each night.

As well as the 2,800 miles separating Los Angeles from New York, I had the intense heat in California, Arizona and New Mexico in the summer months to consider, plus the long stretches of nothing-but-ghost-towns in those states. The challenge started to look almost insurmountable. I pencilled in the dates and places for America, using old Route 66 as the basis, but decided that a closer examination of local conditions would be inevitable once I got there. Once again, sitting in my parents' home in Southend-on-Sea gazing at sprawling maps of America and trying to work out where I would be walking in a year's time was a mite ludicrous.

Finally, the last leg from Land's End back to Buckingham Palace was a doddle to plan and deliberately a doddle to complete. Only one day was set at more than 20 miles, to give me a smooth ride back into the capital. I would be walking - inevitably - for Cancer Research UK, as well as sister charities in each country I passed through. I couldn't exactly ask foreigners to send money to England, so I e-mailed all the relevant charities to tell them of my plans.

After all the planning, I ended up with an Excel spreadsheet filled in for each of the 400-plus days to get from London to London, the long way: starting low, with days of 15 to 18 miles in the beginning, building up to 20 to 25 miles across Europe, rising slightly to 26 to 28 miles across Australia, before shrinking back to 15 miles a day for the first month or so in America, then rising to the mammoth 30-mile days across central USA. When I look back now, the most remarkable aspect of all is that I was never more than two days behind the schedule I had put together on that dining room table in Southend-on-Sea.

With any kind of life-changing undertaking like this, there will always be more that you can do. Another couple of months working will bring in more money for the travel kitty. There could be more media contacts to find with another week of trawling the Internet. You can always be in better shape. You can always make more phone calls, try for more freebies or write more letters asking for support. If I had given in to these temptations to procrastinate, I would probably not have even started my venture yet, rather than be sitting back at home having completed the walk.

It was time to go. The date was set at Friday 29th October 2004. Friends and family had been told. An incredulous agent from Cancer Research UK confirmed that they were sending someone down to see me off. The local newspaper and radio stations had covered the story. No backing out now ...

~ 4 ~
Week One

I woke up and, not for the first time in the past few weeks, I thought to myself, 'What the hell am I doing …?' Friday 29th October 2004. For so long a mere circled date on the calendar, now it was upon me. My mind flooded with a thousand dazzling thoughts, ranging across the dial from great excitement to great anxiety and then, with effort, back to the mundane. Today I would be walking 18 miles to Welling, Kent.

Looking around the hotel room (it didn't take long) I reflected that at least it was good preparation for the rank accommodation that I could no doubt look forward to as I inched my way around the world. Well, what did I expect for £30 a night in London's Victoria district? In the dining room the breakfast of champions was not on the menu as I spooned rather tired cornflakes lightly splattered with tepid milk into my dry mouth. The expectations of friends, family and a band of devoted *Evening Echo* readers weighed upon my shoulders as I prepared to emulate the giants of exploration. I gave my 38-year-old legs a quick pep talk and prepared to leave.

Checking out, I heaved the backpack onto my shoulders and shuffled along to Buckingham Palace, where the sun was threatening to break through the clouds at any moment. At length I was surrounded by friends and family displaying various attitudes between carnival and unbridled terror at the prospect of my disappearing into the ether. The representative from Cancer Research beamed at everyone in the vicinity. My Mum stood, one massive sob waiting to burst free. My dad, stoic as ever, stood with old school friend, Paul, each holding one half of the 'WorldWalker' banner. I moved among my band of supporters, thanking each in turn and trying my best to make reassuring noises about how I was going to be just fine; unfortunately, it's not easy to do when you're not certain yourself.

Our two allocated policemen (kindly donated by the Metropolitan Police for half an hour or so) nodded that the hour was upon us, so I walked over to the gates of the palace and found them - naturally - obscured by a gaggle of tourists. The bobbies came to my aid. "Could you move aside please, ladies and gentlemen," came the authoritative voice, and the waters parted. Crowd dispersed, I moved in to be photographed with my left hand on the lock of the left gate (my successful return to be marked by placing my right hand on the corresponding gate). Some of the tourists started taking pictures. Others broke into applause. Finding a voice at last, I gave myself a '5-4-3-2-1' countdown and then, with great exaggeration, raised my right foot and took the first step. I was off!

That was except, of course, for the fact that I had about 40 people walking in slow procession with me along the Mall. It took an age to complete the mile along to Admiralty Arch, as everyone seemed to want to have a private word with me and say something of significance. The sense of foreboding was palpable - would they ever see me again? Determined to stay chipper, I dismissed this as melodrama and my joke for the day was, "I'm only walking to Welling", to which they all kindly chuckled.

Bidding a final farewell to all at Admiralty Arch, I headed off towards the Thames. My Italian friend, Paolo, who had flown in from Rome for the day, accompanied me along the Embankment, passing Cleopatra's Needle and St Paul's Cathedral as we chatted idly about what might happen, what we hoped would not happen, what would be great if it did happen.

Leaving Paolo at Tower Bridge, I crossed to the south of the river, alone at last. The euphoria of finally being on the road, the wonderful send-off and the excitement of the start of the adventure propelled me through the less-polished London districts of Southwark, Lewisham and Deptford towards the first stop of Welling in Kent. A friend of the family had offered a bed for the night and I was keen to get to Amy's house before the sun went down.

BBC Essex Radio called as I was halfway up Shooters Hill - could I do an interview? Puffing slightly and with calves getting tighter by the step, I said I'd be delighted but could they give me an hour or two please! I continued up and down the other side of the hill and, after some meandering around the small town of Welling, I came to Amy's house. I gratefully unloaded the backpack and slipped upstairs for a bath. I now finally had time to be tired and achy.

I had not eaten since breakfast and wolfed down the chicken and veg meal that Amy put in front of me. After doing the BBC interview, a pleasant evening was spent watching TV before heading to bed at 10:00. The first day of walking had been the ideal blueprint for the next 14 months: off on the road early, only take breakfast and supper, get to the target town before sundown and spend as little money as possible (whilst avoiding getting mugged, run over, arrested or injured). Of course, things would not always go according to that plan.

My target town for day two was Dartford, but after taking an alternative route suggested by Amy's friend, Arthur, I ended up sitting in the Wat Tyler pub in Dartford at 11:00 a.m., sipping a whisky and Coke. I decided to press on.

The Thames was never far from sight and it was alongside the docks of Gravesend that I decided I could walk no more that day. I walked up to a rather fetching hotel overlooking the hills beside the river, but the chap on reception told me that the cheapest room they had was £80 for a double for the night. Damn! I explained what I was doing and - bless him - he asked me how much I wanted to pay. I said that my maximum was £40 for the night. When I told him I was from Southend that clinched it. He was from Thundersley (just down the road from Southend) and he agreed to halve the price of the room for the night as the boss was away.

Setting off for Rochester the next day, I got a call from Meridian Television asking if I would mind being interviewed for the evening news. Were they kidding? Any charitable venture relies on publicity, so I would have dressed up as a banana to get on TV. Fortunately this was not necessary. Morale boosted, I stormed along the streets of Gravesend and into the countryside once again. Listening to the Rolling Stones on my Walkman, I chewed up mile after mile, stopping every hour or so for a swig of water and to gaze at the scenery. With the prospect of being on TV for the first time, nothing was going to slow me down too much. This burst of energy also had the desired effect of making sure that when the cameras were rolling I looked suitably dishevelled, with sweat both caked and moist giving me what I hoped was a heroic sheen. After five hours I arrived at Strood, just across the river from Rochester, and spotted a TV camera, boom microphone and smiling reporter.

Without exception, in all the TV interviews I did during the walk the reporters and photographers were very friendly. I think in the past they must all have been faced with members of the public suffering from 'deer in the headlights' syndrome, unable to put together a coherent sentence when in front of a TV camera. The pattern of questions was formed in that first interview: "Why are you doing this?"; "How are your feet?"; "What are you missing about home?"; "What are you looking forward to?"; "What's the best/worst thing"; and so on. I was very relaxed and answered each in turn - I had been preparing myself for the interview all day and managed to get each response out without tripping over my words, kept the answers succinct and remembered to smile. After that came the surrounding footage to film: "Can you walk towards me"; "Now walk past me"; "Now just your feet"; "Can you take off your hat and take a drink".

It took about half an hour to complete the filming and I then headed off into Rochester to my B&B for the night. I showered and sat waiting for the TV news bulletin. *Meridian News* hit the screen at 5:30 and I sat agog watching myself on the screen. When the programme had finished I had a little one-man party in the room, interrupted by my phone ringing. My Aunt Margaret had just seen me on *London Tonight*! Meridian had syndicated the story and the effect was immediate. The following day, as I walked out of Rochester towards Sittingbourne, drivers were honking at me and waving, bus passengers knocked on the window as I walked along and waved - one woman actually stopped her car and gave me a £10 note to help me on my journey.

Crossing into November meant that the starting gun had been fired to begin the build-up to Christmas. As I made my way through the small villages towards Sittingbourne, the tinsel and Father Christmas figures started to appear in shops windows, and I passed a primary school with the children in full rehearsal for the Christmas carol concert. As the pale sun began its descent, I came up to the 'Welcome to Sittingbourne' sign and eased myself down into a lower gear for the final stretch.

Sittingbourne is one of those inoffensive stops along the A2 between London and Dover. The sheer ordinariness of the situation seemed a long way from the adventure I was embarking on. I think that the following entry from my logbook summed it up nicely:

"I think I'm still enjoying the honeymoon period following the great launch, the relatively small distances of the daily walks, also the familiarity of the route. In the coming weeks I will have the additions of the language barriers, no TV/papers and also the new places. It will be challenging, interesting, scary, getting colder and darker. I shall enjoy this cosy period of Kent whilst I can ..."

Rising early the next day, I went through my normal routine: had breakfast, went back to the room and looked at the map whilst waiting for nature to take its course. I'll avoid being too crude, but during the walking day if I needed a pee it was fairly easy to disappear behind an area of shrubbery. Any other bodily functions would not be so easy to deal with if I was in the middle of nowhere, so I always wanted to get those out of the way before showering and dressing. After a quick check of the room to make sure I hadn't left anything behind, I was out on the road again. I had already decided to walk on today, as Faversham was only seven miles away and Canterbury another 11 after that. If I walked through, I'd get a day off in Canterbury.

Canterbury is a magnificent town, dominated by its ancient cathedral, which has for centuries brought pilgrims from across the world to its door. This particular pilgrim settled in for a day off, but I found myself at a bit of a loose end; it was a little early in the proceedings to be resting, so I was glad to be back on the road the next day to Dover.

Here I found myself on a 'big' road for the first time. The purpose of the A2 between Canterbury and Dover is to propel traffic as quickly as possible from the seaport to the heart of Kent. Four lanes of traffic whizz along and everyone using the road sensibly sits in the comfort of their vehicles. Except me, of course. Walking into the traffic, I now felt the full force of turbulence from every truck that roared past. Cars also became a loud blur as I walked quite alone, separated by less than three feet of hard shoulder from the high-speed torrent of motorised metal. I had to skip onto the grass verge from time to time as the huge juggernaut trucks thundered along, hugging the inside lane, making it into Dover just after 4:00. This pattern of using the main roads was forged at an early stage of the walk, solely for financial reasons. I'm sure I missed some delightful country routes, but the tight budget meant the most direct route from A to B always prevailed.

For years, Dover had conjured up in my mind the images of Britain at war, with the heroism of my recent ancestors never more poignantly illustrated than with the defence of our country from the Nazis on this cliff-faced doorstep. I soon updated this rather rose-tinted image. Seaports are generally fairly rough and ready, but Dover had also been at the forefront of what some of the more provocative media had described as a 'second invasion' of immigrants. The result was an underlying tension in the town itself, whilst Dover Castle and the white cliffs high above and outside the town remained pleasant tourist traps.

Next to the railway station is the Priory Pub/Hotel, which I had earmarked as my last resting place before leaving for the continent the following day. It was a decision I would come to regret within the hour. As darkness fell I walked into the busy downstairs bar to be greeted by wall-to-wall - shall I say - lively characters? Groups of twenty-something young men were busy practising their menacing stances ahead of another unruly Friday night. The beer was flowing, the voices were getting louder and the pool tables were crowded.

Being no fan of macho posturing and even less of a street fighting man, I should have left immediately, but the rooms above were well sectioned off and I was sure that I would have no need to revisit the main pub again that night. I paid the £20 for the night and made my way through the smoke and testosterone up the stairs and into my room. The room itself was huge, comfortably holding three beds. A wall-mounted TV and separate bathroom complemented the ensemble and the din coming from below was tolerably muffled. Then things started to go downhill fast.

I switched on the TV and nothing happened. Adjusting the wires and position had no effect, so I went back down to the bar to ask if there was a special trick involved. "It does work," was the short reply I received from the landlord, and that was the end of that. The window in the bathroom did not quite close and the sound of the trains and streetlife drifted in, along with a chilled breeze. I decided to take a bath and make the best of it. Whilst running the bath I moved to close the curtains facing the street. With one gentle tug I motioned the dust-laden material across the wide bay of the window. And the entire curtain rail came crashing down on top of me and the bed. Half-standing, half-crouching, I considered my situation as the heavy curtain draped over my head, with dust rushing towards my nose. There was no alternative, I had to make a run for it.

I repacked my backpack and arranged my half-eaten sandwich and newspaper on the bed to give the impression that I would be back if anyone came looking. Knowing that I had to go back through the bar in order to escape, I had prepared a cover story that I was going to do some laundry. I trod my guilty way down the stairs and peered around the bar. The landlord was not in evidence and the large TV in the bar had distracted most eyes. I snuck out and disappeared into the night, vowing never to return as long as I lived. Once on the High Street, I found a much more comfortable B&B for another £20 and sighed with relief as my weary frame finally hit the mattress. My last night in England. What a send-off …

Dawn broke the next day with that misty pallor that only a coastal town can muster. The moisture in the atmosphere suffused with the salty air meant that all my senses were imbued with that timeless taste of our island race. I was by no means the earliest riser at 7:00 that morning, but it was still early enough to see the town shake off its slumber to welcome the weekend. My friend, David, had arrived to see me off and we shared breakfast in a greasy spoon café before a leisurely stroll along the seafront. Seagulls swooped and the gentle breeze massaged us into full consciousness as we discussed my impending departure to the continent.

And I did feel excited. For too many years I had been without genuine motivation to get out of bed in the morning. Now I had an adventure completely of my own invention. No company to consult, no committee to persuade, no boss to restrict my intentions. I was free man, shaping my own destiny and doing it with relish. I bade David farewell and stepped onto the Seacat, watching England disappear behind me with a flourishing, frothy wake marking our progress. As I stood on the deck watching the white cliffs of Dover shrinking into the distance, a family stopped me and asked if I was the bloke on the telly who was walking around the world. Yes, indeed, and of course you can have a picture ...

~ 5 ~
Europe!

The ride across the English Channel was routine, but I was still abuzz with the excitement of getting on to the first foreign section of the walk. After leaving the ferry, I looked at the map of the surrounding area to find the best route to Gravelines, that day's target town. Avenue Mitterand appeared to be the one I needed, but there was some manoeuvring required to get onto that road. I set off and almost immediately came across 'Route de Gravelines'. Thinking I had stumbled across a sneaky shortcut I hastened my step, confident to be there in time for afternoon tea. As I strolled ever further, I began to have my doubts. The road appeared to be swinging around to meet with the Channel again. I decided to make use of my French and approached a harmless-looking couple.

"Pardon monsieur, je cherche un rue au direction Gravelines, s'il vous plait …"

Of course, managing to get out a statement in a foreign language does not prepare you for the torrent of the response. The gentleman replied with great gusto in meticulous detail of how I should proceed. I understood not one word of it, but instead followed his hand gestures, which seemed to indicate doubling back on myself. There's nothing more wretched when doing long-distance walking than realising that you have to retrace your steps for several miles and then set off again. I enquired whether there was a shortcut to getting back on track.

"Est-ce qu'il y a un autre route que je peut prendre à arriver sur le rue?"

This time the gentleman looked blankly at me with a faint smile. His lady companion came to our rescue.

"Tu peut marcher à côté du canal …"

Aha! The canal! Now that I could follow (in both senses). They nodded vigorously and I set off with half a sense of pride that I had managed my first exchange in French with some aplomb and half a sense that they had said anything to get rid of me. However, the good lady's directions were accurate as, emerging from the canal, I came across a roundabout with Avenue Mitterand marked as the exit with Gravelines clearly indicated. Yay! Less encouraging was the next sign telling me that Gravelines was in fact another 18 kilometres down the road. I had managed to spend almost two hours advancing just 3,000 metres. Grrrrrrr ...

At least Avenue Mitterand was flat and straight. It looked like one of those diagrams used to prove that parallel lines meet at infinity. I hastened along, aware that time was not on my side if I was to make Gravelines by sundown. With no water, I sped along the road, my mouth getting drier by the minute, but I dared not veer off into the surrounding villages for a drink with daylight fading. I walked furiously along to the little village of Oye-Plage, stopping at a car park to ask a policeman how far it was to Gravelines. He assured me it was only another four or five kilometres. Great! There was another hour of daylight left at least, so I could relax a little. I sat down and drank a bottle of water in about 30 seconds flat, which had the immediate effect of making me sweat profusely. But with a cheery heart I strolled on ... and on and on and on. The hour was up and I was still walking along a very long Avenue Mitterand (if it was still called that) and the sun was just about to disappear. The white line on the side of the road was still leading inexorably onward, but no town was apparent. A little more urgency crept back into my pace as I continued. Angrily I berated myself for not taking the earlier ferry, for being casual about starting off from Calais, for the idiot decision to follow what was clearly the wrong road, cursing the policeman for raising my hopes ... and then I saw Gravelines. The town is perched on the far left as you approach from Calais, connected by a long, thin side road. If it had been situated directly on the main road, it would have been visible for the previous half an hour. Never mind, I was there. I took a room at the Best Western and after a bath, sandwich and cheap glass of wine I slipped into bed and slept soundly.

Progress was much better the following day and I felt decadent enough to have a whisky and Coke at 11:30, which put paid to any hunger pangs and also put a spring in my step for the remaining kilometres. The walk was straightforward and unremarkable except for my brilliant idea to join the main highway leading into town. I quickly found myself walking alongside what appeared to be a Grand Prix circuit, with high walls ready for the reckless to bounce off. This was a little scary. I clambered up the steep grass verge and slithered under the fencing to get back onto the side streets and made my way into downtown Dunkerque. My old favourite hotel, the Tigre, was still standing and still in operation. €37 per night with breakfast thrown in - you can't complain about that. And let's face it - who really needs central heating? France was gone as quickly as it had arrived. One long boulevard took me out of Dunkerque, before a turn to the right led towards the border with Belgium. The road itself was suburban for the first few miles and in a slight drizzle I passed apartment blocks and small rows of shops, getting that familiar feeling of expending lots of effort for very little progress. I grew to hate walking through large towns and cities, where hours can be spent just getting to the outskirts before you see green fields and hills and actually feel like you are making distance. As the road led me south and then east, I walked parallel to the sand dunes, along the road that straddled the two countries.

The border between France and Belgium is now denoted with a road sign the same size as the speed limit badges; I walked past a gas station and was now in Belgium. The rain had eased up and the sky was a clear blue. Confident of reaching the target town of De Panne with ease, I stopped for a drink at a little bar standing merrily on the corner of a street as I entered a small village just inside Belgium.

It was not quite 2:00 by the time I reached De Panne, so I decided to press on. Whenever I was looking at an early finish, I considered whether I should carry on to reduce the deficit and give myself an easier day tomorrow. In this case, I was still feeling fresh and the weather was definitely conducive to more effort, so I carried on. The road alongside this section of the northern coast of Belgium is dotted with seaside strips, which appear to have sprung up for the tourist market. Walk for half an hour and you will see another strip of road with shops, hotels and restaurants stretching for about a kilometre and then you're back on the building-free coastal road. With such a large concentration of 'mini-resorts' I wondered if there were enough visitors to go around, but each seemed to be bustling reasonably, even out of season. Despite the continuing clear blue skies overhead, a keen wind was blowing, bringing a salty assault on my nose and a bracing chill to the rest of me. I decided to be cheerful out of sheer bloody-mindedness and jigged along with the Stones on my Walkman, defiantly singing along, much to the amusement of the drivers rushing past. As I approached Niewpoort, I decided to call it a day - this left a suitably short stroll further along the coastline the next day to Oostende. With a light head and an ever-lighter wallet, I enjoyed a fish supper and slept well.

The next day comprised an unremarkable hike along the coastal road, finally arriving at the huge seaport of Oostende. The sea was whipping up quite nicely and crashing waves along the sandy beach, whilst the clouds hung in the sky like dirty sheep. Coming off the promenade, I walked the final few hundred metres to the Oostende Tourist Information Centre. The staff of course spoke wonderful English and pointed me towards an establishment euphemistically referred to as a 'guesthouse', which would cost me €25 for the night. I set my expectations low and was not disappointed. The floor was concrete, which acted as an excellent conductor of the cold. The heater on the wall was for decorative purposes only and the communal shower room had clearly been modelled on an aeroplane toilet. I reflected that staying in places such as this was 'character building'.

I left Oostende early the next morning for Brugge. Walking out of town towards the train station at the side of the harbour, I was engulfed by a sea mist awesome in its density. Looking behind me, I could no longer see the city buildings and to the front I did not see a large ship alongside the dock until I was almost upon it. Still wearing the first pair of trainers, I felt my footsteps bend into the grooves of the cobbled street leading towards the canal. The cunning mist drew a veil across every angle of sight and I well remember thinking that I was fortunate to be at least threading my way on land, rather than one of the brave souls who would be putting out to sea that day. Even by 9:00 the weak sun had not managed to make any impression.

Rounding the docks and getting onto the canal path that led out of town, I started to get a better view of the quays welcoming ships from all over the world. The mist had cleared sufficiently to see more than 50 metres ahead and I moved from pavement to hard shoulder, then asphalt to the road and river junction that delineated the city limits. A small white picket fence demarcated the industrial canal from the domestic waterway and I strolled happily along the 20-kilometre (12-mile) towpath as the day shook off its chilly start and the sunshine finally broke through. Almost immediately the concrete masses of the city were behind me and I was surrounded by fields, hedges and distant farmhouses. There were clusters of houses along the way at water junctions, but for the most part my only contact with other people was the occasional cyclist whizzing past or the slow, deliberate passage of barges meandering along the canal. Groups of ducks would eye me warily on the banks and fly off as soon as I got too close. As the hours slipped by, I felt a great sense of freedom and contentment: time was on my side, there was no traffic to negotiate the space with, and the day was cold but bright, filling my lungs with fresh country air. I was now heading away from the coast, due east and towards the heart of Europe.

As the shadows began to grow longer with the sun's descent, I came into Brugge, the first place on the continent where I had secured free accommodation from a host on the Hospitality Club website. Erik Broos welcomed me into his huge apartment block, which comprised his family home and several guest rooms. My room for the night had an added kitchenette and luxury bathroom and felt like an apartment - I would have happily stayed for the week! I did my laundry and went window shopping for a new jacket. My hooded vinyl rain jacket had proved functional enough for the drizzle and single-figure temperatures so far, but with the winter ahead, particularly in Eastern Europe, I felt that an upgrade would be necessary. I had heard about this Gore Tex material, which apparently would allow one to swim with polar bears in the Artic with ease. Sure enough, there was a trendy winter gear shop close to the guesthouse where I found the very thing - for €550. Once I had regained consciousness, I triple-checked and my eyes were not deceiving me - this light-as-a-feather jacket would cost me more than £300. I called my mum about what I wanted for Christmas.

The next two days consisted of more canal walking, to Aalter and then on to Gent, where I had another host waiting for me. After a very easy walk in an almost straight line along the canal, I came into Gent and called Rosemarjim from a bar on her street. She arrived with her boyfriend, Matthieu, no doubt summoned to make sure it was safe for her to associate with this British lunatic who claimed to be walking around the world. It turned out that they were both musicians, playing accordion and violin in their own band, with Rosemarjim also supplying vocals. They had a gig coming up and wondered if I would like to hear them play - of course! I was then treated to folk songs from Bosnia, Macedonia, Sweden and Tunisia, with the great gusto of the accordion sympathetically making way for the violin strains and Rosemarjim's sweet voice. After about half an hour, they gave way for me to stand and sing 'On The Street Where You Live' for them - my ever-ready standby for musical evenings. That, I thought, would draw the musical contributions to a close. I didn't realise that I was providing the interval.

Another half an hour of folksy tunes followed my efforts and I began to wonder when I would be able to take a shower and indeed where I would be sleeping. The tone of the songs became progressively more woeful and I began to feel myself drifting into melancholy as another hero's attempts at love were dashed - or was it the woman who had searched for years for her mother, ending up at her premature graveside? Truly folk music was Europe's answer to Country & Western, where happy endings are frowned upon by the purists.

We eventually repaired to Matthieu's house, where I showered and lay back to sleep in his office. Fifteen days after starting out, I was doing okay.

Gent is another city of great sights which entices the visitor to see more. It has beautiful ancient buildings and a wonderful series of main thoroughfares and side streets concealing an incredible variety of shops for all interests. It is also a complete bugger of a place to try to walk out of! Setting off from Rosemarjim's house in an attempt to head east, I stormed off due south and one hour later ended up outside the hotel I stayed at the previous year. This was particularly annoying as it reminded me how long it had taken me to get out of the city last time. The problem with Gent is that it is almost completely circular in its construction; an aerial view would no doubt resemble an onion cut in half, with ever-increasing circles spreading like ripples on a lake. It took me two hours to scythe my way through this labyrinth and emerge on the east side of town. I rewarded my persistence in escaping Gent with a whisky and Coke. Making good progress into Lokeren by 2:45, I continued along to the sweet-sounding but lousy-looking town of St Niklaas. I guess it will be much more pleasing to the eye when the Olympic-sized roadworks have been completed. To add a suitably surreal touch to the proceedings, I laid in bed watching *Gardeners' World* beamed in from BBC2 to Belgium.

My days were now falling quickly into a pattern, which took on ritualistic overtones for a creature of habit like me. After rising early, I would breakfast and shower before checking the room to make sure I hadn't forgotten anything. Then it was off for the daily grind of six/seven/eight hours of walking, followed by the daily search for a place to stay, another shower and then supper. Many people asked if I took supplementary vitamins and carefully chosen snacks to maintain my energy levels; they were appalled when I told them that all I did was have a whisky or vodka midday to maintain the momentum - whatever gets you through the day.

I moved on to Antwerp, where I was to be met by a Belgian host. Approaching the city from the west, you are immediately presented with the Scheldt River with Antwerp located on the other side. Interestingly, there is an underground tunnel exclusively for pedestrians, which added another kilometre to the day's journey, but happily I was met by Olivier and Linda on the other side, who welcomed me warmly to their city and drove me back to their apartment. We chatted well into the evening, when Olivier came up with a novel solution to my accommodation needs for the following night in Oostmalle. He knew of a monastery that offered free accommodation to pilgrims and travellers - this was just irresistible.

He made the call and was subjected to quite an interrogation about my suitability as a guest at this holy place. He obviously made a good case on my behalf, because a promise was secured and general directions obtained. I wondered a little about my suitability as a candidate to stay with these learned, pious gentlefolk, but reflected that the language barrier would provide me with an adequate excuse to avoid extensive theological discussions.

I set off the next day, intrigued.

The monastery was located just off the A42 between Westmalle and Oostmalle. I arrived as the sun was beginning to take its leave, casting a reverent glow above the red brick structure. Day visitors were scurrying back to their cars as I picked my way along the dirt track leading off the main road approaching the large gateway through a modestly sized car park. I pulled on the rope and banged the knocker on the door for good measure. The small viewing panel across the middle of the gate slid open and an elderly monk viewed me through the grating.

"Hello! Mark Cundy here," I said. Without a word, he closed the panel and opened the built-in door to let me in. The entrance hall was dark and a little chilly, although the opposite wall was a glass frontage with French windows revealing the way across a courtyard into the main building. The monk eyed me with a mixture of suspicion and indifference. He raised a hand and pointed to the main building, then indicated I should knock at the door on the right-hand side of the building. I had the impression that I had interrupted his reading of the scriptures or something similarly worthy.

I crossed the courtyard and knocked on door. Nothing. I knocked again. Nothing. I started to circle the building in what was now the twilight. Dreading interrupting my new friend on reception again, I started back, but was caught by an encouraging series of waves from a window next to the door I had previously passed. I went in and was met by two more monks in very splendid robes. They smiled and gestured for me to stand on the left of the reception hall by the stairs.

This side of the building had offices to the left, another exit to the courtyard and stairs leading up to my right. The long panels of heavy wood along the walls and their cousins along the floor, which picked up every careless step, added to the air of great piety. Finally another monk appeared. He sidled up to me, took me by the elbow and said in a very low voice, "You are the Englishman?" I admitted that I was. "Come," he said and made towards the stairs. Squeak, squeak, squeak went my trainers on the polished floor. My new friend turned slightly and looked at my feet with the pained smile of one who has grown used to sufferance in the mortal life and thus regarded my footwear as just another trial.

I went downstairs at 6:15 as directed for dinner, with a significant hole in my belly. Walking into the large dining hall, I made for the serfs' table, but was summoned over by a wagging finger to dine with what appeared to be the head monk. I sat down at a long table with two other monks directly opposite. The chief held out his cup expectantly, so I poured him a coffee. No response. I examined him out of the corner of my eye and saw he was tall, a little portly, and with outstanding eyebrows. Of the two brothers on the other side, one appeared to be hoping to get through life without anybody noticing him, whilst the other betrayed a slightly jolly air - very Friar Tuck. Dinner was then served.

A large tray of bread slices with butter, cheese and ham were placed before us. I fixed a ham sandwich, then a cheese one to follow, but was still the wrong side of peckish. I reached to prepare a third sandwich and felt the eyes of the chief burning into my side. I couldn't exactly put the ingredients back, so I just carried on and wolfed down the third sandwich, trying to ignore my disapproving audience. It's weird how situations of great reverence or seriousness bring out the worst in me. I remember hearing about a relative of mine whose nervous tension manifested itself at a family funeral in the form of hysterical fits of laughter. He couldn't help it, they tell me. So I blamed it on my genes when for no reason the image appeared in my mind of these monks doing an acrobatic routine complete with miniature trampoline with robes flying around in wild abandon. I hastily adjusted my eyes to examine my navel and, with considerable effort, restrained my silent giggles, although I'm pretty sure my shoulders gave me away.

The plates were cleared and dessert followed. A tray containing 24 chocolate eclairs was placed in the middle of the table. Between the four of us, that would be six each, but I resolved to have just two following the sandwich incident. Being Belgian, of course the eclairs were rich and delicious. Having finished my second one I was preparing to make my excuses, but my slightly jolly friend opposite nudged the tray towards me and creased a twinkle out of his eye. He had clearly enjoyed the chief's outrage and dared me to risk damnation by having a third eclair. Sod it, I thought, I'm entitled, and scooped it up. The chief left immediately and Friar Tuck helped himself to another.

I hope I mended some bridges the following morning by helping with the washing-up after breakfast, but I suspect that my stock remained pretty low. I thanked the English-speaking monk profusely and left the order to their solitary existence.

The last day of walking in Belgium was great. Along a stretch of road enveloped by a majestic bank of well-aged trees I stopped off at 'Den Bierpot' for a swift whisky and Coke. I passed through some pretty little villages and was joined by a grinning cyclist who had made a slow approach on my blind side. He explained that he was heading home for Eastern Europe following a celebration for the end of Ramadan with his Muslim friends. Walking and talking, we mused on the directions that our lives went and whether we shaped our destinies or they were preordained. Our discourse was curtailed due to the lateness of the hour and he rode off, after stuffing a couple of Euros into my hand. In the twilight I strolled contentedly across the border and into Holland.

~ 6 ~
Dutch & Deutsch

The little Dutch town of Resusel was my introduction to Holland, just over the border from Belgium. I really wanted to enjoy Holland, having shared houses and apartments with four Dutch people during my time in London and found them always to be the right side of assertive and good fun. Nothing happened to change my mind about the people, but the weather was bloody awful. I think that it rained almost continuously for the entire 96 hours that I spent in the country. Further down the line, I would be togged out from head to foot in completely waterproof gear, but at this stage I was still wearing the blue jeans I had started with and white trainers. The obvious result was that I was a very sodden figure traipsing along the country roads of Holland, jeans clinging heavily to my knees and hips, the tepid rain mixing nicely with the Vaseline on my feet.

The road to Eindhoven gave me 29 kilometres of uninterrupted squelching, although longer distances and adversity seemed to bring out the best in me. I walked determinedly on, making good progress with road signs showing the distance whittling down from 20/12/7 kilometres until I eventually reached the sign welcoming me to Eindhoven. As the fields gave way to suburban and then urban I started to sense that peculiar tension that surrounds big cities around the world. I saw the familiar high-rise blocks of flats, graffiti and broken fence panels. I paid more attention to my peripheral vision walking through these streets and was pleased to see the city centre approaching.

Eindhoven exploded into a major city at the end of the nineteenth century, when the electronics giant Phillips selected it as its base and rapid expansion followed. Once in the buzzing centre of town I started to enjoy myself, slipping into the Tipsy Duck pub. A chirpy young barman called Remo was in charge of both drinks and music, so the bar soon echoed to the Rolling Stones whilst I sipped a whisky and Coke. Remo told me that there were two guesthouses ten minutes' walk away, which would cost me only €25 for the night, so I rashly ordered another drink. Sitting, chatting, laughing, I was very relaxed and enjoying the first social time out since I had started. This was my first mistake.

Always, always secure your accommodation before enjoying yourself. That was the new cardinal rule after Eindhoven. Finally leaving the pub, I made my way to the two guesthouses, both of which were fully booked for the night. I was - probably foolishly - stunned when told this. Now I had to start scouring the streets for a less economic option, with the daylight completely gone - idiot! After another hour of searching, feeling tired, hungry and in great need of a shower, I had no option but to take a room in a very swish hotel, which cost me a budget-busting €85 for one night. My earlier bonhomie was long gone.

I know it's the way of the world, but I always felt slightly cheated when paying a large sum of money for what was essentially a bed, a shower and a television. Fortunately I didn't have to suffer comfort too often, but on a handful of occasions I would sit gazing resentfully at the trouser press, ironing board, wireless Internet connection, drinking glasses made of glass and video/DVD combos. All I wanted was to shower, sleep and move on. However, I needn't have worried, as there were plenty of extremely basic places lying in wait for me.

Eindhoven glided down memory lane as I squelched my way further east. Deurne was the next town on my list and I really must go back there one day when I'm in a better mood. After a seven-hour slog, the rain had penetrated my jacket and cold droplets were running down the skin on my back and shoulders. The toggle strings on the hood of my jacket had left imprints on my rain-drenched face, my gloveless hands were wrinkled and - naturally - my jeans clung tight to the front of my legs. I couldn't have been wetter if I'd flung myself into the nearest canal.

Consequently, I wasn't in the best mood to appreciate the very nicely laid-out town centre, cobbled streets and architecture. I called into the visitor information centre, where a lovely woman told me that there were only two hotels in that locality, both another kilometre down the road on the opposite side of town. I could have cheerfully hit her. On arriving at one of the hotels, I was informed that there was nowhere to get anything to eat in the vicinity and I would have to go back into town where there were plenty of very good restaurants. I struggled hard to recollect what I had done in a previous life to deserve this, but nothing came to mind. I had enough energy left to throw my backpack dejectedly into the room and, still soggy, walk back into town for dinner. Back in the room an hour later, I draped my jeans, jacket and jumper across the curtain rail and showered some feeling back into my hands and feet. I was in bed by 7:45 and felt like staying there for a week. Outside, the rain continued to lash my windows as I drifted off to sleep.

The sun rose on my last day in Holland. I know this, because on looking out of my hotel window I could see the street lights were off. That was, however, the only way of ascertaining that the sun had risen, as it was still raining. The N270 road I had followed from Eindhoven promised it would see me virtually all the way through to my next stop, the town of Well. Like many roads across Europe, there was a cycle lane running parallel all the way. Having spent many years criticising British councils for spending taxpayers' money on building those pesky cycle lanes that nobody seemed to use, I now became a great supporter of the policy. Within a couple of hours I was drenched again, so I stopped off at the town of Venray for some fortification. After a rather disappointing glass of wine, I rejoined the N270 and stepped up a gear. Slowly, a new development dawned on me - there was no cycle path. I was at the brow of a hill on the N270 with large trucks roaring past and about six inches of shoulder to play with. Looking back, I had managed to walk about 500 metres without realising the cycle path had died. The road ahead looked shorter than the dangerous trek back and I didn't fancy trying my luck with the traffic behind me, so I inched over the hill and down to a roundabout. The road ahead was exactly the same with no path, whilst to my left was a huge, muddy field in partial use as an industrial dumping ground. I had no choice. It was time to get muddy.

If I thought the previous day had been miserable, it was only a warm-up for that half-hour trek across the field. The rain was still falling and the only guidance across the field to the side road was a series of tractor tyre tracks, now very soft and muddy with little pools of water residing in each divot. I emerged onto the road on the other side as a bedraggled mess, grateful only that I had avoided falling over. I went into the first pub I saw and got myself a whisky and Coke. Whilst sitting there feeling sorry for myself, a lady police officer darted into the pub, looked around and darted out again. Strange, I thought, but soon lapsed back into my self-commiseration. A few moments later she was joined by a couple of male colleagues, the senior of whom sat down in a chair opposite me.

"Good morning," I said brightly.

"Good morning," he replied without hesitation. Ah, those linguistically gifted Dutch!

I misread the situation spectacularly.

The officer asked me, "What's going on?"

In response, I launched into a no-details-spared explanation of my quest. When the poor chap finally had the opportunity to speak, he asked if he could see my passport. Of course. He handed this to his colleague who the exited the premises, and I sensed for the first time that they perhaps might have business with me.

"Is there a problem officer?" I proffered.

Oh yes, there was a problem all right ...

They were following up on a series of phone calls made to the station about some idiot walking along the very busy and extremely hazardous N270 junction just past Velray. I was positively apoplectic about this, clearly a cautionable offence. As I babbled away I looked for signs on the officer's face that he was softening his attitude in light of my ignorance.

When I finally stopped talking, he raised his eyebrows, looked me in the eye and said, "You won't do this again, will you?"

"Absolutely not, sir!"

All three of them brightened and shook my hand warmly, wishing me good luck for the rest of my journey. I breathed a huge sigh of relief and as I finished my drink I reflected on how it might have been if I'd been facing the police of some of the other countries I was due to pass through ...

I shuffled into Well and headed right towards what looked like a promising guesthouse. It was in fact a restaurant and bar with no accommodation. One of the customers took pity on the bedraggled creature dripping all over the reception area and offered me a ride to the only hotel in town. I accepted gratefully and enjoyed the sensation of being in a car for a full two minutes. She dropped me off outside and I entered the very tastefully decorated small hotel, the Auberge De Grote Waai, carrying my own personal puddle with me. I was ushered upstairs and out of sight of the more distinguished guests, to discover that my backpack was less than waterproof. I decorated the room with the soggy contents and applied the hairdryer to the inside of the bag. This is what it's all about, I told myself, as I lay in the bath a little later, socks and boxer shorts dangling above me. Who'd want to be in a warm, comfortable office drinking coffee when you can be out in the elements, tempting arthritis, pneumonia and careless drivers? No contest.

My mind started to wander to the coming journey across Germany. For several generations in Britain, any mention of Germany had been synonymous with thoughts of the Second World War. The story has been re-told so many times, and watching the History Channel in the UK it seemed that not a day went by without some documentary re-examining the events of 1939 to 1945. However, the people of Germany in the twenty-first century are no more responsible for what happened during the Nazi regime than I am for what the British did in our empire-building days. Of course, the first *sauer* note might shake that enlightened view, but I determined to concentrate on football for lively chats ...

Holland's parting gift to me was a sleet storm and I scuttled through a forested area to emerge onto a small, anonymous-looking road to be greeted by a sign telling me I was entering 'Deutschland'. In ever-brightening weather I soon arrived at my first stop, the town of Sonsbeck. Walking just off the main street I spotted what was essentially just another suburban home, but with a large sign that read 'Zimmer' (Room). I approached a chap standing outside the front door and asked, "Ist es ein gasthaus, bitte?" I had found my first accommodation in Germany. And what a place. I highly recommend the Traumstation guesthouse - just ask for Gerd. The house is decked out in a kind of hippy, New Age, very individual hotchpotch of styles and there is a wonderfully relaxed atmosphere - the perfect antidote to the sterile familiarity of hotel chains. After showering I headed off to a recommended Turkish restaurant down the street for my supper.

Determined to have the whole German experience as soon as possible I ordered Schnitzel. Memories flooded back of my German lessons at school, where Hans and Liselotte would return from the park, back to their *Fahter und Mutter* at the Gasthaus Bauer. And always they would be off to the restaurant to enjoy Schnitzel (didn't they have any imagination, this family? Not exactly a balanced diet). Anyway, I had conjured up in my mind the idea that Schnitzel was a dainty dish, similar to a couple of lamb chops perched on the side of the plate. When the waiter brought over what appeared to be a battered discus and laid it before me, I looked incredulously at the feast before me. It was absolutely delicious and more than I had eaten in one sitting for weeks. In all the time I spent in Germany I never experienced Schnitzel like this again - other restaurants obviously had the mass-storage, slim cutlets defrosted and fried up to order. This had been the real thing. I waddled back to the guesthouse and flopped contentedly on the bed to watch a couple of hours of BBC World.

Those first few days of December were great. I had never been to Germany before, let alone walked through the country; for the first time since leaving London I was now in new territory and genuinely excited. Crossing the Rhein I stopped overnight in Wesel and headed off towards Wulfen. This took me through the much-anticipated forested areas of rural Germany and I was not disappointed. Winding roads interspersed with little villages threaded through the still lush, green fields and long-established woodlands. On more than one occasion I stopped at the side of the road to look front/back/left/right and imbibe the mixture of colours and textures around me. The pale sun illuminating the greyish blue sky threw shards of light through the rich brown frames of the surrounding trees, while the yellowing fallen leaves lay scattered on the green grassy carpet of the forest floor.

Satisfying though this reverie was, I needed to get moving. Wulfen didn't seem to be getting any closer, so I stepped up the pace and eventually turned a final woodland corridor to see a sign telling me it was just three more kilometres to town. Passing a British red telephone box on the side of the village green (what was that doing there?) I made for the Humbert, the only hotel in town, and was greeted by a completely non-English-speaking staff and clientele. I explained as best I could that I needed a "zimmer for ein nacht". Cautious nods of agreement were directed at me, but there then followed a torrent of conditions attached to my spending the night there. I hadn't a clue what they were talking about, but there seemed to be a lot of opening and closing of doors involved and the turning of keys seemed to be coming into the equation. Cursing my lack of knowledge of the German tongue, I smiled my confusion and received a brief smile back. The sun was setting and this was clearly the only place to stay in town, so I was anxious not to upset anyone. The impasse was broken by the arrival of the bellboy, hustled over to me to break the deadlock. Roughly 15 years old, he appeared to have acquired his knowledge of a dozen words in English by listening to pop music on the radio.

Between us we muddled through and it emerged that this was the last day of operation for the hotel for that year. That night they were due to close for the season, but would let me stay; the conditions of my visit being that I would lock up for them when I left. That can't be right, I thought, as I made my way upstairs, but sure enough I was handed a selection of keys with instructions about how to secure the building before dropping them through the letter box.

The next morning I woke up to an eerie stillness. The entire hotel was indeed deserted. I almost trod on the tray sitting outside my door as I went to investigate. Thoughtfully, someone had left me a ham sandwich (now husky dry) an orange (of pensionable age) and a flask of coffee, which had cooled nicely during the night to become undrinkable. A score of 10 out of 10 for effort anyway. I showered and made my way downstairs, wandering freely through the bar and reception. Presumably there would have been nothing to prevent me from staying there a whole week for free, but my timetable did not allow.

I pressed on through the very pretty countryside, stopping off at Dulmen and then continuing on to Muenster. By now I was covering around 20 miles (32kms) per day and feeling distinctly fitter. On a psychological level, I confined my planning to looking ahead about a week or so at a time. If my mind drifted to Australia and America, a grey pall of exhaustion would fall over me and I dismissed them. One thing that I could never quite shake off was anxiety about money. I found myself wandering around supermarkets looking for smaller cuts of cheese and ham to save pennies here and there. The only drink I had was at midday to keep colds at bay and give a kick to the afternoon. I parted reluctantly and infrequently with cash to buy new sweaters and socks; 25 days since leaving Buckingham Palace, my thrifty side was necessarily coming to the fore. One thing I never compromised on, however, was the shoes I was wearing. I would walk them into collapse, but when replacing them I bought the best, explaining why I only used five pairs of shoes during the whole trip.

The road out of Muenster reconfirmed my hatred of walking around big cities. After one-and-a-half hours of criss-crossing the north eastern city roads, I finally emerged onto the main road heading east. As the day wore on, it seemed that I had set myself a town too far, as the target of Bad Laer didn't seem to be getting much closer. I had the assurance of Gerrit, my first host in Germany, lined up, but that didn't make the journey any shorter. Gerrit had arranged for his mother to collect me at a suitable place in town. On and on I strode, conscious that I would now be inconveniencing the whole family if I was late or got lost.

Darkness had fallen and I wandered into Glandorf, the penultimate stop before the target town. In the daytime, I'm sure it would have been easy to get directions and have a sense of place, but the road I had been walking on suddenly became much wider and busier, with what appeared to be several side roads spraying out in all directions. And the cycle lane disappeared. I moved off along a side road and quickly became engulfed in the darkness of German country roads. This is just plain ridiculous, I thought, and I made back towards Glandorf. Standing in the amber glow of the town's first street light, my brain fizzed with anxiety over which way to go, the dangerous roads, the fact that Gerrit's phone number was at the bottom of my backpack and another zillion stresses. I was therefore more than a little glad when my mobile rang - Gerrit in a cheery voice asking me how I was getting on. He told me to stay put and Maria, his mother, would come and collect me. Sweet relief!

Maria arrived shortly afterwards and scooped me up into her car to make the drive back to Bad Laer. We were friends within two minutes, she chatting away amiably and me trying to follow what she was on about, but as always smiles and hugs went a long way to cementing a friendship.

After a delicious meal of pork, spinach and potatoes, Gerritt, his parents and I had a good chat in the kitchen - always my favourite room for socialising. Their house was located in the middle of rolling fields just outside Bad Laer and surrounded by beautiful scenery, which I would enjoy the following morning. That night was very still and silent and I drifted off into a peaceful slumber.

The morning broke with the house redolent with the aroma of sizzling breakfast. The scene was very relaxed and each member of the family drifted in, with Maria bustling around making sure everyone was okay. We had another long and lively conversation, Gerrit telling tales of his travels around Europe, and they all voiced mild concerns about my plans to walk through Russia. As the clock made its way along to 9:45 I knew I had to be on my way. We took photos, hugged and promised to stay in touch and Gerrit drove me back to Glandorf to pick up where I had left off the previous day. Was I sure I didn't just want to start walking from their village? Nope, I must do this properly I said, dutifully remembering my promise on behalf of the charities. However, later that day I wished several times I had just skipped those seven kilometres …

~ 7 ~
All Roads (Eventually)
Lead to Berlin

Sweating, aching, breathing furiously hard, pushing all the nerves and sinews to their limit, I forced myself onwards to the midpoint stop of the day, the town of Dissen. After these metaphorically blistering efforts it was agony to look at my watch to see that it was already 2:00 in the afternoon as I arrived in town. I had no spare time to hang around, but was mindful that more harm would be done with no significant rest, so a 15-minute break in a bar was in order. The fates were not smiling on me that day, because as I emerged at the other side of town the road began to wind inexorably uphill, contouring around the admittedly sumptuous hillside forest. Watching the cars make languid progress through the snaking road, I reflected what a glorious day out it must be to enjoy the area at leisure, recumbent in a car. I really must try that one day.

The hill peaked and, despite myself, I had to stop and admire the breathtaking views to the front and rear. At least now I would be able to wind downhill for a while. Sitting at the foot of the valley was the very welcome village of Wellingholzhausen. After a brief coffee break, I took the Melle road for the final eight kilometres.

The cycle path ended as a long, wide bend in the road swept around a thicket of trees. Just off the road was a gritted side road, which I took to be the alternative cycle/pedestrian route. Big mistake. I ended up on the edge of a field bordering a private farmhouse with no more road and the distant sounds of traffic continuing along the main road. I cut across the thicket of trees hoping that the farmer did not own a shotgun. Raising my steps in an exaggerated fashion, I hauled myself through the trees and shrubbery, finally emerging back on the main road. The late afternoon was assuming an orange tinge as the sun descended and I hastened onwards, cursing the indulgent coffee stop.

Further and further I walked along the road until I saw masses of lights in the distance, which confirmed that Melle was now within my grasp. I had to complete the final couple of kilometres in darkness and stepped gratefully onto the pavement leading into Melle. Finding that the first building in town was a hotel, I looked no further and took a room there.

According to the map I was now on a direct collision course with the first mighty Autobahn on my route. Stories were legend back home of these immense German roads where there was no speed limit. I shrewdly decided to go nowhere near it and located an alternative route that would take me south east of Melle but allow me to cut back northwards towards the target town of Stadhagen. All went well as I saw the hub of the city disappearing over my left shoulder and the green fields beckoned me on. Two hours later I cut northwards. It took more than an hour to reach a suitably large junction signalling the eastward trail, but my heart sank when I saw the accompanying road signs: 28 kilometres to Minden and a further 18 to Stadhagen. I had spent more than three hours advancing only four kilometres. I felt absolutely wretched and was casting around for something to blame - the road, the signage, the map, the weather - but it was, of course, my own fault for trying to be clever without consultation. The final kick in the teeth came when I noticed that there was an excellent cycle path running parallel to the length of the Autobahn. I could have walked straight out of Melle with no need to veer from the direct eastward path. I needed a drink.

I stopped off at a pub in Bunde where an English barmaid gave me a free drink and, in consultation with staff and clients, it was agreed that I should make towards Kirchlengern as the revised target town for the day. I was told that it was another ten kilometres down the road, which was all I felt I could manage. In the event, it turned out to be only four kilometres away, which after the insane meanderings of the morning was a welcome miscalculation. I found a hotel easily enough and set off for a supermarket in the same street.

With a bright and early start the next morning, I confirmed directions and then set out in a huge circle, arriving back at the door of my hotel one hour later. The receptionist waved cheerily at me and I managed a smile through gritted teeth as my eyes scanned the horizon for the comedians who'd given me directions. I started off again, making modest progress along to Meissen. I was now a full day behind schedule but wasn't too worried as I had thoughtfully included a couple of shorter days for myself in the planning stage many months earlier. The Ratsklause guesthouse is really a pub with a few rooms let out almost as an afterthought. It certainly won't be troubling the good people of the *Michelin Guide*, but it was cheap at €25 for the night and the shower was piping hot.

The rain fell lightly on me as I progressed to Bad Nenndorf the next day. After that was the huge city of Hanover. Mindful of my previously angst-ridden experiences of walking through major cities, I determined to get through and out the other side by the close of the walking day. In the end, I settled for being in the heart of town and took a surprisingly cheap hotel in the middle of a busy shopping thoroughfare. It was Monday 29th November and therefore one month since I had started out from London, so I celebrated with fish and chips at a local restaurant. The best part of the day, however, was walking along the main street. Germany does Christmas really well - and Hanover was dressed up beautifully for the party. As expected, a typical Christmas market hogged the angles of several streets, but the best aspect was the dazzling array of lights bedecking each building from top to bottom and straddling the entire main street, looking as though it could be seen from outer space. Thousands of people milled around enjoying the night, despite the chill, with rosy cheeks, gloves and scarves and breath very visible in the illuminated streets. I joined the gaggle of folk savouring mulled wine and felt a warm, festive glow.

Walking the next day to Burgdorf, I became aware that my left shoulder had been aching more and more each day. The backpack was not heavy, but any adjustment to the straps meant that I had to contend with it either banging into the small of my back if loose, or restricting the circulation around my upper body when tight. I mused about getting some wheels, but didn't want to spend too much and also considered that a trolley or pushchair might impede me if I needed to move fast (i.e., jump out of the way of traffic). I pressed on and in the twilight slipped into the town of Uetze.

The town looked reasonably vibrant, but on casting my eyes in all directions there did not seem to be an abundance of hotels or guesthouses. I called out to a woman emerging from the local library to ask her if "der vas ein hotel hier". She started giving me directions, but on seeing my glazed eyes she instead beckoned me to follow her. She climbed into her car and opened the passenger door, inviting me to take a seat. She then drove me about 200 metres back the way I had just walked, smartly switched to a parallel street and stopped outside what she described at the best local guesthouse. After thanking her profusely, I stepped along the pavement and wondered what the odds were of a woman back home in England picking up a complete (foreign) stranger and driving him around town, just as a kind gesture. Pretty remote, I thought, as I entered the guesthouse.

The following day brought me to within seven kilometres of being back on schedule, staying over in Veyhausen and then moving on to Miesterhorst the next day. It was now December and I was making a worrying habit of spending the last hour or so walking in darkness; with no artificial lighting along the German country roads I was walking an increasingly risky path.

I found myself once again wandering along the country roads the following night in darkness as I made my way towards Vinzelburg. Standing perilously on the thin grass verge, between the pathless road and the ditch in almost complete darkness, the way was illuminated only by the headlights of oncoming traffic as the cars roared past. Edging my way along the narrow road, after eight hours of walking I finally saw a sign telling me that Vinzelburg was only two kilometres away. Although only 5:30 in the afternoon, the darkness and the cold indicated a much later hour and my pace had slowed not only due to the uncertain surface under my feet but also the onset of exhaustion. The sweat all over me was now being fanned by the night chill and I shivered slightly each time I had to stop to allow cars to pass. However, the endorphins must have kicked in at the sight of amber street lighting ahead, and I turned the last corner by a group of trees with a flourish, stepping onto the gloriously firm pavement, and entered the town.

And there it was - downtown Vinzelburg: a flower shop, a bank (both closed) and a bus stop; and to the left, rows and rows of residential housing. A moderate thrill of panic ran through me as it became clear that this was indeed it. After wandering around in ever-increasing circles, I came back to the flower shop and realised that, barring an early Christmas miracle, I would not be lying down to sleep in Vinzelburg that night. In desperation I tried to recall the words to 'Silent Night' in German. Positioning myself in front of the closest concentration of houses I began warbling, "Stille nacht, heilige nacht, alles schlaft, einsam wacht ..." The effect was less than dramatic. A couple of dogs barked and one curtain twitched. Then, once again, all was calm.

As I stood in this ridiculous position of finally arriving in a town with no place to stay, my internal voice kicked in with a vengeance. What were you thinking, setting off to walk around the world, with no back-up? Just you, walking alone through countries where you don't speak the language, don't know anyone, never booking any accommodation? What happens if you don't find a place to stay? What will you do if this happens in Russia? At what temperature do the vital organs cease to function? Who will tell your family how you were scraped up off the side of a road ...? And then I saw her.

Moving around her front garden, I saw a figure in the distance adjusting the lights on her Christmas tree. I set off at the best trot I could manage, but seeing that it was a middle-aged woman I slowed to a more measured stride and put on my best pathetic face. In the circumstances, this did not require too much effort.

"Entschuldigen Sie bitte - ist der ein hotel hier?" I squeaked.

"Hotel? Nein ...," she said sadly.

As soon as she said "nein" I knew it was going to be all right. This was not a lady to leave a poor, pathetic soul out on the street. Within five minutes I was sitting in her kitchen, enjoying a steaming hot cup of coffee and a jolly chat in which I managed to convey my mission. A taxi was called to take me 20 kilometres north to the city of Stendal and another was arranged to bring me back in the morning to pick up the walk where I'd left off. The alarm bells were silenced in my head and the clouds of panic, reproach and despair evaporated; As I stood to leave, I realised we had not been formally introduced. I needed at least to know the name of my German saviour.

"Ich heisse Mark," I said, "und Ihnen?"

"Ich heisse Frau Beckman," she replied, and then added with a twinkle, "Not David Beckham ..."

This brush with disaster immediately heralded a change of route to take me through to Berlin. Fortunately this only involved a small adjustment, but it meant I would be heading through larger towns than originally planned, in the hope that this would translate into places where accommodation was abundant. The first new target town was Tangermunde. I took a room at the Gastof Am Rathaus right in the middle of the town, a short cobble-stoned hop from the church and facing the site of a Christmas Festival that was in full swing when I arrived. My clothes were washed and I retired the old sweater I had started out with in favour of a new hooded sweatshirt.

I joined the party inside a marquee erected next to the church and sat munching sausage and cabbage, whilst watching the kids' entertainment on the nearby stage. Multi-coloured lights grew in ambience as the sun descended and families weaved in and out of the shops, loading their cars with presents, wrapping paper, fresh poultry and wine. For the first time it really hit me that I would not be home for Christmas this year. Of course, I had known this months ago in the planning, but now I actually realised it. I reflected that I couldn't really feel an iota of sympathy for myself as I was enjoying the adventure of anyone's lifetime, so missing one Christmas was a small price to pay. In any case, there was enough festive atmosphere permeating each day for me to enjoy.

I was now three days away from Berlin and a family reunion, as Mum, Dad and my Aunt Margaret were making a flying visit. There was, however, plenty to keep me miserable in the meantime.

Monday 6th December was, as noted in my logbook, a "rubbish" day. I woke at 4:20 in the morning and never got back to sleep. Eventually I emerged from the hotel at 8:30 and set off towards Brandenburg, with Potsdam and then Berlin to follow. A sign on the B1 road told me that it was 26 kilometres to Brandenburg and then ... 66 kilometres to Potsdam. Nooooooo! This was disastrous; in other circumstances I'd have shrugged my shoulders, but with the family arriving in a couple of days, failure was definitely not an option.

I headed off knowing I would need to make a serious dent in the overall distance of 92 kilometres to Potsdam. The B1 road was kind in one respect, in that it was one long, straight line with no unnecessary deviations. The next town was not for another 15 kilometres, so I made good progress with no distractions. Unfortunately it happened that this was the first time I suffered a dizzy spell. I had set off with no water and with the exertions of the morning and the anxiety about the distance I suddenly had a peculiar feeling that a giant thumb had pressed down on my head. I wobbled and lurched to the left, holding on to a tree at the side of the road. Steadying myself I turned out all my pockets and came up with a single chewy cough candy, which I popped into my mouth and chewed very slowly and deliberately. This excited some saliva, but a trickle rather than a gush. I walked on in a more measured way until reaching the next town.

I guzzled down a litre of water and felt a good deal better - or was that psychological? Whatever - it worked. I did benefit from the storming pace and found myself entering Brandenburg at 1:45. I knew from that position I could make some serious inroads into the remaining distance to Potsdam. Unfortunately once again I fell foul of a big city - getting out of Brandenburg was like trying to escape the earth's gravitational pull. It wouldn't let me go. By 3:15 I despaired at the fact that I had spent an hour and a half faffing around in the city instead of cutting into the distance to Potsdam.

I finally emerged at the junction of a large road heading east with a southern lilt and thundered off down the road, turning left back on to the B1 towards Potsdam. However, light was fading and I realised I needed to make plans for an overnight stay. Asking a postman where I could find a hotel, he advised me to go on another six kilometres to Gollwitz, where I would find a room.

In the twilight I edged past a huge shopping and leisure centre and then along a narrow stretch of road and had to wait for a train to cross. The lazy barrier rose and I walked on until a sign welcomed me to Gollwitz. Great!

Except … it was Vinzelburg all over again, but without the flower shop. With no carols to sing, I stood despondently under a street lamp, again surveying the rows of houses and wondering, now what do I do? Well déjà vu wasn't done with me yet. Walking down the street towards me was a middle-aged woman with a determined chin. I stepped back off the pavement, staying in the light, and once again assumed my pathetic stance.

"Entschuldigen Sie bitte. Ist der ein hotel hier?"

"Hotel? Nein."

"Kann ich telephone fur ein taxi bitte?"

"Ja - kommst du hier."

And for the second time I was led into a kitchen by a hausfrau who took pity on the sad-looking British chump. Except this time I did not need to wait for a taxi. Her husband was summoned and instructed to drive me to a hotel. He did not look impressed, but managed a grudging smile as he led me out again to the car. I think he had been looking forward to his dinner. "Brandenburg?" he enquired as we drove out. I winced inwardly at the prospect of going all the way back to the city I had just fought so hard to get out of, but with no better ideas I nodded. He dropped me at a taxi rank and I took a cab along to the Sorat Hotel Brandenburg.

The next day was a dream - literally. After getting a taxi back to Gollwitz and walking on, I cannot remember anything about the day until reaching the city limits of Potsdam. This was due to my penchant for daydreaming, of which I am an expert practitioner and strong advocate.

Daydreaming is a very underrated occupation. I don't recommend this when operating heavy machinery or performing surgery, but it is a completely harmless, free-of-charge method of self-indulgence. We all do it from time to time, often in replaying difficult situations where we always emerge triumphant, having got the upper hand and said all those things we should have done at the time! My own daydreams seem to have adjusted with my age; whereas I used to daydream about scoring the winning goal in the World Cup final, I now drift away as the manager of the winning team.

The long periods I spent alone, walking thousands of miles, afforded me several opportunities to slip into the private world of fantasy. On that day, walking through to Potsdam, I was again back in America, working at Disney World. Then I was on stage at Wembley Stadium, replacing Mick Jagger in a Stones concert (the soundtrack on my Walkman helped out with that one). I went on to win Wimbledon and finished off once again managing the England team to World Cup glory. As we were collecting the trophy I looked up and saw a sign indicating that Potsdam was only six kilometres away. I honestly could not remember a single thing about how I got there. No bad thing, I reflected, as it had anaesthetised me against the pain in my shoulder and the day had flown by, as had I by all accounts. I walked well into Potsdam, taking a room at the Hotel Mercure.

En route I had spotted a sign with a bicycle, indicating 14 kilometres to Berlin, so I happily checked my e-mails at a local Internet café, called Mum and Dad to confirm our rendezvous at the Brandenburg Gate the next day and chatted also to Harald, my host in the German capital. After the hiccups of the last week, things were looking up.

I lazily rose and left the hotel the next day and in the process of asking for directions met Michael, a young German chap living and working in Potsdam. Once introduced I told him about the walk and he was very intrigued, to the point that he said this demanded wider attention and he would try to get me into one of the newspapers. This was the first whiff of press attention since leaving England, so I was naturally very keen. To date, my selected cancer charities in Europe had been ignoring me, so I saw the chance to fly their flags even if they weren't cheering me on. We made our way to the offices of the *Potsdamer* newspaper, where I was interviewed and photos were taken. All this was eating into the morning, but I was very relaxed in the knowledge that I had only 14 kilometres to walk that day. Interview done, Michael walked with me to the edge of town. We chatted away about capitalism, globalisation, former East/West relations and the pivotal importance of Potsdam in recent history. I could have talked for hours, but felt I should be on my way. He pointed me in the direction of the main road across a bridge leading to Berlin. And then I saw it - a sign indicating 30 kilometres to Berlin. I felt that sinking feeling once again. It was now 1:15 and I was due to meet the family at the Brandenburg Gate at 3:30.

After a calf-busting two hours, I gave up the ghost, went into the railway station at Wannsee and caught the train into Berlin. I had allocated three days off whilst the family were here and decided that I would rise early on the Friday morning and come back to make up the distance (which I did).

A taxi took me from Berlin's central station to the Brandenburg Gate where after a short wait I heard a familiar voice calling out to me. I hugged Dad, then Mum then my Aunt Margaret. It was so great to see them! Margaret commented that I was looking remarkably fit, which led to enquiries from my parents about whether I was eating properly. After a photo shoot we went off to find a restaurant, but I immediately spotted a television crew filming on the other side of the Gate. I wandered over and introduced myself and explained what I was doing. They agreed to run the story if I could sing a Christmas song for them. So it was that I stood in the shadow of the Brandenburg Gate singing 'I'm Dreaming of a White Christmas' for German television. I then took on tourist duties in my first break since the start of the walk. Over three days we visited the Reichstag Parliament building, went shopping in the world famous KaDeWe store, saw Checkpoint Charlie and ate out to our hearts' content. Unfortunately on the second morning my mum's handbag was stolen, giving us an unwelcome opportunity to become familiar with the German police procedures, although the officer in attendance was very sympathetic.

With the imminent onset of the worst of the winter in Eastern Europe, I also updated my wardrobe with the family's help. Gore Tex boots were now on my feet, together with my new Gore Tex jacket on my back, and to complete the snug, waterproof ensemble, a pair of skiing trousers adorned my legs. Thus set, our minds wandered to the next leg through to Moscow. On Saturday 11th December I left Harald's place and took the train back into central Berlin to begin my trek into the East.

~ 8 ~
Go East Young Man!

The years may have passed since the reunification of east and west Germany, but there remains quite a way to go before the country is one in terms of development. As I left Berlin behind, I could see the same style of road signs, similar advertising boards and common cars passing me, but there was still an invisible line dividing the former communist east and the affluent west. Progress has no doubt been made, but the overall appearance east of Berlin is one of a more drab, weather-beaten land.

I passed through the uninspiring town of Ruderdorf and then set off for the border on the morning of Sunday 12th December. A thick mist hung over the slightly forested area and I crept along the narrow roadway. The day rather suited my mood. Having said goodbye to the family, I was now very conscious that they were heading back to the Christmas festivities, whilst I was left scratching around for cheap motels and a very basic diet in my self-imposed, strenuous exile. That, along with the increasingly drab surroundings, meant that I was in a sombre mood heading towards Munchberg.

My mood was not greatly improved by what I found on my arrival. To be fair, I may have been guilty of looking for things to confirm my bleak outlook, but the town seemed to fit the bill nicely. I took a hotel room in town and dinner at the local Chinese restaurant. My meal would have benefited greatly by being properly cooked, and I later sat despondently watching game shows that I didn't understand on a portable TV with one functioning channel. I was seriously in need of cheering up and vaguely hoped that crossing into Poland the next day would provide a lift.

Setting off at 7:30 the next morning, I walked more or less on automatic pilot through the towns of Jahresfeld, Diedersdorf and Seelow. A long hill descended out of Seelow, but there was thankfully no corresponding rise, so I continued along a long stretch of flat land. As the afternoon wore on, the signs for Kostryn, the first town in Poland, started to beckon me on. Some cars displayed licence plates bearing the Polish flag and, despite my flagging spirits, I felt a frisson of excitement about entering another country. As the daylight became less pronounced I walked across one river bridge and then another, which led to the still-monitored border crossing. The first thing on the other side of the bridge was an advertising board assuring those entering Poland that there was a McDonald's only 500 metres away. This was surrounded by a cluster of ominously grimy buildings.

I had just beaten the darkness, and after slogging through more than 40 kilometres I was in no mood to shop around for accommodation. Fortunately the first building that greeted me on Polish soil was the Hotel Bastion, which thoughtfully had a currency exchange on the ground floor. I exchanged my remaining euros for a fistful of zlotys, which covered the cost of my room and a bite to eat. I could see nothing of Kostryn itself, but could not shake off a feeling of apprehension that my first hours in Poland had engendered. I hoped that things would look better in the morning.

In the event, things were actually much worse in the morning. I got up, showered and breakfasted and then, with no great urgency, headed off towards the centre of Kostryn to find a map and get some money. Walking from my hotel into town, I was taken aback by the dreadful state of the place. The roads were cracked, the buildings were very ugly and tired, and the untreated footpaths gave awkward passage to the locals, who appeared to be wearing the world-weary air that set the tone for this very drab outpost. Welcome to Poland indeed.

Sitting on a bench at the side of a small patchy park, I made a decision: this was the end of the road. The prospect of walking through what would undoubtedly be more of the same for the next two months en route to Moscow would seriously sap my spirits, as well as my bank account. And if there was no enjoyment to be had from the venture, why continue? I still had a few thousand in the bank back home, which would see me through reintegration into 'normal life'. Cursing my own folly in spending so much on this pipe dream, I had hit rock bottom. Walking from London to Poland was in itself a laudable achievement, but it all seemed redundant now; the only thing that heartened me a little was the prospect of being home for Christmas. Whatever it took to be a 'world walker', I simply didn't have it and I accepted that now. The new road atlas of Poland was thrown into a garbage can and I walked back over to my hotel.

Sitting in the bar of the hotel with a whisky and Coke, feeling a conflict of emotions, I did what any other bloke from Essex would do in the circumstances. I phoned my mum.

My own personal quasi-tragedy then turned to farce as my mobile phone cut out twice whilst I was trying to explain in stilted terms my conclusion and reasons for it. The third time it refused to call England at all. I scuttled off to the shop to buy a phone card and then spent another five minutes getting instructions from the bar staff on how it worked. Of all the moments of frustration at the language barrier, this was the worst. I finally got back on the phone to Mum and managed to splurge the whole story out.

Now my mum, bless her, must have felt her heart leap at the prospect of my coming home rather than walking through Russia and beyond. However, she overcame her own feelings to set out for me the consequences of my decision. She painted a pretty accurate picture of me back in England a few weeks later, after the Christmas period had passed and the harsh blast of January reality hit me - the eternal pall of 'What if ...' hanging over me for the rest of my life. And she was quite right.

I strolled back to the garbage can and reached inside to pull out the road atlas. Back in the bar I finished my drink and consulted the staff about the day's walk. They told me that my original target town was very small and in the middle of a forest and they were pretty confident that there were no hotels of guesthouses there. With their assistance I adjusted the route slightly to the north with a new target town of Witnica, which would increase the overall distance but meant that I would only have to cover 23 kilometres for that day. Given my still fragile sensibilities, I figured this was the best course and set off.

Nothing I saw for the rest of the day changed my mind in terms of my initial impressions of Poland. The shadow of communist rule with all the money sucked into Moscow for the space race, then the arms race, is still very much in evidence, with horse-drawn carts on the land, crumbling and derelict buildings dotting the countryside and only nature's hand really showing pleasant views. It was a difficult day for me overall and I replayed the phone conversation in my mind several times, concentrating solely on the short-term aim of getting to Warsaw and then taking stock from there. I did reflect that after the euphoria of reaching Berlin, the family visit and the proximity of Christmas I should have expected a 'low'. It did make me wonder if I would have felt the same if it had been April with no festive season imminent.

I reached Witnica and took a chilly room in a draughty hotel. Nothing really mattered so much at that point, because I had overcome a real psychological test and had just managed to stay on my feet after a significant wobble. The next day saw me walking along grass verges for most of the time, which was not surprisingly heavy going, towards Gorzow WLKP. I believe the 'WLKP' means 'Great', which of course meant that I christened the town the 'Great Gonzo' after the meek little muppet. The town itself was huge, with the consequence that I spent an awfully long time trying to find a hotel. Sadly, the local Poles were not the friendliest bunch, ignoring me as I approached them for help.

Finally one woman pointed me in the direction of the Hotel Mieszko, which apparently was the best place in town. For 180 zloty (£35) I was given a nice, spacious room with the BBC Prime channel on television. The downstairs restaurant was enormous, but the decor hinted more at former glories and the velvet and brass were well past their best. So too were the vegetables I had with my fish, but the vodka made everything just fine.

They are not shy with the vodka in Poland. The next day I was negotiating a potentially tricky road switch to put me back on the original route towards Skwierzyna and stopped at a roadside bar for my usual lunchtime swifty. The barmaid poured vodka from the bottle into my glass until it was more than halfway up. I took the accompanying can of Coke and tried to add as much as possible to dilute it to my taste. The first burning gulp almost came back up again. By the time the whole glass had been drained, I was giddily ready to walk to Moscow that very day, whilst singing *West Side Story* in its entirety. Miraculously, I managed the road switch successfully and Skwierzyna appeared before long. This town, too, looked fairly dilapidated, although some newer buildings towards the river gave cause for hope. It was next to the river that I found a likely looking hotel for the night.

I walked into the Dom Nad Rzeka hotel and checked in. Curiously they did not ask for payment up front as was normally the procedure, but just handed me the key. After showering I was reluctant to pull on my boots again and stepped nimbly in my socks down to reception to confirm they wouldn't mind if I attended the hotel restaurant without footwear. I started explaining my mission to the receptionist and she stopped me mid-flow to tell me that they already knew all about me and the room was free for the night. Eh? Then I remembered. I had recently received a message from a new online friend, Radoslaw, with whom I would be staying just outside Poznan, to say that he had sent around 20 e-mails to various hotels all across Poland requesting free accommodation for me. He had scored a hit with this place and I was ecstatic.

With my recently caned spirits taking a lift, I walked on the next day, up a steep climb and then along flat land towards the next stop, Gorzyn. All the time I was walking through Poland, I benefited from a generous hard shoulder at the side of the road and so didn't need to worry too much about the oncoming traffic. I did, however, maintain constant vigilance of the cars and trucks advancing on me at speed, making eye contact where possible, as it was unlikely they would expect anyone to be walking along the highways. It was my vigilance that saved my skin that morning.

I saw a white van driving at high speed towards me, although I could not see the driver through the glass. About 20 metres in front of me, the van swerved onto the shoulder and was heading straight at me. I had seconds to react and flung myself sideways against the crash barrier at the side of the road. The whoosh of air was inches from my splayed body as I clung to the barrier. Seconds later the van had passed and veered back into the centre of the road. The shock of this near fatal encounter ripped through my frame and I stood momentarily unable to move. Breathing hard, I sank into a seated position on the barrier and felt my heartbeat throbbing in my temples. Sweat trickled down the side of my face despite the cold. To this day I don't know whether the driver had meant me harm or his hands simply followed his eyes in gazing at the strange figure walking along the side of the busy highway.

Composure regained, I continued walking and at length arrived at the little town of Przytoczna. A bar was located and a vodka and Coke very gratefully supped. The road east then became a little more - shall we say - interesting. The flatlands were left behind as the forestry dividing two counties took over. Long, sweeping woods of trees filled the undulating land and the road rose and fell to match the landscape. For the last two hours of the day's walk I saw no buildings and was experiencing the pure, unadulterated majesty of the Polish land. As I scaled one particular hill, my mobile phone rang. It was BBC Essex Radio back in England asking if they could do an interview to update the listeners back home. Of course, but not right now ... why did they always call when I was climbing uphill?

The road finally levelled off and I saw a sign indicating I was entering Gorzyn. I called in to the Zajazd Ostep guesthouse - what a find! - a mostly wooden structure, with a gorgeous little restaurant area with an open log fire. Upstairs I was given the option of a standard room or the 'apartment'. After viewing both and being informed that the apartment was 100 zloty I quickly accepted the latter. Bedroom, lounge with leather seating, bathroom and dressing room - all for £20 for the night. After a shower I wandered down to the restaurant and took the table right next to the fire. A delicious mixed grill followed and the fire crackled merrily as I sat enjoying a brandy whilst watching the highway traffic sweep past. After the wobble entering the country, my sensibilities were restored and I felt good about life in general.

~ 9 ~
Chilled Out

And then the snow came … Overnight, as I slept in the cosy guesthouse, the first snows of winter fell extensively. Stumbling towards the window on waking, I propped my glasses on my nose and gazed out at the winter wonderland. I emitted a slight gasp of pleasure at the beautiful vista before me. About 1½ seconds later, however, I thought to myself, I've got to walk through that.

After breakfast I stepped out at 9:30 and after a couple of manoeuvres that Torvill and Dean would have been proud of, I set foot back on the side of the road. A quick survey of the conditions convinced me that road walking was not an option, so I began the truly cumbersome trudge along the verge, the grass and gravel completely covered by a thick carpet of snow. This naturally made progress very slow and I did not have any handy clumps of grass to sit and rest on. The arduous day ended at Pniewy and I hoped there would be no more snow for a while.

In the event, of course, the next day we got more snow. Not at first though. I was given a clear two hours of walking along the slush-laden highway before being forced inside for a Coke stop at Podrzewle. At that point the light, dusty sprinkles of snow gathered pace sharply, but fortunately my new outfit of head-to-toe Gore Tex kept me toasty warm and, equally importantly, dry. I sat mulling over my Coke with the other good folks. We all seemed to be gazing out of the window wondering when would be the right time to set out again. At least they all had vehicles to get into.

Back on the road, each footstep brought that familiar creak of body weight crushing snow and as I looked around it really was quite a view, with the fields and upcoming forests dressed in their winter finery. I had been primed by an old Polish friend back in England to expect freezing temperatures and, this being one week before Christmas, I wasn't too surprised. It did present the most hazardous passage I had faced so far since starting out almost two months earlier.

The town of Bytyn was my chosen midday break spot and I was relieved to see the signs indicating that the distance was now in single figures. Alas, as I walked along a particularly challenging road with a wide ditch at the side, the snow returned with a vengeance. The sky above, the path before me - dammit my own personal space - was invaded by a furious rush of thousands of snowflakes. I could not see more than a few metres in front of me, the flakes thrown by the increasingly strong breeze into my face. I spat them out, blinked furiously as they assaulted my eyes and finally halted, turning my back on the road ahead to get some relief. Looking sideways I gained a perspective of the snow storm that had descended and into which I had walked. It was relentlessly smothering the land all around - nature's caress compared with the hammering hail or sleet I had seen before, but just as perilous. Just ahead I saw a gas station with an adjoining café and with very careful steps I inched towards it.

In the entrance to the gas station shop I shook myself like a dog and watched the flakes cascade off me before stepping inside. I took a miniature bottle of vodka and a can of Coke and sat to watch the storm. It was as if the gods were having a huge pillow fight, scattering the feathered debris across the landscape. I ruefully felt that it would be impossible to continue and wondered about my next move, as the last town had not presented any accommodation options. As my mind started to wander towards taxis, the snow stopped abruptly. The air was instantly clear, but the downpour had softened the soundtrack to this scene. I left my drink and walked out to survey the road ahead. Tricky, but with no further snowfalls it was possible. I set off.

Three hours later I was still walking, on the road when it was clear, and scrambling onto the bank when traffic came along. The day's exertions were really taking their toll on my body and spirit and I decided not to worry about making the target town of Tarnowo Podgorne, but instead get into the next hotel or guesthouse that I saw. The locals in the small villages that I passed through were unwilling to offer help, so I carried on relentlessly until I saw a sign telling me that the 500 Hotel was two kilometres away. Sweet relief. I was walking on empty at that stage, with any nutrients from my breakfast long exhausted and the kick from the unfinished vodka and Coke worn away. My right calf was aching terribly as I scaled a rise in the road and I groaned audibly at the top. A long downhill stretch before me was supplanted with a long incline up the other side. I made my weary way down and, at a very stilted pace, heaved myself up the other side, and then felt a final injection of adrenalin as I spotted the hotel entrance sign just ahead on the left.

As I trod those final steps I glanced across the road and saw a sign welcoming travellers to Tarnowo Podgorne - I'd made it! The most challenging day so far had ended in triumph and I hugged myself as I bent my stride up the steps and into the hotel. To add to the bliss, tomorrow would be the day I finally got to meet my Polish champion, Radoslaw, and Poznan was only 22 kilometres away. A meal and bath later, I lay on the bed thinking of nothing but the twisting fortunes of the day.

Arriving in Poznan the next day, it was immediately obvious where all that 'new investment' in Poland had manifested itself. Forget the small towns and villages with their cracked concrete streets and crumbling buildings - here was a first-class precinct of modernity. The hotels, restaurants, squares and avenues smacked of new money flowing in. Keen-as-mustard investors had identified Poland as a place with great potential for growth, which for many means an inevitable replication of the capitalist pyramid of the masses making money for the few. Others offer the pragmatic view, that rising employment levels and standards of living outweigh the disparities.

All of which brought me to sipping a very expensive vodka and Coke in a sumptuous hotel bar in downtown Poznan. Having checked the map, I saw that I had a few kilometres left to walk in order to reach Swalzedz and my much-anticipated meeting with Radoslaw (from here, referred to as Radic) and his family.

Across a bridge and onto another long, winding road, I made my way to the far side of the provincial town and, in failing light once again, looked along the road to see, standing sentry on the far edge of Swalzedz, a collection of identical apartment blocks arranged in uniform rows with a labyrinth of walkways and built-in shop units on the perimeter of each. As I approached and made my way into the concrete warren, I felt a little unnerved to be wandering around these monolithic structures, which in England would often conceal the grubby race of drug dealers and their clients.

Radic later explained to me that these were a hangover of the Soviet influence. The workers who flocked to the city needed somewhere to live, so this ugly, soulless linear mess had been thrown up with no consideration of the requirements of human habitation beyond the functional. They stood as testament to some 'revolutionary' architect who no doubt planned with great relish the vertical estates in the classic sixties drab fad, which we too had suffered from in Britain. It almost goes without saying that the architect would have had no thought of living there himself.

I was still early for my rendezvous with Radic, so I took a seat in a hotel bar adjacent to his block. Outside, the streets looked so very cold, with snow lining each walkway and well-wrapped locals scurrying along, their hot breath pumping out like chugging miniature steam engines. Radic arrived a little while later and we shook hands warmly before making our way back to his family's apartment, where I met his parents and his younger brother, Marek. The apartment was identical to all the others in the block but, like the other families within, they had furnished and decorated it to put their own stamp on the place. One large rectangular lounge/dining room with a small bathroom and bedrooms off the hallway, with plenty of family photographs and a multitude of books and knick-knacks dotted around, made for a very cosy family home and I was made most welcome.

Radic and I chatted long into the night about the post-communist era, the dawn of European Union membership, our respective tales of travelling and the niceties of our own societies. The Polish people, he confirmed, can be a little insular at times, not wanting to mix much outside of their own social circles. Not unheard of back in England, of course, but I admitted I'd experienced quite a lot of cold-shouldering since arriving in the country; conversely, I'd also been treated to some great acts of kindness. The latter was certainly true of Radic and his family. His mother was anxious that I should be able to wash my clothes and be sure of where I was walking the next day, insisting that I run through the map with them twice. She also gave me a beautifully illustrated card depicting St Christopher to keep me safe. Radic's father was a little more reticent, perhaps being of a generation that did not easily trust strangers, but he dutifully shook my hand and wished me good luck in German. As I prepared to leave them, Radic gave me details of two more hotels that had agreed to give me free lodgings, on the portentous dates of 23rd, 24th and 25th December. Now I knew I had a place to stay at Christmas.

I walked on through Nekla and Wrzesnia towards Slupca, where in a very short space of time I experienced both extremeties of Polish attitudes. A long, hard walking day came to a close when I entered Slupca, a grimy industrial town annexed by a small consumer shopping quarter. Passing the factories on the outskirts, I saw a blue street sign with a picture of a bed on it - the international sign denoting a hotel ahead. Walking into the main shopping street, I went into a store and asked were the hotel was. "No hotel" came the reply from a pair of giggling teenagers. Well, kids being what they are sometimes, I headed across the street and made the same enquiry of a pair of gents in their forties working in an opticians. Same reply and louder laughing as I left. Strange, I thought, in a land that makes so much of wearing its Christian values proudly, that they would be so rude to a stranger clearly in need of help.

Cold, tired and hungry as I was, I stopped at a taxi rank and asked the driver if he could take me to the nearest hotel. He fairly bounced out of his seat, took my backpack and rested it carefully in the back, and then held open the passenger door for me. He scrabbled around in his pile of music cassettes, finally finding a tape of Elvis Presley, presumably for my benefit. 'Hound Dog' came roaring out of the stereo and he cranked his neck to give me a gappy smile, before joining the King for a chorus.

His shoulders jigging in time to the music, he roared, "Yew ain nuthin bit a hand dawg ...!", and glanced once again over his shoulder at me, with a look of keen anticipation. I felt compelled to react favourably to the first friendly, if a little frantic, face I'd seen for days.

"Jus cryin alla time!" I bellowed back. And the pair of us chugged our jolly way along the freezing streets of Slupca. As the snow began to fall once again, the filthy air ran thick with industrial fumes and the tired fairy lights in the little town square failed to brighten the overall view. It didn't matter. I was bouncing along with the Polish Elvis, belting out the tunes and giving the rest of the town the old V-sign.

Time was marching on and, to keep pace with it, so was I. On the next day - 23rd December - I decided I would walk on to Konin as planned, but would then take the train on to Kutno on Christmas Eve to take up the kind offer from the Hotel Rondo for a festive two-day break. This would mean another train back again to pick up the trail and fill in the missed two days of walking. The day of walking to Konin was anything but festive, as the rain came with a vengeance. The snowy road became slushy very quickly and by the afternoon great puddles of water lined the way. Up, down, up, down I wended my way along, getting filthy in the seeping mud as I passed one dreary village after another. Finally the large city of Konin loomed into view and I checked into the Hotel Fugo for my free night, safe in the knowledge that there was no more walking for me for the next two days.

Ah, Christmas. My favourite time of the year. I always enjoy Christmas, with carols, food, family, friends, gifts and extending my own volumes of goodwill to all men (and women). Luckily I found kindred spirits at the Hotel Rondo. I took the train from Konin to Kutno and a taxi to the hotel. On arrival I was told by the receptionist, "Everything is free for you." The owner, Mr Zylak, was Father Christmas himself, not only providing me with food and accommodation on the 24th and 25th, but also contacting the media, with the result that I was due to be interviewed on Polish national television on Christmas Day. Excellent!

I unpacked in my room and went straight into the dining room for a very tasty fish lunch. A trip into town brought a large bottle of vodka, a carton of orange juice and a selection of chocolate bars. Back at the hotel, I sank back onto the bed and, to my unmitigated delight, I found that British Sky News was beamed direct from the UK. I spent three ecstatic hours glued to the cyclic news bulletins, watching and listening time and again about strikes by postal workers, last-weaved Christmas shoppers at the Bluewater shopping mall in Kent, the Government's Christmas 'Don't Drink and Drive' campaign and all the glorious Year In Review shows. As someone who had not seen anything of the news from back home for so long, I drank in every detail, combined with a couple of vodka and orange cocktails.

Christmas Day! I woke and stumbled out of the hotel room to find that all the staff were working normally and had prepared some yoghurt, toast and coffee for me in the breakfast room. As I was sipping my coffee, the chap on reception politely asked if I could go downstairs, as the TV people were in reception. I bounced down and did an interview, with my new friend on reception translating the questions and my answers as best he could. We then went out into the street to film some action shots, culminating in my walking into another room in the hotel, taking off my boots and lying out on the bed. Later that evening, the feature was run on the evening news on TVP3 across the nation.

I spoke with all the family and some friends on the phone and, following a quick e-mail, also got a mention on Sky News beamed across Europe. In between lunch and dinner, I lazed around in my room, slowly drinking most of the vodka until I lay quite sated, thinking of a relatively early night ahead of being back on the road the next day.

At 8:00 in the evening, I heard a knock at the door. The first lady I had met on reception stood there and told me that the owner and his wife sent their compliments and would like to invite me to a Christmas Day supper. Naturally I accepted, but first had to stick my head under a lukewarm shower to try to shake off the effects of the vodka. Thus refreshed, I walked out of my room, down the corridor and into the restaurant.

Mr and Mrs Zylak sat waiting for me, together with the receptionist who was there to act as translator. Mr Zylak had a little English, but his wife was bilingual in Polish and Russian only. The table was full of every kind of snack you could imagine, which I was not exactly ready for - the sudden intake of three meals that day after a couple of months of only two meant that my stomach felt fit to burst. I bravely attacked the sandwiches and chewed slowly to try to give the impression that I was eating constantly. We chatted about the economic prospects for that region and Poland in general, until at a suitable pause in the conversation Mr Zylak looked at me with a little smile and said,

"Vodka?" Having already sunk enough that day to make an elephant languid, everything inside me screamed "Nooooo" - but of course I politely agreed.

At 11:00, our little party broke up and I managed to thread my way through the tables and chairs of the restaurant without incident. Trying each corridor in turn, I finally made it back to my room, which I had wisely left unlocked. There is a stage of drunkenness in which lying down makes the entire world spin faster on its axis than nature ever intended, but merely sitting down had that effect on me. I opened my eyes as wide as they would go in a strange bid to minimise the spinning and my left contact lens promptly fell out. Staring down dumbly to see where it had gone, I inadvertently achieved a closer examination of the floor with a gentle thud. I took the other lens out for good measure and felt my way along to my backpack containing my glasses. In the bathroom I guzzled several glasses of water and took a long, hot shower. I dried off and sat on the bed once again. My next memory involved daylight breaking through the curtains.

~ 10 ~
Happy New Year?

Ah, those traditional Boxing Day walks ... were never like this! After missing the first train back to Konin, which left at 9:20 (grrrr) I had to wait around until 10:50 for the next one, with the result that I didn't start walking out of Konin until 11:45. This was not a good start.

The A2 road led out of town and once again eastwards. The road was very undulating and amid the ups and downs I found it very difficult to get back into the swing. The combination of two days off and the usual Christmas excesses compressed into those two days meant that it was very heavy going. Kolo wasn't that far and the day would obviously have been a good deal calmer if I had set off at 9:00, but the late start meant that the daylight was always against me.

Coming along the approach into town, I passed the Europa hotel. My puffing, struggling frame dearly wanted just to call it a day and flop onto a bed, but I kept going as there were still another eight kilometres to go. I finally walked off the main road and into Kolo at 4:30, which all in all wasn't bad going. I sat on a bus stop bench briefly, and then made a leisurely stroll into the main town. By now the sun was gone and the familiar amber shades illuminated the town centre, but all the shops were closed and the place seemed pretty dead. I stopped to ask a gentleman where I could find a hotel. With the language barrier at its highest point once again, he gestured to me with a sweeping hand that the next hotel was way down the road ahead. How many kilometres I asked? He held up all fingers of both hands. Ten kilometres? Here comes that sinking feeling again.

The gent asked me to follow him, which I did. We arrived outside his house and he asked me to wait for a moment. A few minutes later he emerged with his English-speaking son who explained they would give me a ride to the nearest hotel. The state I was in, I agreed with thanks. Off we went, with son asking his own curious questions and translating his father's. However, when

58

the car swung out onto the road, we were not heading east to the hotel he had previously referred to. Nope, we were heading back the way I had come and arrived soon on the doorstep of - you guessed it - the Europa hotel I had passed a couple of hours previously. I didn't care. I thanked them and headed in gratefully.

The next day was a 40-kilometre slog to Krosniewice. With seven kilometres to go, I arrived at the little village of Czarwonka and with a very thick mist gathering I decided to take a room in the little motel on the side of the road. In reality it was a gas station with a crummy café attached and a few rooms thrown in. I checked in with a very young receptionist, whom I was clearly inconveniencing just by being alive. The room cost me the equivalent of £12. Now, although I was always looking for a bargain, this place fell below the minimum line. It was absolutely freezing, with no heat coming from the heater; the portable television had wires hanging out which crackled menacingly even after I had switched off the set and the shower was cold. I went down to confer with the surly girl behind the counter, stating I wanted to call a taxi to take me into Krosniewice. I was then subjected to a series of facial expressions to indicate that this monumental task was quite beyond her.

At this moment, Damian introduced himself. He was sitting with his wife and young son having a meal in the café and, on hearing my pleas in English, he asked if there was anything he could do to help. He did his best to raise a taxi for me, but with no luck. Eventually he said, "We can take you into Krosniewice if you like", and half an hour later he dropped me off with a smile and wave outside the Rubina hotel in town.

The hotel also housed a restaurant with a dance hall, which that night was playing host to a party for a large group of the town's young folk. I sat eating my dinner, watching the teenagers drink, dance and practise their cool. The scenes that unfolded before me could have been replayed with a group of teenagers anywhere. The fat kid was popular, but not fancied; the three untouchable ice maidens looked down with magnificent disdain on all they surveyed; the hunk wandered around in a t-shirt to emphasise his muscular build; the two sweethearts looked like they'd rather be alone, but felt obliged to stay. With my thinning and greying hair I was safely detached from the proceedings, although I was incongruously wearing the same uniform of jeans and hooded sweatshirt. They partied on whilst I made a weary trudge back up to my room.

Walking back into Kutno the next day, the Hotel Rondo welcomed me once again with another free room for the night and food. As I walked into the now-familiar town square again, a group of boys, no more than 10 years old mobbed me - they had seen me on TV!

"Can you speak English?" I enquired.

"Yes," came the reply from the boldest.

"My name is Mark," I said. "What is your name?"

"My name is Dominic," he returned.

"How do you do, Dominic?" I said in an exaggerated greeting and shook hands with him.

"How do you do?" he replied, grinning. They then all ran off laughing and pointing back at the famous British explorer. Sweet.

Relaxing later back in my hotel room, I tuned in once again to Sky News, looking forward to seeing the preparations for the New Year celebrations around the world. What I saw to my growing horror was the ever-burgeoning tragedy of the Asian tsunami. Any trials and tribulations I was facing instantly shrank into the minor irritations they truly were in comparison.

The next day I walked on to Lowitcz, just a couple of days away now from Warsaw where I had arranged a rendezvous with the Russian Embassy. The requirements for obtaining a Russian visa are quite straightforward, but I had been told I cannot apply and be granted my visa less more than 26 days before I was due to enter the country. So I had made arrangements with a specialist travel agency in London to pick up the visa at the Russian Embassy in Warsaw.

Lowitcz was a pleasant town and I had the bonus of staying at the Zajazd Lowicki hotel, just off the highway. Agnes on reception was very excited about having me as a guest after seeing me on TV and she immediately called the local newspaper. The owner of the *Lowitczer* newspaper, Worjiech, duly came out, interviewed me and took pictures for the next issue. He gave me a tour of the town and explained how once Poland had been freed from communist control in the '90s, the newly free press meaning that he could set up his own local newspaper. It's another of those things that so many of us have taken for granted in our lives, that a newspaper will succeed or fail as a result of public response rather than state control. We wished each other well and parted.

I spent the last day of 2004 walking along a seemingly endless, uninteresting road beneath a dull, overcast day. No great scenery distracted my mind from the mundane process of putting one foot relentlessly in front of the other. The E30 road offered no bus shelters with benches to rest on, so I continued on my solitary way through the delicate rain, which was busy banishing the last vestiges of the snow to oblivion. I spotted a sign on the side of the road announcing the 3-Star Hotel Chopin in Sochawecz and concluded that this sounded like the kind of place I would like to spend my time seeing in the New Year.

I got a twin room at the Chopin and immediately dashed out to get in the essential vodka and a few chocolate bars for the evening's celebrations. The shops were closing fast and I had to plead to be allowed in, but managed to get those essential items to see in the New Year with elan. Back at the hotel I took a roast turkey supper in the room, as there was a private party under way in the restaurant/ballroom. BBC World kept me entertained for the evening and the town's fireworks ensured there was no sleep until after midnight. I linked my own hands together to sing 'Auld Lang Syne' alone in my room. Happy New Year!

I spent the first day of 2005 trekking along what appeared to be a never-ending, uninspiring road under yet another grey sky. Arriving in Blonie, a taxi driver pointed out the nearest hotel, which was standing in fortressed majesty akin to Fort Knox. Buzzing me in through the high metalled fencing, I was greeted by a manager of immense personality. After securing me in the hotel's clutches he was not going to allow me to stay anywhere else. With a booming voice he explained the hotel policy in excellent German, allowing me to understand one word in every five. I eventually surmised that the hotel was locked up for the night at 8:00 and was not unlocked again until 8:00 the following morning. What kind of a town was this?

The restaurant was closed, but rather than let me out to go in search of food they thoughtfully scraped up a collection of leftovers from the previous night's New Year party for my supper, which was duly washed down by a very warm but much appreciated glass of wine. After showering, I stepped out into the lobby which was now shrouded in darkness and all doors were indeed locked up. As I sat watching *Batman* in Polish, I wondered what would happen if a fire broke out, as I didn't fancy the 30-foot leap out of my window.

Setting off the next day for Warsaw, I couldn't help feeling a little chuffed that I had overcome the major wobble a couple of weeks earlier and had managed to stiffen my resolve and make it through to the capital. The day was essentially a trawl through village after village, until the landscape on the horizon grew steadily more urbanised. The raggy pathway became more regular, the two-lane highway grew to four lanes and I saw in the far-off distance the monster shoeboxes of apartment blocks and in their midst some glossier skyscrapers. Suffused with a boosting vodka and Coke, I walked in sunshine to the heart of the Polish capital, almost 1,000 miles from London to Warsaw now completed.

I had previously made contact with a new friend on the Internet, who had agreed to accommodate me in Warsaw, but I had no contact details and no apparent Internet café presented itself. I therefore settled for a room at Days Inn with a comparatively astronomical cost of 250 zlotys for the night (£50). The sting of that cost faded quickly as I sat in the room, showered and rested easy on the bed.

A curious feeling of fate laying its hands over my plans crept over me as I dozed, contemplating the next stage. I don't claim to have any sixth sense, but something told me the task of getting my Russian visa the following day and then continuing eastward would not be as smooth as I would have hoped. It didn't matter that night. I had walked from London to Warsaw and was feeling more than a little proud.

The next day, armed with a tourist map of Warsaw, I made my way towards the Embassy district. The Russians had granted themselves a very grand building to house their Embassy staff and I let out a low whistle at the splendour. Things seemed very quiet. I peered through the gates and a young immaculately uniformed Russian soldier asked what I wanted. I muttered "Embassy" and "visa" and he directed me to the next building. Strolling along, I noticed that the gates were also locked up at the front of this wing of the complex. A small, handwritten sign was stuck on the bars written in Polish and the peculiar Cyrillic Russian language. I could not read a word of it, needless to say, but the date of 17th January leapt off the page. I pressed the buzzer and a voice barked a volley of Russian at me. I yelled into the box, "English!", and he came back to me with one word: "Closed".

And so it was that I learned the Russians take an extremely long New Year break. The Embassy, with the instructions to grant my visa tucked inside one of their pigeonholes, was closed until 17th January. With five days' processing time, this meant that I could not set off for another 22 days. The significance sank in very quickly, as did my reflections on the days missed, which had put me behind schedule - if I had arrived a few days earlier, this would not have been a spoiling issue. I realised that I had three basic options: stay put in Warsaw for the next three weeks until I could collect my visa; carry on walking and try to get my visa in Lithuania; or return to England and get matters sorted at the London Embassy.

In view of the price of hotel accommodation, staying in Warsaw was immediately dismissed. With my tight budget, I could not afford it. The second option of walking on to Lithuania bounced around my mind for a while, but the logistics of getting to the capital, Riga (way off my walking route), and trying to co-ordinate the re-sending of my authorisation from

Warsaw to Riga via the London travel company left too many uncertainties. The last option became the only option: fly back to England, rest up with my parents and then, with visa in hand, return to Warsaw to pick up the walk a few weeks later.

The prohibitive price of flights from Warsaw to London meant I ended up taking a train from Warsaw to Berlin, staying overnight in the German capital and then flying out on a budget airline, arriving back at London Stansted on 3rd January 2005.

Despite the disappointment of the sudden halt in proceedings, it was not without a little pleasure that I stepped off the plane in London to be greeted by my parents. Back in the family home that night I sat chewing a bacon sandwich, 48 hours after arriving in Warsaw.

~ 11 ~
Back on the Road

My stopover back in Britain was slightly elongated, firstly due to the five visits I had to make to the Russian Embassy in London and then by the horrendous weather conditions gripping Eastern Europe. Temperatures plummeted and television reports showed Poland in particular being deluged by snow.

One significant development was that I had visited the charity shops around Southend and emerged with a second-hand baby stroller/buggy for £10. Now I could rest my aching back and shoulders, pushing the backpack along. The Pram had joined the Man. I also invested in a bright yellow fluorescent workman's vest and wrote on the back 'World Walker for Cancer Charities' with details of the route - good not only for promotion of the cause, but also for visibility.

Unfortunately, as the plane touched down in Warsaw the snow was still very much in evidence, with more swirling around as I made my way through Customs and out onto the streets outside. I had finally been able to contact my host, Wojiech, who came to pick me up from the airport and took me back to his apartment in the city. It was quite a pleasure to meet such a jolly Pole, who fed and watered me whilst earnestly telling me to buy a Kalashnikov rifle before setting foot inside Russia. The following morning Wojiech escorted me to the outskirts of Warsaw and, after several weeks of inaction, I started back out on the road again.

I was terribly excited about using the baby stroller for the first time and it all went very well for the first 30 seconds. However, I then hit the first trench of snow and slush and the thing skidded in all directions. Looking down in front of me, I saw the front wheels shuddering and the small metal rod rattling in protest. How long is this going to hold up? I wondered. Passing through the town of Marki, I progressed onto Highway 8 and hit a clear patch of road and shoulder. Now I romped along, stroller cutting a bold path before me, with a quiet hum of wheels on tarmac as we raced along. At that point I experienced the first instance of something that would continue for many months to come - the horrified stares of drivers rushing past me, wondering what on earth that idiot was doing pushing a baby along the highway. This gave a little light relief to my efforts, which were pretty strenuous on the first day back. I made it to Radzymin at a little after 2:00, which was great going in the circumstances, and headed for the Hotel Duet which Wojiech had kindly arranged for me.

After the long lay-off, I experienced all the delights of life on the road revisiting me in one fell swoop that day. My legs, back and feet all ached as I slumped into the room. The shower was freezing, so I used it for my lower half only and washed head and torso using the sink and flannel. The TV was Polish language only and the fold-out table was for entertainment purposes only, as there was no catch to prop it up. The room temperature was marginally greater than that outside and the mattress could have doubled up as an ironing board. Apart from that the place was great ...

I went berserk the next day, covering the target distance by 12:45. I sat rather bemused in the town of Zabrodski, wondering if I could possibly call it a day. I didn't feel exhausted by any means, so after a well-deserved vodka and Coke I decided to press on. It was nice to be ahead of schedule for a change. The road continued to be easy going as I rolled along, finally arriving in Kryszkow. I asked a taxi driver to take me to the cheapest hotel in town and he whisked me off northwards, dropping me outside a building that bore more than a passing resemblance to a derelict hospital. As I stepped inside, it would not have surprised me in the least to see the corridors resplendent with patients and trolleys, but instead the hallways were adorned with peeling wallpaper and evidence of long untreated damp. Down the largest hallway I unearthed the reception desk and was heartened to learn that one night's accommodation would cost me the equivalent of £8.

Just across from the hotel was a huge supermarket, with a series of smaller shops attached. I emerged with a loaf of bread, cheese spread and a pack of sliced ham which was remarkably devoid of taste. I also picked up a pack of plastic knives, as I knew I would be having similar meals in the future - not exactly nutritional but certainly functional and cheap. I sat in the hotel room, with cellophane wrapping scrunched over the dressing table, and prepared my modest supper. The TV crackled into life and a documentary about the wolves in Poland gave me pause for thought. I had already spent a few weeks walking through remote areas with forests all around. Was I passing through wolf territory? I reflected that attacks were rare, the traffic probably keeping most animals away from the road and, anyway, I now had my plastic knives for defence ...

Ostrow was a 35-kilometre hike the next day, followed by a slightly shorter trek to Zambrow. Now I think it's fair to describe Zambrow as a city, due to the boldness of its name in the atlas, together with the conurbation shading on the map. It was certainly big enough to spend an age walking around. After asking three times of the locals where the nearest hotel was located, I had added another hour's toil on my feet. I finally asked a taxi driver to drop me at the door of the hotel. He protested, waving his hand to indicate it was so close as not to be worth his while. Then I made my first mistake - pulling out a 20 zloty bill as an inducement to get him to take me. He gleefully pocketed the money and drove me for about 30 seconds back down the town entrance road and left me outside the cleverly disguised guesthouse. I walked into reception and up and down a few narrow corridors, but not a soul was around. Disgruntled, I knocked on the door of the café below. A woman came out and via wild eyes and a wilder array of hand gestures I got the gist of it - the guesthouse was not open for business.

I trudged back up the road into town again and swear I saw the same taxi driver licking his lips as I reappeared. He knew what was coming next and offered to take me to another hotel in another town, but I'd have to pay him 30 American dollars. He pulled out a threadbare map from the glove compartment and pushed a stubby finger along the page to indicate the town of Lomza. I checked my own road atlas and noted that whilst I would be taken badly off course by this I could rejig my planned progress for the coming days to compensate and still stay on schedule. Besides, I had no choice. With no Polish language and knowing nobody in the region, this git had me stitched up like a kipper.

He dropped me at the Gromada hotel in Lomza, which on an unlimited budget would have been my hotel of choice in town, but was painful with my limited funds. I handed over the 30 American dollars as agreed and made my way up to my room, punching the wall to vent my spleen at the day's events. Roll on the end of Poland.

Things went from bad to farce the next day. Highway 61 took me out of Lomza and after a massive dip and climb in the road, I was rewarded with a shoulderless stretch to Stawiski. Whilst grinding my way through, trying to keep self and stroller safe from oncoming traffic, I came into a particularly thick area of woodland. There appeared to be one of those unofficial footpaths trailing parallel to the road, so I rattled along that for a time. However, I reached a point where enough twists and turns had left me unsure of my directions. The compass gave a clue, but it appeared I would need to double back and try again. This was not an attractive option, so I cut through the trees and came upon a road. It was impossible to tell whether it was the same road I had left, but I followed my nose again and embarked on another undulating, tree-lined mystery tour. It was only midday, but the mist was already - or perhaps still - threading its way from one side of the road to another, reaching deep into the surrounding woods.

Soon a truck stop appeared and I was glad to see a couple of trucks and a parked car. On my side of the road a couple of women were taking the air. Putting on my non-threatening, pathetic face again, I approached the two ladies and beamed a greeting at them: "Excuse me, is this the road to Stawiski?" One of them looked at me rather disdainfully, but the other gave me a sly nod to confirm I was heading in the right direction. I decided it was time for a rest anyway and engaged the friendlier one in a chat. I remarked on the beautiful forest, the narrow road and pointed to the back of my vest to try and convey my walking mission. She listened and smiled politely, letting out the occasional "Ah" as I carefully made each point. As I babbled away, the miserable one got a ride into town, which seemed a little unfair on my new friend, so I felt obliged to stick around and keep her company. She took a photo of me with the stroller against the forest backdrop, and after I had finally elicited a smile for one particular remark I felt my duty done and made to leave. She gave me a little wave and a wink as I stepped off.

It was a good ten minutes down the road before it actually hit me. They were prostitutes. Why else would a reasonably attractive pair of women be hanging around the woods? They certainly weren't dressed for the weather. And there was I, babbling away about what a lovely forest it was and - gosh - isn't it a narrow road ...? I must have looked and sounded like a really goofy teenager. I was glad I hadn't asked them where I could get a bed for the night ...

That was just as well, as the stretch of road through to Szczuczyn was incredibly long, the route consisting entirely of forests and fields with the occasional small village. The rain began at around 3:00 and did not let up for the rest of the day. I eventually found myself walking into Szczuczyn after dark and saw every kind of conceivable shop and service except, naturally, a hotel or guesthouse.

I stood, a disconsolate figure in the increasing rain, once again with no apparent source of assistance. Was this the night when the wheels truly came off? A quick glance across the other side of the busy road suggested maybe not.

A Union Jack. The glorious red, white and blue icon of my country beamed proudly across the top of a store. I hurried across the road to discover that this was the British School. I manoeuvred the stroller through the doors, relieved to see they were still open. As I stood in the reception area, I noticed there was an open door to the main room at the rear, occupied by a group of youngsters sitting around rows of desks. A woman came out and before she could say anything I jumped in with my best BBC accent.

"Good evening. I'm sorry to trouble you but I'm British, I've just arrived in town and don't speak Polish. I'm trying to find a place to stay this evening."

She introduced herself as Maria and said she would consult her students as she did not live in the town. I think they were somewhat excited that an actual Brit had walked into their British School. After an abortive attempt to find somewhere, Maria phoned her husband and said they would make sure I was okay. I felt a sob of relief and gratitude rising in my throat, choking me for an instant and pricking my eyes as tears welled up. I managed to thank her and sat down in the reception hall.

Her husband, Pawel, arrived a little while later, greeting me with the smile of a man who was used to being roped in to help out life's waifs and strays. Maria locked up and with a cheery grin said we should go to their car. At this point another slice of farce was added to the day. Bless them, they had one of those miniature European cars that looked like two shopping bags would fill the rear. I folded up the stroller and this was rammed into the back seat behind Pawel, who sat scrunched in the driver's seat with his chin resting on the steering wheel. I climbed in behind Maria and wrapped my ankles around my neck so she could take her seat in the front.

We called into a couple of shops in town and obtained the locations for the three local guesthouses, two of which were full and the third had a single large room with eight mattresses sprawled across the floor to share. Maria sympathetically suggested this was not quite the thing I was looking for and she was spot on. Finally she turned to me and said that she knew of four hotels in their own town and they were not too expensive. Would I like them to take me there? I was very mindful of the fact that these good people were no doubt wanting to go home for their dinner (it was now 7:30) as well as of my own fatigue and so I readily agreed. I had no idea where they lived or its proximity to my walking route, but I didn't care.

As the little car wheezed along, Maria turned to face me. She asked if I had any children, to which I replied, "No", but added that I did have a niece. She then enquired whether I had any pictures of her. "Yes," I said, cursing the word as soon as it left my lips. That was a real foot-in-mouth moment, which given my position at the time was physically quite possible. Now I'd have to retrieve the bloody mini photo album from my bag. Inverting my frame and ferreting around by my feet I just managed to avoid an impromptu self-castration, finally pulling out the tiny album and handing it over. "She is so cute!" said a delighted Maria. "She certainly is," I squeaked.

Eventually we arrived outside the Hotel Rydzewski in the town of Elk. Maria went inside ahead of me to check whether they had rooms available and the price. She also obtained details of the bus service to take me back the following day.

The next day I studied the atlas and saw that I had been moved slightly to the west by this detour. It wasn't horrendous, but I had finished up closer to Germany than when I had started out the previous day. However, I was a little further north, so with some fancy reworking of the route I could stay on track. For some light relief I took the bus back to Grajewo and walked the 20 kilometres back to Elk to fill in the gap.

My next stop was Augustow, during which I encountered the worst snow storm of the whole trek (and that's saying something). A bitter wind was blowing the snow at a 45 degree angle into my left side as I walked along Highway 16. "Think of the charidee ... think of the charidee ..." I muttered to myself as the stroller weaved its own way along, displaying decidedly rebellious tendencies.

I stayed in the Gosciniec Ostoja guesthouse in Augustow, which I found very difficult to leave, as the bed sheets were unquestionably the snuggliest I had encountered. What did they wash them in? They also provided reading material for every visitor language, the English offering being Dante's *Divine Comedy*, which gave me some very strange dreams that night. Fortunately the clouds had snowed themselves out and the following day's walk to Suwalki was completed in a blissfully dry and bright climate.

My last full day in Poland was a tough one. The road leading towards the target of Szypliski was very undulating, with a few more z-bends than seemed necessary. It was on this day that I started playing truck tennis. The first semi-final was between Scania and Volvo. Every time a truck roared past bearing the crest of one of those companies, they scored a point. The first team to reach 15 won the set, with the best out of five sets winning through to the final (you can see how extended exposure to long-distance walking affects the brain). It was nail-biting stuff, with Scania taking the first two sets easily, then Volvo punching back to square the series at 2-2. In the end, Scania walked off with the fifth and deciding set and advanced into the final.

DAF versus Honda was the other semi-final, which took an age to resolve. In between, the Scania trucks just kept coming and I became despondent about the chances of whoever won through to the final. In the end, Honda edged it but were trounced by Scania, who took the trophy. All of which riveting action killed a few otherwise uneventful hours bringing me into the small town of Szypliski at 3:30.

Wojiech back in Warsaw had been surfing the Net trying to find accommodation for me for the remainder of my time in Poland. He had called that morning to confirm he had made a reservation for me at the improbably named Malibu Motel in town. It was a symphony in brown, with a nice enough twin room for the bargain price of 60 zlotys for the night. In keeping with the name of the motel, someone had stuck a promotional poster of a Caribbean island on the wall of the room, which served only to emphasise the bleak caramel backdrop even more.

Safely installed, I made my way ravenously downstairs to the dining area, where the very jolly receptionist/waitress/barmaid (and, for all I know, cook) decided that I should have the daily special. Gazing at the wall menu in Polish, I had to admit she was probably right. I took my place in the empty dining room, at the spot where the tablecloth had fewest holes. In the blink of an eye, a steaming hot bowl of spinach and potato broth was placed before me and it was delicious. Before I'd had a chance to finish, the main course arrived from my breathless friend - kidneys with mashed potato and cold coleslaw on the side.

Now I do take a little pride in being able to eat most things that are placed before me and certainly on this trip I could rarely afford to be choosy, but the sight and smell of kidneys have always sent me running for the hills. However, she was so keen for me to be happy, and I so wanted her to be happy that I was happy, that I started wolfing down the awful dish, spreading as much mashed potato on my fork as possible. I didn't quite manage to convince myself that this was in fact steak I was chewing on, but I managed a respectable share of the offering and had the added bonus that any hunger pangs had truly disappeared by the time I had finished. I swore to learn the word for 'chicken' in every language I would ever need from that day forward.

~ 12 ~
Into The Baltics

On Wednesday 23rd March I walked the final couple of miles from Szypliski to the border town of Budzisko. The sun had kindly made itself available as I prepared to enter Lithuania, the seventh country on my quest.

Crossing the border, the diligence of the Polish border guards contrasted starkly with the nonchalance of the Lithuanian border guard, who was too busy with his cigarette and simply waved me through. I walked on my way towards the first target town of Kalvajinski. My first impressions of Lithuania were very positive, not least because the sun was radiating something peculiarly like warmth; not anything to slap sunscreen on for, but, for the first time since October, I walked along without gloves. The widening fields before me certainly had snow on them, but large patches of green were clearly visible and I allowed myself a silent hope that the big thaw was finally on its way. By early afternoon, I was crossing a raised bridge over a shallow valley next to the town. A car rushed past and then doubled back, turning to face me. As it slowly approached me I saw two young lads with shaved heads and a tattoo or two between them. Wondering if I could really defend myself with a plastic knife, I stopped to face them as the car ground to a halt alongside me.

"What you do?" asked the first, revealing that the Brits certainly do not have the worst teeth in Europe. I explained my quest and, in retrospect, a little foolishly turned around so they could read the route on the back of my vest. Laughing, they told me that I was crazy, but wished me "Guten luck" and then drove off. My first experience with the Lithuanian people and very sweet it was too.

I left Kalvajinski and the charming town of Marijampole behind me to tackle the monster 40-kilometre slog to Kaunas, the former capital of Lithuania. Exiting Marijampole, I walked into a maelstrom of bridges, junctions and joining roads and had to complete some nifty manoeuvres to stay on the right track. Eventually the road straightened out and I had a long, long hike through small villages and country views.

The final approach to Kaunas was pretty thrilling - a wide descent around a mountain to see the city perched on the opposite side of a flowing river. From first sight to actually getting into the city took almost two hours and I was feeling rather weak from the day's efforts when I finally hit the streets. Almost immediately I came upon the tourist information office, which to my good fortune was still open. The agent was very interested in my mission and searched not only in Kaunas but also in the next few towns for the cheapest accommodation. She turned up a twin room in a hotel right in the middle of the city for just 70 litas (£14), which I readily took.

I was absolutely exhausted, but not so much that I couldn't appreciate the main street. A church stood majestically at the head of the main boulevard, and the long, wide, tree-lined passage reminded me slightly of Paris. It was very clean, abuzz with the old and the new in terms of architecture and shops, cafés and bars. This section of the city was really alive, but not too westernised. It displayed a modern 'take' on its own dynamism and is a firm favourite for revisiting in the future. As I left Kaunas the next day, I had that rueful feeling that would hang around my shoulders from time to time about how nice it would be to have a day or two more to spend there. The very nature of what I was doing meant this was never possible, and conversely there were also places I couldn't wait to get out of too! The road beckoned me on ...

Jonava was the next stop, at the end of a long, boring stretch of road. On arrival I asked the local police where I could stay the night and they directed me to the Jovindiana guesthouse, which appeared to be run by, and exclusively for, teenagers. A few giggling exchanges between them as I checked in were immediately excused, as the role of people over 30 is of course to provide fodder for youngsters to make fun of. I did it in the past and now it's happening to me. Long live the generation gap.

I called into the tourist information office the next day and a woman of considerable girth assured me there was an excellent hotel in my next stop of Ukmerge. The road planners of Lithuania had not spared too much thought to the likelihood of someone walking along the main connecting highway, so I spent a large proportion of the day walking on the road itself, skipping to the side whenever traffic appeared. Several small settlements hinted at civilisation throughout the morning, but I had to make it into the afternoon before I came upon a bus stop with a bench and shelter. As I approached I noticed about half a dozen people waiting for the bus and a young retriever yapping around. Initially he bounced over to me, but jumped away as I turned to smile.

I absolutely adore dogs. They are funny, lovable and great companions. If it had been possible, I would have had a canine sidekick with me for the whole walk, but for obvious reasons that just wasn't practical. The bus collected the passengers and as it departed I noticed the dog was still on the roadside. And that's where the trouble started. I had thought he belonged to one of the people waiting for the bus, but evidently he was out for a wander and had scampered along to the bus stop to be friendly. Now it was just him and me. I deliberately ignored him and walked off. Unfortunately he was not to be shaken off that easily.

I walked and walked, mile after mile and every step of the way the dog (who I inwardly called Skip) was chasing around me, tail wagging and bright eyes trying to catch mine. I tried ignoring him but this was not working, so in the end I turned to him and shouted, "Bad dog! ... Go home! ... Get away!" I hated doing it, especially as his ears drooped and he cowered away from me as I shouted, but I had to shake him off as I was now going far away from the area where he picked me up. But nothing I did seemed to discourage him. In his youthful zeal he was running from one side of the road to the other, into the fields and then back to the road again, always keeping me in sight, always scurrying back to my side. When I sat down to rest, he found an old sock by the side of the road and started grabbing it in his mouth and flinging it over his head to entertain me.

In the end, I decided to wait at the next bus stop and take the bus for one stop to leave him behind. It would mess up the walk for the day, but only by a mile or so. I saw a junction ahead with a few houses and made for it. As I crossed the road towards the stop, I heard a screech of brakes behind me, followed by a sickening thwack. I didn't need to be told, but looking over my shoulder I saw the crumpled frame of Skip lying by the side of the road. The only movement was a weak flapping of his tail as his contorted body sprawled the pavement. I felt ill. I felt awful. There was nothing I could have done to stop him following me or to prevent the accident, but I still felt dreadful. Most of all, I wished I had made a fuss of him when we stopped, to give him some affection before this. Two days later I was more concerned about suffering the same fate myself.

Walking out of Anyszcai towards the border with Latvia, I needed to head 11 kilometres east, before joining Highway 120 to take me north towards the town of Utena. The smaller road east rose up before me with no shoulder and narrowed as it surrendered to the clutches of an all-embracing forest. Walking slowly up the hill, I was constantly peering along the road and listening for traffic. At the top of the hill, the road revealed itself to be following every contour of the meandering landscape. Thick ice still clung to the roadsides and my feet slipped as I nervously made my way along. Skidding to a better view of the road, I discovered it didn't get any better. This was majorly hazardous. I stood for several moments weighing up my somewhat limited options. In the end, I concluded that with trucks and cars darting around every corner I could not proceed. If it had been summer, if I did not have the stroller with me, if there was a viable alternative - all the ifs buzzed around my head like flies I could not brush away.

I felt wretched. For the first time in more than 1,000 miles I had to concede. I could not walk this stretch. I made my way back into the town and sat at the bus stop. As the bus rolled its winding way along the road, I felt weighed down by anguish. The road actually got worse as we went along. The forest cleared, but the road shrank to no more than a single lane for traffic in both directions, with the same frosty icing. After an 11-kilometre (7-mile) journey I disembarked and stood at the junction with Highway 120. A cloudy mood was not one I wanted to continue walking with, so I reminded myself that I had previously said this was something I was going to do, "or die trying".

Fortunately I had much to cheer me up later in the day. I reached Utena and the tourist information centre found me a home-stay for the night. Several families in the area rented out rooms to foreign travellers - usually students - but this particular family had agreed I could stay the night at their farmhouse home for 25 litas (£5). Yes pleeeease! The only downside was that it was another four kilometres down the road, but I took that as penance for the bus ride.

As I approached the farmhouse, a young man called out: "Hello Room!" I confirmed that I was indeed the room. As we walked up to the house, we chatted away quite happily, not understanding a word, but with the waving of arms and slapping of thighs we managed to get along famously. The farmhouse was everything I would have expected, with stone floor meeting the panelled stairs and a narrow wooded hallway on the first floor, leading to three small guest rooms. As I made my way down to the other family business - a roadside café - the young man introduced himself as Tardis (at least that's what it sounded like to me) and, together with his father, we sat in the little cabin where I had a meal of sausages, mashed potatoes and onions washed down with strong coffee. We laboured through a conversation where Tardis's father related the struggles of maintaining the farm, which explained the need for additional income via the café and taking guests.

I was by now 48 kilometres from Zanasai, the last town before entering Latvia. On advice from Utena tourist information, the journey had been split into a 32-kilometre trek to Dagulie and then a pleasant stroll of 16 kilometres to Zanasai. The reason for the stop at Dagulie was that they had found for me a log cabin park overlooking a lake - by itself a good reason to head there - but also it was the only place in between the two where I could find any accommodation.

I busted easily through the 30-kilometre barrier and arrived at the log cabin park a little after 3:00 the next day. I trawled through a muddy path, avoided the barking guard dog tied to a tree and knocked on the office door. The 'park' turned out to be two large cabins for hire with a small clubhouse, set in several gorgeous acres of forested land and overlooking a small lake. No doubt anticipating future foreign business, I was escorted to the larger of the two cabins, which could have comfortably housed four people, comprising two double beds and huge bathroom upstairs and a kitchen/diner occupying the ground floor. The cabins were constructed entirely of wood, polished, varnished and sealed, and with lake views from all angles - and I paid £12 for the night. After taking supper in the clubhouse I retired to my cabin and sat contentedly watching CNN.

A little after 10:00 I climbed the stairs and prepared for bed. As I looked out of the window, I noticed the owner closing up the clubhouse and driving off. I was suddenly struck by the fact that I was now quite alone in this forest, the only signs of other people being the distant glints of lights from cars passing across the fields. What was beautiful by daylight had instantly become a little spooky in the moonlit glow. I scrambled into bed, turned out the lights and pulled the covers up, attempting to relax into slumber. Ten minutes later I almost jumped out of the bed.

BANG!

A mighty whack on the side of the cabin rocked every timber. My eyes flashed open, my whole frame tensed and I forced myself to breathe. Hairs spiked in fear all over my body as the awful stillness returned. In the near distance I could hear the park dog barking frantically, still tethered to his tree. I lay frozen in fear for the next development. Oh to be in a noisy, bustling hotel in the centre of a town! If I ever got out of this one alive, I would never, ever sleep alone in a forest again. My muscles began to loosen a little, as whatever it had been seemed to have moved on.

BANG!

Another cabin-shaking jolt and I was immediately out of bed, reaching around for my clothes. Shaking, I slipped on my trousers and sweatshirt. I can't say how, but I knew that was definitely not an animal stumbling around - someone was having a laugh at my expense or, more sinister, meant me harm. I threw on the light switches all over the top floor and stomped down the stairs with a very macho stride, giving out the clear message that whoever it was would do well not to mess with me. With no other way to demonstrate my feigned toughness, I very purposefully picked up a pen from the coffee table and stomped back upstairs again. I dragged the second double bed across the room to cover the door and hoped that my posturing had caused my tormentor to think twice before incurring my wrath. I derobed and slipped back into bed.

Two minutes ... five minutes ... ten minutes went by with no disturbance, and whilst the silence was by itself quite unnerving I began to feel my ordeal may be over.

BANG!

The biggest shudder yet shook the whole room and I dived beneath the covers, promising to get the first plane back to England and never venture outside my hometown again. And then it hit me - the noises and shudders were the heating and water system cranking into life ...

I felt a sense of relief washing over me, as if I had been dipped in a huge vat of warm honey. After that came a fit of the giggles as the nervous tension was released and finally, finally the sinking into a deep sleep.

Wishing for no further excitement for a while, I set off the next morning back down the side road to emerge at Highway 120 just after noon. I easily chewed up the 16 kilometres to Zanasai in less than three hours and looked forward to an early finish. The highway bent into a final curve and below me was the town. Walking along the final approach, I was passed by a couple of lads who called out to me. Reading the message on the back of my vest, they were delighted not only to meet somebody from England, but also one was doing such an incredible journey - could they have a picture please? Of course - and can you take a snap for me too please? No problem. Looking back on that snap now, with one of the lads standing with me, I realise from my suntanned face how much the conditions had changed since the snow-laden greeting back in Poland. I took a motel room for the night on the far side of Zanasai and with a customary cheese and ham sandwich supper, I settled in for the last night of my eventful passage through Lithuania.

~ 13 ~
Latvia

There was no time for a long goodbye to Lithuania - as soon as I passed the last group of buildings in Zanasai, the border was upon me. Once again, the Lithuanian guards were very relaxed and waved me through, but it was a very different story when I reached the Latvian checkpoint. The Latvian guards called me across brusquely. One in particular seemed to take an interest in my stroller and backpack. Fearing I would have to open it up and spill the contents, I gave my broadest beaming smile and announced loudly that I was British and could not speak any Latvian. This had the desired effect of sending him off to get another officer.

The next chap to come across appeared to be the chief and he addressed me in English, requested my passport and, with a non-smiling but not unpleasant expression of enquiry, asked my business in Latvia. I produced my passport and explained my mission of walking from London to Moscow and beyond. He looked at me incredulously, so I fished out the itinerary and quickly became the talk of the border, with truck drivers leaning over to listen in to the now-translated story about the crazy Brit walking around the world. The chief waved me on - with a real smile - and wished me good luck.

Taking my first steps into Latvia, I was soon passed by those same truck drivers, who honked loudly and waved as they went by. A very nice start, but this was to prove the highlight of the day.

The road from the border to Daugavpils ranks alongside the American Midwest and the A-roads of Cornwall as the toughest walking I had to do. The road was up and down, nothing extraordinary about that, but it just went on and on climbing and falling, with each rise in the road seeming stiffer than the last. Each time as I leant on the stroller in a final effort to reach the peak, I said to myself, "Please let this be the last one…", and promptly ran up against another huge trough. I had no water with me and felt my tongue sticking to the roof of my mouth as all moisture evaporated and, most seriously, I stopped sweating. I took frequent rest breaks at the side of the road, which were vital but of course prolonged the journey.

The road did finally plateau and I gazed into the distance at a large city, sitting on the opposite side of an approaching river. A very fetching tree-lined road led the way, but for ages the river did not seem to come any closer. Walking under a railway bridge, I eventually turned into a street that stretched alongside the river with a small village overlooking the riverbank.

Sadly, there was no walkway on the railway bridge across the river, so I had to walk around a large bend in the river to reach the traffic- and footbridge to cross into the city. After seven hours on the road, I finally stumbled into Daugavpils and propped myself up on a street bench. The city was really very pretty. As with Kaunas before it, I had arrived in a very well-developed, clean and vibrant district with a Baltic flavour seasoning the modern facilities. As I had no cash, I hastened to the nearest bank and withdrew a fistful of lats. For the first time, I had no currency conversions to worry about as the Latvian lat was at parity with the British pound. I called into the Sia Verina hotel and took a room for 30 lats. The young man on reception was charming and after checking me in he called after me, "We have BBC!", which pleased me no end.

Crossing the street from the Verina, I was delighted to discover that the Latvian tourism industry was run with the same great gusto as their Lithuanian neighbours. The lady I spoke with was most anxious that I had every little scrap of information to ensure smooth progress through her country. However, that included a serious shift in my route through Latvia. I had originally chosen to walk through, among others, Dagda and Rundani. With no hotels in those towns or their vicinity, she devised an alternative route covering the same distance through the more visitor-friendly towns of Rezekne, Ludza and Zilope. The only problem was that I would need to start more than 60 kilometres north of where I currently was. There was no option. We agreed that I would walk on to Kraslava the next day, come back to Daugavpils, and then take a bus north to get onto the route to Rezekne the next day.

Two days later I disembarked at a suitable spot from the bus and walked on to Rezekne. In the late afternoon I checked into the Viesnica Latgale hotel and sat in contemplation of my imminent arrival in Russia.

As a teenage schoolboy in the 1980s, I had grown up in the midst of the Cold War, with NATO and the Warsaw Pact countries watching one another like hawks and steadily building up enough nuclear firepower to obliterate each other and the rest of the planet several times over. Whilst the rhetoric cranked up and we all lived with the idea of SS20 missiles pointing at us, I was never convinced that oblivion was a heartbeat away. It all seemed to be happening at a higher level and, even with the massive protests happening across Europe, it appeared this chapter in history would play itself out whilst the rest of us got on with our lives. In the school playgrounds my friends and I discussed what we would do if the four-minute warning came. I seem to recall our views ranged from a visit to the local glassware shop with a hammer to a resolve to lose our virginity.

During those days our only insights into life in Russia were the images played over and again of queues of drably dressed people lining up to buy a loaf of bread or a few vegetables in sparsely stocked shops. In fascination I watched BBC correspondents reporting from Moscow with the Kremlin in the background. I just had to go there one day. I did have some apprehension, because it was unlikely that the Russian authorities had been able to shake off 70 years of communist state control and the engineered suspicion of foreigners. Well, in 72 hours I would find out for myself.

As I crossed a railway line the next day, a car pulled up on the side of the road in front of me. There was absolutely nothing else around, such as a café or rest area, so the car had definitely stopped on my account. Approaching, I tried to make out who might be stopping for a chat. It was there and then I met Natasha, the next angel sent to look after me. She worked for the local authority with responsibility for visitors to the area and also submitted articles for the local newspaper. Her English was excellent and she was quite taken with my mission, displaying an immediate feel for my anxieties about entering Russia.

After a quick chat, we agreed that I would keep walking on to Ludza and she would meet up with me on the outskirts of the town. This we did and photos were taken for a newspaper article. I then walked on into the main part of town and Natasha took me along to the local hotel - at which I was the only guest! Later that night, she returned with her husband and they took me out to dinner and then for a tour of the town. We walked high among the ruins of an ancient castle, strolled past the nearby lakes and saw the church where they had been married a few years earlier. It was once again nice to have the opportunity of actually seeing at leisure one of the places I was passing through. After that, it was back down to business.

The next day I would walk on to Zilupe, the last town in Latvia before crossing into Russia. After long discussions, Internet searches and consultations with travel guides, we concluded that it would be madness for me simply to walk up to the Russian border pushing my stroller and asking if

I could come in please - not to mention the fact that there was no hotel in the remote vicinity of Mogili, the first village I had earmarked in Russia. The only option was for me to take a train across the border to facilitate my entry, disembarking at the city of Vyliki-Luki where we knew of two hotels. I would then use one of the hotels as my base for walking the first section of Russia.

Natasha checked the train times and ticket prices and telephoned the cheaper of the two hotels in Vyliki-Luki to make a reservation for me. To my consternation, the trains out of Riga to Moscow ran only during the night, with my arrival in Vyliki-Luki scheduled for either 2:00 or 4:30 in the morning. I opted for the 'earlier' train.

After walking to Zilupe I took a bus back to Ludza to meet up with Natasha and her husband for the final supper. They very kindly drove me to the railway station and waited with me for the train to arrive. Rumbling along the tracks came an iron behemoth, grinding to a halt next to the darkening platform. My chin was roughly at the same level as the tops of the wheels and I arched my neck to see up to the curtained windows.

The enormous train harked back to an earlier era, not of romantic steam but of heavy industrial efficiency, and the patrolling guards seemed keen to maintain the tradition of strict efficiency, inspecting each passenger, bag and ticket before allowing anyone to climb the steep steps onto the carriage. Natasha waved me off from the platform and I gazed at the darkening skies as the heavy wheels ground their way into motion. I watched the town of Ludza disappear behind me and the overhanging trees fanned a farewell as I surrendered myself to the inexorable passage into Russia.

~ 14 ~
Здравствуйте Russia!

The train rumbled along its majestic course as darkness fell and the only view in the window was my own reflection, a face trying to maintain its quiet optimism whilst contemplating emerging onto a no doubt deserted railway platform in the middle of Russia at 2:00 in the morning. As I sat sipping mineral water, I scanned the handwritten notes that Natasha had carefully prepared for me in the Russian script. They read:

- "Hello, I am English and do not speak Russian. Can you tell me when the train arrives at Vyliki-Luki please"; and

- "Hello, I am English and do not speak Russian. Can you please take me to the Lukee Servis hotel please".

So that was successfully getting off the train dealt with and hopefully also arranging a taxi to drop me at the hotel. I consulted my BBC Russian phrase book entitled *Get By In Russian*, which offered social insights and useful phrases, plus a section detailing the changes in the country with its 'new' leader, Mikhail Gorbachev. It might have been a good move to get a more up-to-date version, but at least the essential words and phrases were listed.

At length, the train slowed to a stuttered, sluggish progress. Glancing out of the window, I saw that we were inching our way past a vast, heavily bricked barrier wall. We had arrived at the border. Graffiti adorned the imposing structure and barbed wire was visible as the lights emitted by the train gave a reasonable view of the mighty demarcation between the European Union and Russia. We were heading in.

I stepped up my rehearsal for greeting the legendary border guards. Over and over I kept repeating the phrase, "Dobri vie chyer" (good evening) in a bid to win favour. After I thought I had mastered the phrase, I moved on to "Pa zha loo stah" - a useful phrase that means 'please/there you go/you're welcome'. This was recommended for when handing over papers and the likeliest phrase to extract a smile.

At a straightening on the line, the train finally stopped. A stillness prevailed as I sat motionless, listening for any sign of officialdom. Outside the lights of the siding bays illuminated the signposts indicating this was the main Customs area. Far away, I heard the sound of crunching footsteps. These got closer and closer and I then heard low voices exchanging greetings with the train guards. Several pairs of feet were now boarding my carriage and making a shuffled way along the corridor. My senses were now fully alert to every sound, as the carriage floor creaked under the footsteps and the voices became louder, stopping in turn to question the passengers in the enclosed compartments. I opened my cabin door so that I could hear their final approach and also as a 'nothing to hide' gesture.

Silently I kept practising my 'good evening' phrase over and over: "Dobri vie chyer ... Dobri vie chyer ... Dobri vie chyer ..." The moment arrived. The guard finished with my neighbour, rapped on the door of my cabin and walked in. With great ceremony I stood to receive him and uttered with great gusto: "Bore da!"

To this day, I have no idea why the only Welsh phrase I knew suddenly leapt out of my mouth. Understandably, the guard looked as confused as I was. Trying to save the situation, I muttered something close to "Dobri vie chyer" but the moment had passed and I meekly offered my passport. (I later found out that, as well as being Welsh for 'good morning', the phrase 'Bore da' means 'beard' in Russian ...)

I was soon in the company of three border guards, who inspected my passport with great interest. Sitting as nonchalantly as my nerves would allow, I peered out of the cabin door to see they appeared to be trying to authenticate my visa by stretching my passport against the fold and slipping fingernails under the sealed plastic. Be careful with that please! Eventually they were satisfied that all was in order and I had been forgiven my lapse into Welsh. Another starched uniform barked a word that sounded like 'declaration', so I held up my backpack and pointed to the stroller and shrugged my shoulders. Nothing to declare, sir. He, too, was happy and the Customs and Immigration grilling was over.

I could now forget about officialdom and turn my attention to worrying about stepping onto the deserted platform. This was Friday night going into Saturday morning, which I presumed would mean that I would be visited by the party crowds and attendant boisterous behaviour. I had a vague map in my head of the hotel's location, but trying to make my way from the railway station at 2:00 in the morning was not going to be easy. As the train gathered speed once again, I looked out of the window at the inky black night, with few clues as to the landscape. Once again that question rang inside my head, "What the hell am I doing?" I knew nobody in Russia, had no clue about the language and did not anticipate finding too many good Samaritans at this hour.

Finding it impossible to relax, I stood up and walked out into the corridor. Standing in the division booth, I stared hard at the window to try to get a better perspective. To my alarm, I saw the land was on fire. Great roaring flames reached into the night sky, with the occasional outline of a person skulking in the shadows. Both sides of the train revealed the same sight, as the Russian land all around the train's path was aflame. All I needed now was the music from the 'March of the Valkyries' to kick in and my horror show would have been complete. I didn't know it at the time, but they were burning the spring grass, providing me with a dramatic backdrop for my ill-timed entry into Russia.

Time marched on and the guard poked her head around the door to tell me that the train would be arriving in Vyliki-Luki in ten minutes. Troubling though the journey had been, I had at least felt a degree of comfort in being on board; now I was to be cast out into the night. The city's outlying buildings came into view, the train heaved itself to a grinding halt and my time was up. Carrying my backpack and stroller, I climbed down the steps and onto the platform. The guard gave me a nod in farewell and I stood stone-like on the platform as the train started chugging away down the line.

Senses sharpened, I skimmed the platform for trouble. Dim lights in the main station building gave shape to some other late-night travellers - or were they settling down for a snooze on the benches inside? The platform was long and wide, and midway along it was a footbridge leading the way out of the station at height, with what was clearly the main urban street on the other side. Making my way towards the footbridge, a girl appeared in front of me and demanded something in Russian. I nearly jumped out of my skin. No doubt she was after money, so I shrugged my shoulders and carried on walking. I scaled the steps and walked along the dark metal corridor, darting my eyes down to the platform behind me. The lights of the city glistened in the near distance ahead of me, although I could not see the end of the footbridge clearly. I descended and found myself in a small clearance with several market stalls wearing tarpaulin covers. About 30 feet in front of me was the main road and I now found myself in the blaze of the early Saturday morning, with cars whizzing past, people leaning out of the windows shouting boorishly and others staggering in and out of a couple of bars to my left.

I approached the roadside and concluded that the road directly opposite, leading north away from the station, was where the hotel would be situated. However, I felt very exposed and vulnerable with the revelry going on all around me. With my backpack secured on my shoulders and my stroller folded under my left arm, I stepped out into the road and rushed to the other side. Right in front of me was a large red sign displaying a yellow hammer and sickle. Welcome to Russia. Now I was in the thick of it. People walked past, some paying no attention to me, others eyeing me curiously before wandering off. I had no reason to think that I was in any danger but, let's face it, turning up in the middle of a big city in the small hours and encountering drunken locals is not good in any country. I had to get to the hotel. I walked northwards up the road and stood in the gutter waving at passing taxis. After a few passed me by, one stopped. Interestingly, he already had two people in the back. The driver looked as drunk as the passengers and retched out something in Russian. I waved my hands horizontally in front of me and said "Don't worry" with a daring smile. Fortunately he drove off. Moments later, another taxi stopped and this one was free. I dug out Natasha's note asking to take me to the Lukee Servis hotel.

The driver gave me a pained grimace and pointed down the road as if to say 'it's only just down the street'. With a pleading look I said, 'Pa zha loo stah' and, bless him, he agreed. I jumped in the back, with my backpack still on, crushing me against the stroller and his headrest. He turned the car around, drove for about 30 seconds and pulled up outside the hotel. Okay, so it was really close, but I gave him 50 roubles for his trouble.

Out on the street once again, I moved sharply into the courtyard surrounding the small hotel. I pressed the buzzer and had to say "Mark Cundy - the Englishman" four times before the door vibrated in response to the release button being hit. I entered and took the first room offered, so relieved to have made it off the train, down the street and into the sanctuary of the hotel in one piece. Five minutes later I sat on the edge of my bed, drenched in sweat, not through walking this time but due to the release of the nervous tension that had been building since the train pulled out of Ludza. Now, much relieved, I was able to relax - safely delivered into Russia.

I allocated the next day to orientation. After a very late finish and my concerns about how things worked in this strange new land, it wasn't feasible just to get the train back to the border and start walking. I had already decided with Natasha and her Russian husband to use Vyliki-Luki as my base for the next week or so, taking a train or bus out in the morning, doing the day's walk, and then boarding another train or bus to bring me back. Firstly, I planned to head for the town centre to get my bearings and transport information.

The small hotel was situated in a side street, with a road leading to the railway station at one end and a junction to a larger road at the other. Walking the short distance to the junction, I was immediately struck by the filthy state of the street. Rubbish was strewn across the road itself, which was lined with crumbling buildings and a dirt track either side instead of a pavement. The junction yawned out into a very wide road and I turned left. The immediate neighbourhood comprised a succession of rows of housing, which can at best be described as a collection of patched-up shacks; single-storey affairs with corrugated iron roofs and non-tarmacked tracks threading in between, with rusty cars and vans catching most of the gravel and dirt. Beyond this neighbourhood stood a few large factories, stained by years of chemical or coal-burning output. The grime was ingrained into the walls and the massive frontage stretched imperiously across the landscape, emphasising the heavy industrial roots of the city. And, of course, there were the inevitable Soviet-style blocks of apartment buildings: tower after tower of miserable vertical living for the masses - except this was of course the land that first spawned the bland structures before exporting the idea to the rest of Eastern Europe.

The centre was somewhat better, with wide avenues boasting a few trees along the way and the occasional small square displaying greenery within. My first job was to phone home to tell everyone I was in Russia and in one piece. The receptionist at my hotel had told me to go the 'Phone House' and thoughtfully drew me a little map. I found the building easily enough and joined the queue of locals wanting to place long-distance calls. I was delighted to see that the 'Phone House' looked the same as it must have done several decades earlier. The internal decor was a marvellous sheen of grubby granite and the wall of one half of the huge room was occupied by tellers sitting behind glass booths. Watching other people, I quickly saw that you had to approach the tellers, inform them of your intentions (e.g., call your Aunt in Moscow) and hand over an appropriate sum of money. You would then be allocated a number relating to which telephone booth you should use. After the call, you then had to return to the tellers and either pay any additional monies due or collect the difference. So far, so easy. When my turn came, I presented a piece of paper on which I had scrawled down the number I wished to call, assuming that the '00 44' would tell them it was an international call to the UK. I handed over a bunch of roubles and was told to go into booth number 9.

I went into booth 9 and smiled at the rotary dial telephone on the wall. Calling my parents, I got their answering machine, but decided not to leave a message. Instead I called Paul and Lisa to say hello and pass on the news to Mum and Dad. Ring, ring ... ring, ring ...

"Hello?" I heard Lisa say.

"Hello!" I chirped back.

"Hello?"

"Hello!" I said a little more loudly.

"Hello?!" repeated Lisa a little testily and then decided she had had enough of this crank caller and the line went dead. I tried again with the same result. Shuffling back to the queue, I waved over the heads of the people in front of me, who did not look too impressed. Smiling in an apologetic manner, I repeated the 'Hello' sequence followed by a confused look. The woman behind the booth put her finger in the air and made a pressing gesture. Ah! I have to press the button to speak. Righto, many thanks. A gentleman in the queue, sensing my confusion, then explained to me in Russian with the same pointy gesture and a chuckle. Thanking him, I stepped back in and successfully called Lisa with the news.

Walking around the streets of the city centre, I discovered a number of indoor markets, selling clothes, household items, car spares and electrical goods. To supplement the food supplies available in the markets, a number of country folk sat or stood on the pavements, with wooden crates, baskets or even buckets of food produced on their land. One babushka (grandmother) stood staring as if in a trance, with several layers of clothes wrapped around her against the chill and a plastic bucket at her feet, full to the brim of potatoes. I felt a painful sympathy for them all, but this lady in particular. How would I feel if I'd seen my own late grandmother spending hours on a very cold day just standing in the street with a meagre armful of spuds to sell?

Getting back to business, I now had to get details of the times and costs of trains and buses. With no skills in the language, I took two sheets of paper from my logbook and drew a little picture of two trains/buses, writing the names of Vyliki-Luki and the destination towns in Russian script under each train/bus. Directly beneath I had drawn a little clock and a question mark, and below that the symbol for roubles. The unsmiling but efficient clerks at the railway and bus stations started telling me the answers, but I swiftly uttered the useful phrase "Ya anglee cha-neen" (I'm English) and they duly scrawled down the train times and prices on my makeshift timetable.

Later, as I sipped a very agreeable vodka and orange in my hotel room, I gazed at the laminated pages of the Russian road atlas I had bought in London. The following day I would take the train from Vyliki-Luki back to the border Customs station of Sebez and walk on towards Ulyanovsheena. Once there, I would take another train or bus back to Vyliki-Luki and repeat the exercise each day for the next week. In theory, it was a great plan.

~ 15 ~
Getting to Know You

Sunday 10th April. I was standing once again on the railway platform at Vyliki-Luki, but this time in reassuring daylight at 8:30 in the morning. I was not alone on the platform, as several locals and transit passengers waited with me to take the train towards the border. Uniformed officers came and went, but paid little attention to the travellers; in fact they appeared as many other officials in Russian life, gainfully under-employed and bored. A statue of Lenin kept an eye on proceedings as the train rolled into town.

The countryside that chugged by was nothing spectacular. At last, we arrived at Sebez and, together with the remaining passengers, I disembarked and made my way along a narrow wooden walkway in between trains to reach the station building. As I proceeded I was aware out of the corner of my eye of the figure of a man who seemed to be watching our progress. As I stepped onto the platform, I felt a tap on my shoulder. I looked around and it was the same gentleman who had been observing the arrivals. A little shorter than me, as slim as a jockey and dressed entirely in black, sporting a thin moustache, he looked like one who had loved the shady officialdom of years gone by as a boy and was disappointed that those days had passed by the time he was old enough to enlist. He pointed to the office attached to the side of the station building and I bent my steps to follow him inside.

I had managed to get out my most useful phrase - "Ya anglee-cha neen" (I'm English) - but he merely nodded and pointed me towards the door. We entered a small side office with one table and a couple of chairs facing the resident official. The gentleman sitting behind the desk was wearing a perfectly starched military uniform with a magnificent peaked cap, under which he could easily have concealed a water melon if he had chosen to. He nodded to the moustache like a chief acknowledging a serf who had brought him a sacrifice. The chief sat back in his chair and rested his hands on the desk in an expansive gesture of stature and asked me something in Russian.

"Ya anglee cha-neen," I said again, following up with "Nyet russkee", which was my attempt to indicate that I did not speak Russian. Simultaneously, I pulled out my passport and handed it over with an indulgent smile. Whilst the chief was examining my visa, the room suddenly filled with six junior officers in full uniform. This was slightly unsettling, but they seemed relaxed and were chatting to each other and paying little attention to the potential James Bond in their midst.

"Sebez," said the chief, showing a masterful economy with words. He no doubt figured that keeping the conversation restricted to a few choice words or phrases would facilitate a speedier conclusion. In this case, he questioningly mentioned the name of the town with eyebrows raised at me. Clearly - what was I doing in Sebez? I decided to follow his lead in keeping the answers succinct, drawing on the few words I had learnt and covering the considerable gaps with gestures.

"Touristee" was my opening gambit, followed by "Gasteeneetsa [hotel] Vyliki-Luki" and showed him a card from the hotel I had resourcefully put in my pocket that morning. He nodded his understanding but returned to his original query, "Sebez". I don't think he really suspected me of any kind of sinister intentions, but this was the main Customs district in and out of Russia. By this time I also had the attention of the audience of junior officers. I repeated "Touristee" and said "Sebez" and looked around the office in an exaggerated fashion to indicate I wanted to look around the town. Finding this less than convincing myself, I thought I had better add some more, so I made a circular knife-and-fork motion with my hands just below my chin and a munching sound to indicate I'd also like to sample some of the local food. I've no idea if Sebez is held in reverence for its culinary delights, but that was the best I could do at such short notice. The idea of trying to explain the walk was just not feasible.

Some words were exchanged, a copy of my passport was obtained and notes were made of my name and the visa reference number. The chief then raised an open hand indicating the door and I was free to go. Whew! Quite how much trouble I would have been in if the chief had been in a bad mood I don't know, but I decided that that was the closest encounter I ever wanted to have with the officials. There was nothing untoward in the interview itself, but I was now immediately made aware of the differences between my total freedom of movement across Europe and the attentions that I could attract here.

Hanging around outside, I knew that setting off for a walk was not an option due to the lateness of the hour by now and the knock-on effect with the train that would take me back to Vyliki-Luki. One of the junior officers appeared beside me and mimicked my eating motions. I nodded, feeling that a bite to eat and a drink would be excellent. He suggested I wait a moment and dashed back into the office, emerging a moment or two later with the moustache, and he told me that the man in black would give me a ride to the nearest restaurant. The irony was not lost on me as I gladly accepted.

So, the man who had fingered me on emerging from the train was now driving me in his own car to get something to eat. I'd like to know how often that has happened with Customs officials. Dropping me off at the restaurant, he also asked me if I'd like him to wait and take me back to the station. I declined with thanks, wondering if he was now off to hide in the bushes to see what I did next.

I reflected on the train back to Vyliki-Luki that, all in all, this had been an abortive start to the walk in Russia, although I was aware that I had been lucky to find myself in front of an official not of a mind to make life difficult. If I tried again I might not be so lucky, so I mentally deleted that first stretch of walk off the list, not wishing to arrive in Sebez again the following day. They'd never believe the meal was that good.

The next day saw me on the much more agreeable bus route. Perched inside a single-decker coach, I'm sure the rest of the passengers like me were collectively hoping that the ramshackle vehicle would make it all the way. On those potholed roads we bumped our way together through the countryside westwards once again. I had originally asked a gentleman if he could tell me when we arrived at Eedreetsa; he kindly passed the message on to another passenger when he got off, and I went through three new friends as we weaved our way along. It was midday by the time I emerged into another rather run-down town, roughly 20 kilometres down the road from the prying eyes of the Sebez crowd.

I immediately began walking back the way I had just come, joining with the M9 and storming down the highway that would eventually take me all the way into Moscow. The brush with officialdom the previous day stayed with me as I began walking along the road. I held a sense of apprehension all the way, fearing that I would suddenly be confronted with a car full of ex-KGB officers pinning me down and taking me off for interrogation. Nonsense of course, but I was not walking with the same ease as on my previous passage through Europe. This was a day of walking simply to be completed, not enjoyed.

Back in the hotel I showered and prepared to face the nightly task of ordering something to eat in the restaurant. I was presented, as always, with a menu on which the only part I understood was the prices. The cost was never an issue, as the meals were uniformly cheap across the land, outside of Moscow. I was by now also accustomed to the fact that good service and subsequent tipping had no place in provincial or rural Russia. You said what you wanted and it was brought to you with no gushing smiles or subsequent checking that the food was okay. If you were lucky, the food remained on the plate after it had been thrown at you. On the one occasion that I did leave a tip, the waitress tetchily chased me out of the restaurant to give it back to me.

This particular night, I fancied some chicken. The waitress, who was reassuringly rotund, waddled over to the table and took her position with pencil and pad poised. I thought I'd try first of all by asking in English. "Chicken?" I enquired brightly. Shake of head and a sigh. Okay, time for charades. I stuck out my elbows and wagged them whilst making my best clucking sound. Aaah! The penny dropped and I finally got what I wanted. I beseeched her to write down the Russian word for chicken and then say it a few times so that I could ask for it by name next time. I had chicken every night for the next two weeks.

I also struck up a friendship with the young woman on hotel reception. She smiled brightly whenever she saw me and in between her duties, which she took very seriously, she used to stop for a chat. She had been born in Vyliki-Luki, but told me very proudly that she had been to Moscow several times and had even taken a holiday to the Black Sea. The job in the hotel had attracted hundreds of applications and she had been thrilled to have secured it. Her face was still very young and full of optimism as she wondered aloud to me if she could finally leave her hometown to live and work in the West. She then smiled sadly and remarked that it was all just a dream; she would no doubt marry somebody local and have her own family. I told her that anything was possible - look at me! However, her expression changed again to reflect the wisdom of one who accepted her fate.

I grew in confidence over the next few days, walking through the small towns of Matsumovo and Novosokolyneekee (wouldn't you just love to play Scrabble in Russian?) as I sewed up the first section of the modified walk through Russia.

The final link from Novosokolyneekee back into Vyliki-Luki was troublesome, as the M9 actually bypassed my base town. The day started badly with my missing the early bus and having to wait around for another hour-and-a-half for the next one. Arriving in Novosokolyneekee, I walked steadily for an hour until reaching a bus stop that did not look familiar from the morning's journey. I enquired of the people waiting about the right road back towards Vyliki-Luki and they all agreed that I should take the bus. I explained as best I could that I wanted to walk. The response to this appeared to be them telling me not to worry as the bus would be along shortly. Smiling valiantly, I stood on the street walking on the spot with a big grin on my face to indicate that walking made me happy, so I didn't want to take the bus. Unfortunately, I think this behaviour slightly alarmed them and they all began to move away. A couple of children laughed and aped my walking/smiling routine. I smiled back and did it again to their delight.

With a sigh, I headed off across a field and then another, following a scattered lines of trees. With a final flourish, I edged along the side of a river and, with the railway line coming into view, stepped back into the outskirts of town. From that moment, I resolved to stick to the M9 with all its deviations, deferring any more adventures through the Russian countryside to an unspecified future date.

The next stage was easy, heading east from Vyliki-Luki, and at last I had the impression of making progress. There was a regular bus leaving at 9:30 each morning to take me along to each of my target towns and another to bring me back later in the day. I had the quaint notion that I might strike up some friendships with the regulars on the bus, but nobody was particularly interested in their usual fellow passengers, let alone me. To be honest, I was just pleased to be making quiet, modest progress towards Moscow. The M9 passed directly into the little target towns each day, so I was not left wandering around trying to find my way back too often. Once I had progressed as far as Abakonovo, I reckoned it was time to move on to my second city base of Rhzev.

I found myself once again preparing for a late-night train journey, checking out of the hotel and heading down to the railway station. I would be getting on the train at 2:00 a.m. this time and travelling another 200-plus kilometres to Rhzev, my new home for the next week or so. The train chugged in more or less on time and I took a seat in the standard-class carriage this time together with the other late-night travellers. I felt silently thrilled about this ride across Russia in the dead of night, evocative of all those Cold War spy novels, imagining the real covert journeys that must have been made on trains such as this, with agents seeking to slip through the shadows, under the watchful espionage radar.

The train stopped at intervals in what appeared to be the middle of nowhere. Several passengers climbed off, crossed the rail line and began walking down dirt tracks no doubt towards tiny villages beyond the illuminated plains. Watching their slow progress as they shuffled along, I thought more and more about the hard lives down the years of the inhabitants of this massive country.

The Romanov dynasty, which had provided one Tsar after another and presided without too much apparent benevolence over the masses, had been violently overthrown in the October 1917 revolution, to be replaced by the workers' Communist Government. Time had worked its inevitable effects and no discernible improvements had manifested in the lives of the downtrodden, with the added afflictions of war and then state-controlled tyranny. With the final collapse of the USSR came a new promised land along the twin paths of democracy and free market economics. The stilted steps towards this had faltered, however, and the masses found themselves disenfranchised more than ever, whilst a small band of entrepreneurs became the new elite, no more philanthropic than the Tsars or Communist chiefs.

My mind swam with these thoughts as the train rumbled on, finally arriving at Rhzev at 7:30 in the morning. Relieved to be arriving in daylight this time, I stepped out to view my base town for the next ten days. The railway station and the bus station were situated next to each other at the far south end of town. A taxi took me into the main centre, where the Hotel Rhzev stood as another fast-fading majestic edifice next to a broad stretch of the River Volga. I checked in, subjecting myself to the now familiar passport check and general charades. The room was located on the seventh floor and had an excellent view of the whole town. I had a comfortable bed, en suite bathroom, writing desk, big television and a fridge for £6 per night. Bonus!

With great discipline, I rose early the next day and after breakfast and showering made my way down to the bus and train station to get the times for transporting me back and forth for my daily walks. This was a doddle and I was cheered to see that I could take a bus to Nylidovo the right side of midday.

The road out of Nylidovo was another small yellow one according to the map, so I took the laminated pages with me to avoid any later confusion. The bus arrived and I got on board. It was another bone-shaker and trundled along the still potholed M9. The landscape swept past as we gained speed outside of the town and I reflected that the worst was over in Russia, as I had scheduled myself shorter days leading into Moscow. Something deep inside told me that I'd pay for the smug grin that covered my face at that moment. I didn't have to wait long.

The bus pulled into the first main stop and quite a few of my fellow passengers got up to leave. There was something familiar about the name on a couple of signs I had spotted on buildings in the little town. I pulled out the map and, sure enough, we had arrived in Zubtsov - the first town east of Rhzev. I had taken the wrong bus and spluttered away in the opposite direction to the west path not yet trodden. I joined the throng of people spilling out onto the street. I decided to make the best of it and walk back to Rhzev - a walk that was not due for a few days yet, but so long as I covered the distance I felt compelled to be relaxed about the order in which these were completed.

As the walking days were usually over by mid-afternoon, I had the opportunity to look around the large town of Rhzev and make some modest attempts to get to know the locals. My favourite waitress in the restaurant behind the hotel would greet me with a knowing smile and waggle her arms as she approached the table as a means of enquiring whether I wanted chicken again. Opposite the hotel was an outdoor market, where a brisk business was done selling slippers - at least five stalls selling them, all of which seemed to be doing okay. The fruit and veg lady, with thin greying hair pulled back under the same scarf each day, smiled as I approached and had my apples and oranges ready before I had to ask.

As my daily back-and-forth bus/walking trips came towards their end I began contemplating my imminent arrival in Moscow; significant not only for the pleasure of finally seeing the Russian capital, but also for marking the conclusion to 'Part One' of the world walk. Even allowing for the enforced stopover back in the UK, it was coming up to six months since I had started out from Buckingham Palace. It was perhaps indicative of the daily efforts that my fondest thought about the landmark arrival was that I could have a few days off! Back to the present, and with the walks between Nylidovo and Rhzev completed, I now turned my attention to making progress eastwards.

I took the now familiar bus ride to Zubstov and walked off towards Dmytrovo. The M9 threaded a fairly straight route through the countryside, which was chronically dull and it was several hours before I came across any sign of civilisation. As I made my way along, with the standard fare of large trucks, rickety buses and small private cars rushing past me, I felt that I had now fully relaxed into walking in Russia. Watching the smaller cars lurch across the road, one could have been forgiven for thinking that there was an excess of tipsy drivers on the loose. The reality was, however, that even the M9 major road had some pretty awful potholes along its surface.

The roadway became marginally more interesting as I approached Dmytrovo, but annoyingly the town itself was set back roughly three kilometres off the highway. I had little choice, however, as the plain road offered no bus stop and if I wanted to get back to Rhzev I'd have to go into town. After a brief rest, I turned up the small side road. Almost immediately I had company. A gentleman stopped his car and leaned out the window, asking me something in Russian.

"Ya anglee cha-neen," I said for the umpteenth time that week, thinking I really must expand my vocabulary.

"Eengleesh?" he queried, following this up with "Helloooo" and a broad grin.

I entered into the spirit and nodded, saying, "Da ... da."

Sadly, just as I had exhausted my mastery of Russian, he too had used up all his English. Nevertheless, he was determined we would be firm friends. We established that I was trying to make my way back to Rhzev and he insisted on driving me. Not one to look a gift horse in the mouth (where does that phrase come from?), I agreed and expressing gratitude climbed into the passenger seat. I told him my name and he replied that his name was ... well, it sounded like 'Margo', but that couldn't be right. Never mind. We lurched out into the road and I was immediately grateful to be sitting down at last.

Margo kept looking across and smiling away, and we experienced one of those moments when there is a need to turn general bonhomie into spoken communication, even on the smallest point. I tried talking about Spartak Moscow, but he was not a football fan. He looked to tell me about the countryside and I nodded and raised my eyebrows at what I thought were the right moments, but I think we both knew that nothing meaningful had really passed between us. It was not helpful that he kept leaning across to rub my forearm to make a point. The physical contact wasn't a problem, but the swinging of his car across the lanes definitely was ...

Finally, a light seemed to flash across his head of something we could talk about. This was instantly replaced by a very doleful face and I wondered what was coming next. He looked at me very sadly and said, "Eengleesh. Princess Diana." And there it was. We had a genuine connection. Neither of us needed to say any more, but we were united at that moment. I was aware that Diana had been very, genuinely loved by the Russian people, and the obvious, honestly felt sadness from this man living in rural Russia paying tribute to someone so far away in every sense was a bittersweet moment. He turned the car into Rhzev and dropped me outside my hotel.

~ 16 ~
Moscow in the Spring

The remaining days leading up to Moscow followed a similar pattern. I was navigating what the Latvian tourist office had described as the 'hungry road' through to the Russian capital, with little evident prosperity. My developed-world eyes frequently despaired of the drab views afforded by the little towns and villages along this route, but in trying to maintain an open mind I found myself lurching from one attitude to another.

Firstly, the natural reaction I felt was: these poor people - living in conditions of such destitution, waking every day to the grind of an existence in a dusty, undernourished life. Then I moved on to: if you are born into such a world, then you don't know any different and accept that this is how life is. From there, I considered the abundant satellite television dishes perched outside the houses and flats and the fact that images from Europe and America must be beamed into these homes, as well as the magnificence of the better cities in Russia, so they could not remain wholly ignorant of the better world out there. The next twist was that the Russians remain a proud people, often for good reasons of stoicism and a strong sense of identity. For example, one afternoon I returned to Rhzev and saw in the modest city park a group of maybe 40 youngsters raking up leaves and clearing fallen branches. In my time, I have witnessed groups of youths coerced into community toil, resenting every stroke of work they were forced to do. In this case, there was no sense of that - there was camaraderie and the kind of convivial good humour in doing a job well that I had only witnessed in much older volunteer workers in my experience back home.

The Russians with whom I had direct contact were bluff, lively characters. There was a great energy about them, in the way they walked, talked and indeed how they helped me along the way. On one occasion I had asked a gentleman where the nearest 'gasteeneetsa' (hotel) was. "Gasteeneetsa?" he roared back at me and then grabbed my shoulder and spun me round to face the other way. With his arm still on my left shoulder, his other hand pointed down the road and indicated the second turning on the left, all the time barking out instructions and giving me a short, sharp squeeze to emphasise each point. Releasing his grip, he looked at me expectantly and I said, "Spa see ba" (thank you), at which point he grunted and clapped me on the back as I walked off. Never in all the time I spent in Russia did I feel in any way threatened as I strolled from town to town. Once I had got over my brush with the authorities, I found myself in a land of undoubted harsh conditions but tough natives with good hearts.

Having scheduled myself shorter and shorter days leading into Moscow itself, the last leg was a mere 19 kilometres from the suburban town of Krasnogorsk to the gates of the Kremlin. In spite of all the great sights and wonderful experiences I had had during the entire walk, nothing compared to that day. Rural Russia was well and truly behind me as I walked through the now entirely urbanised streets and avenues of the capital.

Sometimes when walking I like to see the great sights from afar and watch them grow before my eyes. On other occasions it is better to turn a corner and - bam! - be hit by an amazing vista. Moscow saved up the grand prize for me until I approached the bridge spanning the Mascva River and, pushing the stroller onto the final straight, I was suddenly presented with the magnificent Kremlin and St Basil's Cathedral before me.

My pace slowed until I stood quite still halfway across the bridge, not quite believing that I was finally standing in front of the superlative building/monument that had captivated me for so long, so many years ago. The red brick fortress stretched far along the riverside, topped with dozens of towers and displaying a stern majesty that effortlessly exuded: power.

Shuffling along the bridge, I was oblivious to the passing traffic or anyone else who might have been walking alongside. Drawing my eyes away from the Kremlin's edifice, I concentrated on its neighbour, the incredible St Basil's Cathedral with weirdly curvaceous turrets - an architect's wildest musings made real. Ivan the Terrible had apparently poked out the eyes of the architects of the Cathedral shortly after completion so they could never again produce a building of such beauty. As I made the final approach to these two awesome structures, I took the mandatory photographs, resigned to the knowledge that they would never capture the experience of actually being there.

Red Square itself was sadly closed off due to the imminent Second World War anniversary commemoration services. This did mean that I was able to see hundreds of war veterans, now somewhat aged but sporting their best jackets and with medals on proud display, the ribbons and metal providing mere token reminders of the considerable sacrifice made during those dark years of the mighty struggle. With days to go before the ceremonies, some of these old soldiers may well have been making their last visit to the capital of the country they fought so hard to defend. I made my way back to the bridge.

Crossing back over, with the Kremlin now behind me, I could not resist gazing back once again and sat for a good 20 minutes emblazoning the view in my memory. I may never return, but when I close my eyes now I still recall every detail of that remarkable day.

Beaming, I made my way to the neighbourhood of Kolomenskaya to meet up with my Russian host, Tor. It turned out that he was still at work, but I was welcomed into the flat by some friends who were visiting. Tor and his girlfriend, Mary, were the principal tenants, with others staying over for long or short periods by arrangement. The short-term-stay visitors were in town for a church bell-ringing convention (that was a first for me) and did not have a great deal of English between them. Another young man, who seemed to be hanging around to bum cigarettes, food and drink from everyone else, was the only one who spoke a little English and he assured me that Tor and Mary wouldn't be long.

Tor was a chap of 30 years, with a large frame and a warm manner. He was every inch the convivial, gentle Russian bear. Mary was a slight, very sweet lady and they made a great couple. Their flat was of a reasonable size, with a large lounge doubling as Tor and Mary's bedroom, two further bedrooms, a small kitchen and smaller sole bathroom. With the number of people living or passing through from day to day, a degree of tolerance and patience was clearly required, but everyone seemed to rub along just fine.

Tor took hosting seriously, and when I mentioned I had almost run out of toothpaste in the early evening of my arrival, we set off to remedy the situation. We walked long and far around the immediate and surrounding neighbourhoods. This part of Moscow lent itself to good walking (even though I'd had enough just recently!) but Tor was keen to point out the areas and places of interest, which I appreciated. His English was not extensive, but better than most. Whilst telling me about one particular building, he called Mary on his mobile to confirm a particular word he was scratching for to finish the story. At length, we approached the undoubted highlight of the mini-tour: an 800-year-old monastery that had survived the communist attempts to eradicate organised religion in the country. The main place of worship sat between two streets, with a large area of courtyards fenced off and humble living quarters set to one side. We approached and Tor crossed himself on entering the ancient building. Once inside, my senses were immediately assaulted as never before in any church or other place of worship.

The inside of the church was exquisitely decorated, maintaining reverence not only for the iconic symbols of the Russian Orthodox Church, but also for the quiet nobility of the building's age. The pungent aroma of incense flooded my airways, but the most arresting impact of all was the sounds: the priest was singing a sermon with great feeling whilst waving the incense burner and the congregation was singing along with lusty voices reaching to the rafters. It was absolutely magical in its energy and I stood, smiling involuntarily at the sheer compulsion of the synergy between priest and congregation in this amazing place. The time to go was far too soon, but I had to consider Tor's long working day and we left with the sights, sounds and smells lingering with me still.

Back at the flat, I enjoyed the traditional gathering of the household in the kitchen for eats, drinks and chat. The table sat along the wall under the kitchen window, with a pot of leafy tea regularly refilling our cups and a large cake was sliced up between us, as the bell-ringing visitors, my hosts and I discussed in detail my walk so far and my plans for the next stages. This was truly what I had set out for; not anonymous hotels and endless days of speaking only with service staff. I wanted to meet the people of each place I went through, sit and eat and talk, wash the dishes together and hear about their lives. Unfortunately, on most occasions the conversation was dominated by discussion of my walk, which I understood because it was such a novelty that anyone would do such a thing, let alone a British man with few language skills and no more resources than a small backpack and stroller. I had intended to donate a bottle of vodka to the proceedings, but found out that neither Tor nor Mary were great drinkers of alcohol, apart from occasional glasses of wine. I learnt that day that Russians are very appreciative of large cakes and so provided a delicious fruit sponge for all following my next visit to the local supermarket.

This being midweek, everyone was working, so I was left to my own devices for the next day, which I spent again seeing Moscow on foot. I attended one of the better art galleries and visited the Bolshoi Ballet HQ, before heading for Pushkin Square for an appointment with an Australian journalist living in Moscow to do an interview for the English-language *Moscow Times*. I met up with Greg and we took a coffee in a little café just off the Square. He asked all the expected questions and I gave what I imagine were all the expected answers and then, with business concluded, we relaxed into a chat about our lives. He was still quite young, in his early 20s, and into his second stint of living and working in the Russian capital. In a very short time, we agreed that I would go round to his apartment and stay there for my last full day in Moscow and he kindly offered to see me safely onto the Trans-Siberian train on the Saturday morning.

I hope that Tor was able eventually to understand my reason for switching hosts. He asked me if there was a problem with his home, which I emphatically denied, expressing my genuine gratitude for having the opportunity to stay with real Muscovites. I left a little ruefully, but did in fact have trickier problems to resolve. The previous day I had gone to visit Intourist, the Russian national tourist centre in northern Moscow, to pay for and collect my ticket for the mammoth Moscow to Vladivostok train journey. It turned out that Intourist did not accept payment by credit card - cash only. Incredulous that the twenty-first century had not been acknowledged by the state's tourist department, I made two ATM visits in two days before finally picking up my travel documents. A shopping trip to the renowned Arbat Street followed, where I picked up three Russian nested dolls for my three-year-old niece. Also on offer for sale were a variety of fur hats, military regalia and, sadly, veterans' medals. I declined the opportunity to invest in a vintage cosmonaut's spacesuit.

I went along to Greg's apartment and met with him and his two flatmates, one German and the other Australian. A little after 11:00 they all decided I needed a night out on the town, so the four of us descended out onto the street.

Getting around Moscow is not difficult, with the excellent subway system. If, however, you don't want the hassle of making your way from station to station to reach your ultimate destination, just hold out your hand at passing cars. There are hundreds of private citizens who drive around looking to give paid rides to people who are not bothered about using regular taxis. We ended up getting a lift with a chap doing the rounds in his own car. Price fixed and agreed, he drove us into town and dropped us off close to our destination, the Hungry Duck. Jackets dropped off in the cloakroom, we made our way upstairs into the main club. It was a large main hall, with disco lights illuminating the proceedings. In the centre of the hall was a raised oblong platform area and a couple of bars in a side room to the left. Drinks acquired, we moved into the main hall again just in time to see a young lady step up onto the platform and begin removing what little clothes she was wearing. Up stepped a young man dressed as a cowboy, who started removing his shirt. Inwardly I sighed and just managed to stop my eyes rolling. Many people go through the stage of wondering what it's like to be in a strip club, but I had passed that stage many years ago. Call me a killjoy if you want, but on the few occasions I've been in such places, I have found them curiously devoid of any kind of eroticism. With no mystery, no chase and certainly no subtlety, it's just boring to me. Others will see it as harmless fun, which it surely can be, but I decided to take the air instead.

Outside on a very wide balcony area, I passed the time chatting again with Greg and we were joined as time went along by Russian, Belarusian and other European visitors. Enjoying once again the chance of a night out, I drank a little more than I should have, but reflected it was the first time since the New Year, five months earlier. Greg and I left and arrived back at the flat as the clock registered 5:00 a.m. Finally I laid down on the bed and dissolved into a contented sleep.

The next day Greg and I shared a farewell drink and made our way along to the main railway station. I took a last look at the amazing city of Moscow and climbed aboard the Trans-Siberian train. Next stop - Vladivostok.

~ 17 ~
Trains & Planes

The Trans-Siberian journey from Moscow to Vladivostok - unbroken - is an endurance test. As you would expect on the longest single train journey in the world, there's lots to see as you chug along, but to spend six-and-a-half days on a train is quite testing. I boarded to leave at Moscow and the train pulled out at 9:30 p.m. on Saturday 7th May.

One special treat is the official Trans-Siberian video. It runs for about 20 minutes and is absolutely priceless. It appears to have been shot entirely with hand-held camcorders, with all the disjointed poise of an amateur wedding video. Interspersed with the blurred shots of the landscape flying past are interviews with the staff, who clearly have not been trained for this sort of thing. We are then treated to the sight of the lengthy process of a member of staff emptying the garbage at the side of a platform, at which point the camera then shifts to dwell over a bucket of dead fish. The elegant strains of Shostakovic crash into pop music and back again and I seriously wanted to get hold of a copy. If you ever do the trip, demand to see this video and make sure you are alone when you watch it.

The guards on the train were all female and there was absolutely no doubt about the fact that they were in charge. I caught mine on the first morning gazing wistfully out of the window, no doubt reminiscing about her Olympic shot-putting days. Clearly there is a minimum weight requirement, with none of them coming in at less than 200 lbs. I feared that if two of them were hurrying down the corridor in opposite directions at the same time, we would soon need the fire department with cutting equipment.

The daily treat was the twice-daily leg-stretching break, where the train stops for 20 minutes, usually at the larger stations, so passengers have the chance to nip out and buy in supplies for the rest of the day. One particular aspect of these stops was the locals who appeared out of nowhere to set up little trestle tables next to the train and try to catch your eye and sell you foodstuffs as you got off. My guard would occasionally arch an eyebrow at me if I looked as though I was straying too far too close to departure time. I am certain that the train waits for no one.

The fourth day of the journey brought one of the real highlights of the 6,000-mile trek, as we passed by Lake Baikal, and it was a pity that we did not have any time to get out and take a longer look at this natural wonder. Apparently, 20 per cent of the world's fresh water is located in this one lake, which by itself is a staggering fact and the people of this region are very proud of it. My brief glance as the train rolled by revealed a view of what looks like an ocean, with a flat horizon stretching beyond the perception of the naked eye.

The train moved on, snaking in between huge snow-topped mountains and hills, rising to meet the lower peaks and offering more glimpses of attempts to colonise the land. More evidence of the contrasting climates came a couple of hours after the snow-laden hills, when I saw a bare-chested man digging his small allotment beside a wooden shack, with his wife following behind him, planting seeds in the newly dug troughs. Clusters of these shacks were lined up together, with dirt roads providing the borders and alleyways in between. Once again, several satellite television dishes protruded from the roofs and I wondered what might be the villagers' response to the images beamed into this little corner of the earth they occupied. Envy of the far-off lifestyles or relief to be so far away? Now that would be an interesting conversation to have.

The journey ended on Saturday morning at 9:30, exactly six-and-a-half days since setting off from Moscow as the train pulled into Vladivostok. I climbed a flight of metal steps up to street level and looked around as the early morning rain began to fall. The city was clean, bustling and full of Chinese tourists. A taxi took me to a beachside hotel with faded grandeur and cracked walls for $30 per night. This was the one for me. In reception the three attendants had roughly 20 words of English between them, so I handed over my passport and prepared to fill out the registration card.

"Nyet!" came a sudden exclamation. Was there a problem? Oh yes, there was a problem all right. I was apparently in violation of my visa and had to report immediately to the police - no hotel in the city would touch me until I had rectified my appalling abuse of the terms of my visa. I had that sinking feeling once again. The upshot was that whilst travelling through Russia the hotels at which I had stayed should have stamped the card stapled into my passport as confirmation that I had stayed there, effectively accounting for my every movement in the country. No stamps, so I was technically illegal. It's

The pram makes a run for it along
the Hume Highway (Australia)

The dry, dusty highways of Australia

The endless road leading towards
Junee (Australia).

Barry, the middle-aged rocker who gifted
me a can of Wd40 for the stroller (Australia)

Setting off on another day's plodding after
a free night at the seven creeks hotel

Cadillac Ranch, just outside Amarillo

Elation at finishing part Two in Sydney

A great day off at the Grand Canyon

The wilderness of Arizona

In the mid-way Point café in
Adrian, Texas. The café
sits exactly halfway along route 66

The end. My Dad and old school friend Paul hold the
banner as they did more than a year earlier

Doing an interview
(and singing "White Christmas")
for German TV

Leaving Potsdam on my
way into Berlin

Poland dressed for the winter

The treacherous conditions along the
Polish highways

44 days in -
Arriving at the
Brandenburg Gate!

Germany gets ready
for Christmas! (Stadhagen)

The lovely, flat landscape of
Belgian canals (Brugge)

Leaving the White Cliffs of Dover
(and the wrecked room) behind me

Walking across Tower bridge
(day one again)

October 29th, 2004 - setting
off from Buckingham Palace
with police escort (right)

Stating part Four - Lands End on
a blustery December day

A very happy man, winding
up part Three - 2,800
miles from the beaches of
California to downtown Manhattan

Interview for ITV News
at Admiralty Arch (last day)

The family join me for the final week
at Salisbury. A back up team at last!

Walking back along the Mall

Alanreed's official census results, posted for all to see

About to be rescued in Princetown, New Jersey. A member of staff in the property shop offered me dinner and a bed for the night, 5 minutes after saying "hello"

The name of the gas station doesn't begin to describe it! (Ohio)

Ohio in fall. Where I felt the real sense of freedom

Another TV interview in Joplin, Missouri

Buying some nested Russian dolls
from Father Christmas

Looking contented in Kaunas, Lithuania

Russian common-folk
gather along the street
to sell their wares

The "Hungry road" - the M9
which took me all the way to Moscow

Waiting for the train to take me on the fateful ride into Russia

not really the kind of thing that you want to walk into a Russian police station and admit, but I had no choice if I wanted to sleep in a bed that night.

I set off into the centre of town and located the police station. Opening the door, I found the reception area with glass frontage and to the side a small metal desk, reassuringly occupied by a uniformed man holding a semi-automatic rifle. I approached the man with very open hand gestures and uttered my usual opening gambit, "Ya anglee cha-neen." Quickly establishing that neither of us spoke the other's language, he picked up the phone and dialled through to a colleague, whilst looking me up and down with deep suspicion. A brisk woman, with hair pulled severely back into a bun, emerged from the side door and barked at me: "Yes?" I explained in faltering tones that there was a problem with my visa. She took my passport and her eyebrows shot up in an accusing manner. She gestured that I should follow her through a metal-barred cell door, but not before my backpack had been emptied on the desk to confirm I had nothing sinister lurking within.

The metal door clanked shut behind me and I descended concrete steps down below street level. An impending sense of doom gripped me as another metal-barred door was clanked shut behind me and I wondered when I would see daylight again. We made our way into an interrogation room and I sat with mounting unease on a small wooden chair next to a metal desk. The lady clearly had other cases to work on and she was in no hurry to attend to my issues.

Eventually my case bubbled to the surface of my interrogator's attention and she turned to face me and snapped, "Don't you know our laws?" I was at a loss as to how to respond when the door opened and the latest of my angels appeared, right on cue. Anya swept in with the one facet that had been conspicuously missing in all dealings with Russian officials to date: a smile. She had been sent for as the best English-speaker in the station and effectively became my defence lawyer in this impromptu hearing. Quickly familiarising herself with the circumstances, she sat back to listen. The interrogator returned to her line of questioning, namely, "Don't you know our laws?" Anya with great speed and feeling retorted, "Of course he doesn't - how could he?" At that point I just wanted to hug her. The rest of the hearing was conducted between the two of them, with me nodding in contrition at the appropriate moments.

Eventually Anya explained to me that I must fill out a form admitting that I understood I had done wrong and, whilst pleading ignorance, must apologise emphatically in writing and then pay a £20 fine. I can do that! Anya escorted me back up the stairs, through the cell door, into the street and along to the bank to withdraw some money for the fine. We chatted about my walk and she marvelled at the adventures I was having. Apart from a few trips within Russia itself, she had not ventured beyond China. With the fine paid, we went back into the station and got my passport stamped. I said goodbye with thanks and went to check into the hotel.

Vladivostok itself was a very well-presented city, with an attractive harbour and purpose-built beach. I sat eating a sandwich in reasonably warm sunshine and watched the locals, daytrippers and tourists going into the little theme park with modest rides, the children taking donkey rides along the promenade and the hastily set up beer tents which acted as magnets for the Chinese visitors. I was reminded of Southend-on-Sea, except there were no fish and chips on offer. Vladivostok had been closed to any outside visitors until the early 1990s due to its sensitive military importance, which made it all the more remarkable that it had been scrubbed up ready for tourists in such a short time. Italian and French restaurants offered alternatives to the local and oriental fare and any kinds of designer clothes were on offer in the city's main shopping area. Nevertheless, I made sure I was back in the hotel as darkness fell. My phone rang at 8:00 and a voice asked if I wanted a Russian girl for the night. No thanks ... Moments after I had replaced the receiver, the phone rang in the unoccupied room next to me. Someone was doing the rounds.

Hot on the heels of a six-and-a-half day train journey I now faced a very convoluted series of flights to put me into position to start 'Part Two' of the walk. Korean Airways would take me out of Vladivostok to Seoul, then Japanese Airlines to Narita, Tokyo. The next day Qantas would fly me out of Tokyo to Brisbane, then bounce me from Brisbane to Adelaide and finally Melbourne. This would be trying for the most seasoned traveller, but I had one additional issue to jar me: I'm terrified of flying.

Can I just say that, statistically speaking, someone is more likely to get a smack in the eye from me if they start a sentence with the phrase, "You know, statistically speaking ..." Wherever you are, mention a concern about flying and some smug git will rattle off the trite customary reference to flying being statistically the safest form of transport. YES - WE DO KNOW. And it doesn't help; it doesn't make any difference. Do these people think we've never heard it before? Do they think we will suddenly relax on hearing this revelation?

In my younger days, as already mentioned, I had flown all over the world with no qualms. But I can trace my anxiety back to a flight with China Airways from Taipai and Bangkok in 1993, where the turbulence and cabin crew's reaction to it convinced us all we were going to die. My phobia has, of course, attracted the waggish observation more than once that people now understand why I walk everywhere ...

The routine for me is becoming all too familiar now. Find the seat and strap myself in as tight as the belt will allow. Clasp hands firmly on the hand-rest and try to think of what I will be doing later in the day when the terror is all over. The plane begins to taxi across to the runway, with each bump and shudder of the fuselage reverberating through my body. The plane comes to a rest and I experience the awful last moments of safe stillness before the inevitable mighty thrust into the ether. Then the sound of the engines cranking up and the plane lurches forward, faster and faster and faster. The tyres rumble insistently along the ground until the propulsion becomes too much for gravity to contain. The first lifting from the ground tingles my shoulders and the pit of my stomach sinks. Eyes closed, hands gripping tight, every muscle tensed, a flush of heat bringing a rash of itches that I cannot release my hands to scratch. The plane climbing, climbing, rattling overhead lockers and the high-pitched whining of the engines giving voice to the internal scream I manage to suppress. The shaking of the aeroplane's tail as the maelstrom of air currents outside torment the metallic invader of their skies. And then the engine noises regress, maintaining a quieter hum as the plane levels off and begins its long course at great speed. Seatbelt signs go off, people move up and down inside the cabin and the crew begin their rounds. This should, of course, be a moment of sweet relief as the take-off has been successfully executed. For me, however, it merely confirms that I am now trapped for the entire duration of the flight, condemned to feel every nuance of turbulence and hear every rattle and change of engine tone. My initial valium and vodka is used to get me onto the plane, but the take-off usually negates the effects and I keep the tablets handy for more fortification as the journey progresses.

Undertaking five flights in 48 hours should really, I guess, have worked as some kind of shock therapy for me, but I was as spooked by the fifth as the first. After an hour in Seoul I was off on the long flight to Tokyo, which then required me to stay over one night in Japan as the connection couldn't be guaranteed. Flying out the next day, I cursed that I had slept so well in the hotel in Tokyo - I was counting on a restless night to render me unconscious for the next big flight, but no such luck.

Australian immigration admitted me into the country at Brisbane, then it was two short internal flights to Adelaide and finally into Melbourne. At the end of this tortuous haul, I stepped gratefully off the last plane, collected my bags and walked out of the airport into the night to catch a bus to downtown Melbourne.

~ 18 ~
G'Day All!

Oh joy! Oh unreserved, unfettered joy! Smiling faces, great service, clean sheets, upbeat people, beautiful weather, lovely buildings AND everything in English! Street signs, menus, newspapers, magazines, television, conversations in the street - all in English!

I felt positively giddy with glee when I stepped off the first plane in Adelaide and on clearing Customs I made my way to the customer service desk and a broad-smiling Aussie bloke uttered that immortal phrase, "G'Day mate. How's it going?" I knew that wherever I went from here I was back in the English-speaking world, and whilst there were bound to be trials and frustrations I could at least explain myself confidently. I had cherished all the experiences in Europe, but felt so very, very happy to be in Australia.

Ahead of me lay 550 miles to cover from Melbourne to Sydney in just over a month. I had in my sights the Hume Highway which stretched the whole way, built to iron out the contours of the land mirrored by earlier connecting roads. Being now in the Southern Hemisphere, arriving in May meant that the days were getting shorter as Australia headed through autumn into winter, with accompanying temperatures in the 60s ideal for walking. My mighty pound was also going to get me roughly $2.50 in Oz, so I hoped to bump along on a modest budget before heading off to America. I rattled off a couple of e-mails to the Victoria and New South Wales Cancer Councils to let them know I was heading their way.

Kicking off Part Two in Federation Square was very different to the start of Part One. With no time to organise any advance press coverage or appeals for the charities, nobody knew who I was or what I was doing. With no ceremony I started pushing the stroller towards Elizabeth Street and out of the city. The good news was that for the first time I managed to negotiate my way out of a major city without going around in circles. Elizabeth Street took me past the very attractive Princes Park and on to Royal Parade, leading out onto the M31 highway. The end of Melbourne was denoted by the start of Brunswick, with narrow streets and tightly packed shops making progress a little slow. Eventually the road widened and suburbia receded, leaving me walking along the main highway.

At 3:45 I came upon the 'Welcome to Cragieburn' sign and gratefully made my winding way into the little town centre. I asked a couple where the nearest, cheapest motel was located and inwardly groaned as they told me there were no motels or other accommodation in town. Disconsolate, I stumbled across into the small shopping arcade and into the Salvation Army shop for their advice. The lady told me the best idea would be to go back to Brunswick and stay at the F1 motel. This was several miles - sorry kilometres - back. I accepted my fate and they kindly called a taxi for me. My first day of walking in Australia and I had to double back for a motel, spend money on a cab and then get back here early the next day to keep walking. Grrrrrr …

Things picked up from there, as the F1 gave me a free room. After showering and packing up the next morning, I went downstairs to Hungry Jack's and had a plate of grease for breakfast.

I had various suggestions for how to get back to Cragieburn, involving train stations some way off the main road and bus services that seemed sporadic at best. In the end I found myself walking the same road I had trodden the day before. When a taxi finally appeared behind me I almost leapt into the road to flag it down. $10 later, I found myself back outside the Salvation Army shop and popped into the café for a sustaining coffee before heading off towards the day's target town of Wallan. The error of this decision soon came back to haunt me, as the milky coffee stimulated the greasy breakfast, leaving me on the open road to Wallan in need of a toilet.

With nothing but fields and sprinkled wooded areas all around I walked on gingerly, feeling the pressure on my bowels and trying to think of something else whilst scanning the horizon desperately for some sign of civilisation. The combination of this pressure, plus the anxiety of finding a suitable spot and the constant walking motion led me towards the dreadful thought that I may suffer the most unfortunate accident imaginable. Left, right, left, right and try not to think about it - I marched ever onwards, pushing the stroller and checking how many tissues I had in my pocket. Just as all seemed to be lost, I spotted a sign at the side of the road ahead - a gas station! With a steady pace and an increasingly mincing motion, I pushed open the door, rolled the stroller (backpack and all) across the floor of the shop and dived into the toilet, making it with only seconds to spare.

I emerged a few minutes later, business attended to, and sat gratefully on a bench outside the shop. No more coffee at crucial times of the day and no more breakfasts after my daily ablutions had been completed. I pushed the stroller back onto the road.

The next four hours were spent in a constant battle against a fierce wind. The road to Wallan took in some lovely scenery and the Hume Highway did iron out some of the worst dips and dives, but in some sections the planners appeared to have built in swoops and swings so drivers could capture the best views. At one point I was coming around a rising bend into a full-face torrent of wind and virtually ground to a halt. The force of the wind was equal to the force of my efforts walking into it and every step had to be fought for. At least I was brightening the day of some of the motorists who shook their heads with a smile at my efforts.

Wallan's motels were full for the night, so I breezed on to Kilmore, with its plethora of motels and camping sites. I settled for a motel on the edge of town for $55 and after checking in I made the delightful discovery of what would be the pattern in motels across Australia. As well as a queen-sized bed, television and en suite, as expected, you are supplied with a kettle, fridge and toaster. What a treat! Probably reflective of my ever-lowering expectations and increased appreciation of crumbs of comfort, I was delighted by these homely touches. Bread, butter, cheese, ham, bananas and oranges were bought at the local store and I sat down to the first decent cup of tea I'd had for months. The weather was warm enough for me to take my tea outside, where I sat on the porch chair, sipping away and watching the sun descend.

Checking my map for the next day's walk I saw that, following the extra distance covered, I was only a short stroll from the next target town of Broadford. Allowing myself a lie-in, I set off briskly at 10:00 and on an unremarkable morning arrived in Broadford a little before 1:00. Having got ahead of the game so well, I decided to press on for the next target town of Seymour, a further 22 kilometres on.

As I walked back to rejoin the Hume Highway, I passed a group of around a dozen teenage lads who looked at me curiously as I passed. Can't imagine why - a bloke pushing a stroller with a backpack in it, wearing a canary yellow workman's vest with 'World Walker' written on the back ... The spokesman for the pack yelled out to ask me what I was doing. I briefly explained, to which he replied, "Bull****." I shrugged my shoulders and smiled as only an older cool guy can in that situation.

That stretch of the Hume Highway was enclosed for several kilometres by wooded areas and I found myself once again facing down the traffic hurtling along. Covering a day-and-a-half's worth of walking, I pressed on, feeling the strains of getting my body back into the real swing of things. With no town or villages crossed by the road, I had to rely on a bottle of water and the fruit candies I had in my pocket for sustenance. As the road rose to open up quite a swathe of open countryside, I felt once again the pressure to increase the depth of my breath, the old familiar trickles of sweat running off my forehead and down the sides of my body, and forced myself to push through the pain barrier and onward. Three long hours later I came to the Seymour service station just outside town, where I bought another bottle of water and rested up on the wooden decking next to the car park.

I then shuffled along to the first motel I found and the owner very magnanimously told me that if I continued another 100 metres on the left there was a much cheaper motel for me. Good on you! I took a room and peeled off my clothes, which were absolutely saturated with sweat. I just about managed to stay awake long enough to eat my dinner at a nearby restaurant and stumbled back to my room, then sank into a deep sleep.

The local tourist office found me a motel room in the next town of Avenel for a bargain $20 and recommended that I should go to the local newspaper, which kicked off the low-level publicity that would eventually grow into national coverage by the end of my time in Oz. I often had the impression that I was the biggest thing to happen locally for years and the papers gave me great coverage, more than once making me the front page story.

One week into Oz, I was not only making good progress but actually enjoying the experience. I had increased the distances covered each day, and the knowledge that I could now speak the language along with the friendly reception I got everywhere meant that I walked with an easy mind and a level of confidence I had not felt since the familiar surroundings of south-east England. Life was great and I looked forward to more of the same as I headed further north out of Victoria State towards New South Wales. I upped the pace again with a 36-kilometre stretch to Euroa, then walked on to the sweetly named Violet Town. On arrival I had in mind that a European Cup final was being played that night in which Liverpool were featuring for the first time in more than 20 years. I took a room at the Frances Ellen hotel, which did not reduce its pricey $70 for the night, but I did have the compensation of a spa bath and a separate lounge area from where I could watch the footie. I went out and bought the usual bread, cheese and ham plus a few cakes and biscuits for the anticipated party I would later enjoy.

Waking at 3:30 the next morning, I sat down with a few slices of toast and a pot of tea and got ready for the action. I had the volume turned down, as there was a couple in the room next to me and a trucker on the other side.

When the referee blew the half-time whistle 45 minutes later I felt like going back to bed. The Italians of Milan had completely dominated the first half, with the result that Liverpool were losing 3-0 with no apparent prospect of getting back into the match. However, after seven crazy minutes in the second half, the match was squared at 3-3. I was bouncing up and down on the sofa, silently screaming my delight so as not to wake the neighbours, but after Jerzy Dudek saved the fifth penalty to bring us final victory, I could contain myself no longer. "YEESSSS!" I screeched, safe in the knowledge that we were now approaching 7:00 in the morning and any respectable person would be up and about by that hour. I danced twice around the coffee table and brewed up another tea to celebrate. All this, and I still had to go out and walk 30 kilometres ...

As I approached Benella later that day, I broke my journey at a rest stop and met a genuine bushman: whippet thin, with a few possessions arranged around his body and an assured air - I was going to say sun-kissed skin, but this guy had gone way beyond the kissing stage with the sun. I asked him what time it was and he replied happily, "Haven't a clue", before wandering off into the wild. After Benella, I was heading for a rendezvous with a certain Mr Ned Kelly ...

Glenrowan, my target town for the next day, was where Ned Kelly made his last stand. Of Irish descent, he remains one of the most colourful figures in Australian history. In the latter years of the nineteenth century he rebelled against the unfair treatment of the poorer sections of Aussie society and became a kind of Robin Hood character with many sympathisers helping him stay one step ahead of the police. As his behaviour became more extreme, he and his gang armed themselves to the teeth and made their own form of armoury to protect them from the numerous shoot-outs with the law. His last stand in Glenrowan sealed both his legend and the town's status as an historic byword. The town's prosperity is built almost exclusively on maintaining the legend.

The main street stretches not quite a mile, with restaurants, tea rooms, pubs and even a charming animatronics museum dedicated to the memory of Kelly. Outside the post office stands a huge, colourful statue of Kelly, a good 30 feet high, dressed in the iconic helmet and brandishing a rifle. I took a Devonshire cream tea in Billy's Cafe, listening to 'Waltzing Matilda' playing on the stereo, and couldn't resist going into the museum to enjoy the animatronics show. It won't give the people of Disney much to worry about, but its charm was perfect for the place.

~ 19 ~
Fame at Last

My schedule for the next week or so demanded that I walked high 30s/low 40s in terms of kilometres each day, getting on for roughly a daily 26-mile marathon. That was fine, as I was certainly back into the routine by now. After doing an interview for the *Wangaratta Chronicle* newspaper I headed out onto the road again, finding the route to Chiltern remarkable for its scenery but not exactly peppered with distractions like cafés, bars, shops, etc. It was therefore a steady progression that brought me along into Chiltern just before sundown. The next day was pretty similar as I pushed on to Wodonga. Coming into town I spotted the offices of the *Border Mail*, which I had been told was a high-distribution newspaper and definitely one to be seen in. Interview done, I crossed the bridge dividing Wodonga from its twin town of Albany and simultaneously stepped over the state line into New South Wales. As darkness fell, I made my way to the Chiltern motel and after a shower popped into the pub next door and tucked into a plate of bangers and mash.

Before setting off the next day I rushed to check out the *Border Mail* newspaper. They had squeezed me in on page 7 with four paragraphs on a slim ¼ inch column. Never mind - I had made it into a larger circulation paper and with this happy thought I walked up to the offices of ZAY Radio and knocked on the door of the studio. One of the engineers let me in after I assured him I was not armed and certainly not dangerous. He gave me a cup of tea and went in search of the station manager. He repeated the 'not dangerous' phrase by way of introduction when the station manager appeared, who greeted me with the phrase, "Ah no, he's a bloody pomme," to which we all laughed.

With the morning show's time running a little tight, they decided in the end to put me in with the DJ and do the interview 'live'. Thus it was that I sat with ZAY broadcasting across both states, telling my story on air. Interview concluded, I headed back to get on the road.

The media coverage gave me a spring in my step as I headed northwards out of Albury. It was just as well, because the road became somewhat protracted with little relief to a lonesome walker. The landscape was once again great, but man cannot live by views of trees, fields and mountains alone. A little café is always appreciated. The temperature was still up in the 60s, which made for pleasant strolling, but as I stepped up the pace I felt myself overheating from time to time. At length, I came along to the intersection between the mighty Hume Highway, which I had followed since day one, and the Olympic Highway, which I would now take to head more or less due north.

The most sensible thing would have been to follow the Hume all the way through to Sydney. This came in at exactly 860 kilometres (500 miles). However, whilst I was still planning the route back home in England I had fired off a scattering of e-mails requesting a place to stay through the Internet. One reply had come from John in Wagga Wagga, who not only had invited me to stay at his family home but also had taken the time to break down the distances of my planned route and suggest alternative stops. Now anyone who took that much trouble to look after my welfare following a single e-mail demanded my respect and thanks, so I bent the route to incorporate Wagga Wagga to meet up with him.

I turned up the Olympic Highway and began the trek on to Gerogery, another 12 kilometres down the road. The effect of switching highways was immediate. The traffic flow dried up to a trickle and I walked hour after hour with only occasional cars rolling past. The side of the road was now covered in dried-up grassy clumps, which rustled and shook a little worryingly as I passed. Whilst panting my way along this rather deserted road, I remembered a statistic given out on the Discovery Channel a while back, which advised that 90 per cent of the deadliest creatures on the planet are located in and around Australia. I encroached a little further onto the road surface, away from the clutches of the mysteriously lively grass, and hastened my steps.

As I came into Gerogery, a car stopped and a travelling businessman got out to shake my hand. He had been listening to the radio broadcast that morning and wondered if he would run into me. That sort of thing happened all across my slice of Australia following a media spot, with people stopping their cars and coming out of shops and offices to wish me well, and occasionally pressing a few dollars into my hand 'for a beer' or to help with other costs. A few moments later, I arrived in Gerogery.

It was little more than a single-street village, but in tandem with much of Australia there was always a pub with rooms attached. As I was the only guest for the night, I got a large set of rooms with a double bed in the main area and six singles in the adjoining room. Whilst spacious, the room was absolutely freezing, so I commandeered two extra duvets from the spare beds to cocoon myself for the night. Hopping gingerly out of bed the following morning, I made my shivering way into the bathroom. After exchanging pleasantries with the spiders, I blasted myself on full jet power to shower some feeling back into me.

I cracked along at a romping pace the next day, chewing up mile after mile, reaching Culcairn at 12:30. I stopped off at the Culcairn pub for some refreshment. After chatting about my mission, MJ behind the bar gave me a free can and one of the locals suggested the television news should be made aware of my exploits. In a jiffy, phone calls were made and Prime News promised to come and look for me along the road. After drinking everyone's health I set off at an even brisker pace, propelled along by the imminent TV coverage, the bonhomie from the bar and, naturally, the tipple.

On and on I steamed, finally coming along to the small village of Henty where I would spend the night. I took a room at the Doodle Cooma hotel before stepping out for chicken and chips at a local café. Henty was a small outpost of civilisation, perched on the Olympic Highway between the larger towns all around. It had a sleepy air of quiet existence for those either wanting respite from the higher-octane pace of their working lives or those just wishing to live out a rural life with modest amenities close by.

The fickle finger of fame furnished my flush face the following day. Prime News made good on its promise as I walked through Yalong Creek. Belinda and Matt introduced themselves and set up to record an interview for transmission that night. We did a 'straight' interview with face to camera, and then Matt shot me walking along chatting with Belinda. Then we added the comedy touches, with me dashing behind a bush apparently to commune with nature. The whole shoot took around 45 minutes for about five minutes on the news bulletin, punctuated by my appeal for donations to Australia's two principal cancer charities. I continued on my way, finally arriving in a small town interestingly called The Rock, and took a room at the local motel for $55. I watched myself on the news and danced a little jig around the room. To celebrate, I went into the bar, where the owners gave me my $55 back to support the cause.

As I slowly walked back to my room, I gazed up into the night sky. It was a fresh, cloudless night and the stars looked incredibly clear. Apart from the muffled voices from the bar, all was still. The night sky looked curiously artificial as it might to a habitual city dweller, with no pollutants to obscure the view. I was tired, but very much at peace. I had told myself during the snowy, drab, frustrating tribulations of Eastern Europe that there would come a day when I could relax and smile about all the anxieties I had been going through. This was that day.

The effect of my TV appearance was immediate. Walking on towards Wagga Wagga the next day I was honked, waved at, stopped for chats and, it appeared, taken to the hearts of all who saw me. With the bit firmly between my teeth I powered on, enthused by the response of the great Aussie public, and to my astonishment arrived at the halfway town of Uranquinty two-and-a-half hours later. That was a distance of 17 kilometres. I refused to believe it. The timing was quite correct, having left at 9:00 and arriving at 11:30, but I checked into a pub to make sure of the distance. Sure enough, all confirmed it was at least 15 kilometres, maybe a little more. Grabbing a can, I sat out on the porch to watch the traffic for a while and rest easy.

The approach road to Wagga Wagga goes on for ever. Just as the signs beguile you into thinking that you are about to hit town, another stretch of open road laughs at your premature relief. Walking along the final section of the main highway, I crossed into town and paid a visit to the *Advertiser* newspaper and finally met up with John, my champion of middle Oz, more than a year after our initial e-mails.

I spent a very enjoyable evening with John, family and friends that night, including that tried and trusted Australian tradition, a barbeque. With all my clothes handed over for a wash and spin, I was offered a complete change of wardrobe for the night, but happily wore my trousers without undergarments ahead of their turn to spin. That turned out to be the biggest mistake of the entire walk.

The next night, whilst taking a shower, I felt a small lump that had appeared on the lower right cheek of my backside. An old familiar medical complaint had come back to haunt me at the most inappropriate time in my life. I had sustained my third perianal abscess. This condition is caused either by grit or an ingrowing hair, leading to the development of an infection beneath the surface of the skin that grows by stealth until the abscess is the size of an egg (sometimes larger) and the pain is unbearable. Not to put too fine a point on it, sitting and standing become excruciating. By not wearing any undergarments beneath my trousers the previous night I had caused this myself. I was aghast. If anything was going to torpedo my ability to complete the walk, this would be it. On that first evening of discovery the abscess was not even the size of a pea, but I knew from bitter experience how things usually developed.

I ran through my options: carry on walking and hope for the best; check into hospital and try to get it removed immediately; or go back to England for treatment and once healed get back on the road.

I knew that no hospital would drain the abscess at that early stage. The whole point of treating them was to allow them to manifest and then drain before healing could begin. Going back to England was really unattractive, as I was having such a great time and making real progress - and the cost of flights would have probably sunk my chances of getting back on the road to finish. I settled for the first option, to carry on walking and hope for the best, although I did plan to take medical advice whilst still in Australia, thereby avoiding the heavy bills of healthcare in America.

John dropped me off the next morning on the road leading out of Wagga Wagga, to head on to the next big town of Junee. This was a real endurance test, as the road wound long and free along a pretty deserted part of the country. I had set off with three litre bottles of water, but with the warmth of the day still belying the onset of autumn these did not last as long as I had hoped. I felt sluggish as the day wore on and cursed the 40-plus kilometre target, but in reality there was no alternative stop in between Wagga Wagga and Junee. A young lady stopped in her car, concerned about the baby in the stroller, but realising there was none she then switched her concern over to me. I looked a little peaky apparently. I grinned through the aches and resisted the temptation to flop on the passenger seat.

I finally saw a sign ahead telling me that a gas station was imminent, with the unmistakable faucet sign to indicate water was available. I happily glugged a few mouthfuls from the water bottle and stepped up for my prize, except ... the gas station was deserted; the shop attached had a sign they were closed due to illness. Muttering darkly, I spotted a tap on the side of the building and went over to get a drink of precious water at least. No go. The tap had spiders' webs dangling from it and had apparently long since gushed its last drop. Now what? Well, looking up and down the road I could not see any other sources of refreshment, so I applied the TINA principle (There Is No Alternative) and carried on walking.

I was dry, oh ... so ... dry. My tongue began making subconscious contortions around my mouth, trying to extract moisture and playing on the body's sense of dehydration. I stopped sweating and began to feel the beginnings of a headache. I resolved that from that day forward I would carry more water than I could possibly drink. The hazy sun, not really so hot but nevertheless insistent, continued to cast a challenging sheen across my path. I still had the can of Southern Comfort and Coke stuffed down inside the stroller, but knew better than to apply alcohol to a dehydrated body. And still, the relentless road refused to offer up a village, a house, a shop or a well. I had perhaps a quarter-inch of water left in the last bottle, which I rationed to a sip every ten minutes. (What the hell am I doing …?)

Finally, finally I approached the turn-off to Junee, and seated at the top of the road was a shop with café attached. I sucked in air to let out a whoop of delight, but found that this wiped the remainder of saliva out. I literally staggered through the gate, up the path and into the shop. I bought a litre of Gatorade and two more bottles of water, then sat down outside the shop, not caring about the remaining distance into town, and guzzled. The Gatorade lasted around two minutes and half of the first bottle of water followed it down quickly afterwards. Breathing hard, I slumped my head between my knees and closed my eyes. Rising back up, I stretched my arms above and then to the side, before arching my back and then relaxing back into my seat. This had been a tough day and it wasn't over yet. I had completed 32 kilometres (20 miles) and had another nine kilometres to walk into town. And the really bad news was the extremely steep hill that I could already see in the middle distance. Nothing for it, I had to move on.

Walking along the road leading towards Junee, I passed several fields that were parched dry. The soil had been turned over, but it appeared to be a process of churning dust into the wind. Australia had been suffering a crippling drought for several years, with the result that I had unbelievably heard about children of three years old who had never seen rain. The country's plight had made water one of the hottest political and social topics on the national agenda. Various approaches were debated, from price hikes and rationing to desalination of seawater. Sustained rainfall was what was needed, but there was little evidence to suggest that an end to the drought was likely. I was quite touched to learn that Wagga Wagga, which does not have specific water issues, nevertheless introduced restrictions in solidarity with the surrounding areas of the east.

Leaving the dust fields behind me, I began the climb of that hill leading into Junee. I could no longer see the little shop and café where I had stopped, so felt I must now be getting close to town. The hill was a monster - some are short and steep, others long and gradual. This seemed to combine the worst in both. I stopped several times to catch my breath and was taken aback that I was now halfway through the last bottle of water recently purchased. Upwards and upwards I struggled, pushing the stroller ahead of me, leaning on it for support and in the process twisting my back into all kinds of unhealthy angles. Finally the summit was in sight. I pushed the last 20 metres with legs of jelly and stood to survey the town of Junee, which was positioned just the other side of another hill. Okay - shoot me now. I don't care.

The 'hill' was actually one of those optical illusions, because there was the downward slope of the hill I had just climbed and then a much smaller rise to cover before arriving in town. It was only from first glance that the second 'hill' appeared to be in the way. I walked through the town and out the other side, taking a hotel room right on the road leading back onto the highway for the next day.

In the local grocery store I bought myself a pack of Tetley tea bags and a carton of milk and proceeded to have four cups of tea back in my hotel room with my supper. Rehydrated and finally relaxed, I tuned in to the new series of *Dr Who*.

~ 20 ~
Wet Wet Wet

I didn't sleep well in Junee. It was nothing to do with being scared by *Dr Who*; my mind was churning around the usual concerns about money, the daily walking distances, the weather in America in the summer and, now, the abscess.

I made sluggish progress out of Junee towards Bethungra, although I was cheered up by further honks and chats with people who had seen me on TV. I eventually turned into the very small village of Bethungra and hastened along to the Shirly hotel. After a brief chat with Lorraine on the desk, she offered me a free room, with $20 to cover the cost of dinner and breakfast. Great! After showering I came down to probably the best meal I had enjoyed since arriving in Oz: roast beef with a plateful of broccoli, spinach, beans, carrots and nicely roasted potatoes. Recipe from home, flavours from Oz - I was quite sated. Joining me at the dining table was Barry, a slightly grizzled-looking old rocker who sat, Jack Daniels in hand, with his grey beard and shock of white hair, t-shirt and tight jeans. He looked exactly how I wanted to look when I hit 50. We sat in front of the open fire and chatted about my walk and his life. There was something of the nomad or gypsy about him, enjoying freedom, but he was also an affectionate and proud father. I wish I'd seen him on his motorbike to complete the picture. I mentioned my concerns about my squeaky and ever more rattling stroller and he appeared the next morning with a can of WD40 as a gift, bless him.

The next day was thankfully shorter, although straining up and down the increasing convolutions of the Olympic highway made me feel at times I was due for a medal. Three weeks into the Australian leg of the walk, I was seriously looking forward to getting back onto the Hume Highway. I checked my weight for the first time since starting out, and discovered that I had now dipped below 12 stone, having shed 15 lbs since I was in England. My 34-inch waist trousers were now hanging off my hips and I was running out of belt notches to hoist them up.

I presently came into the neat little town of Cootamundra and headed straight for the tourist information office, located in the town's train station. The office was an add-on to the station café and I sat down for a coffee whilst explaining my mission to the officer in charge, Wendy. She logged on to her computer at the counter and started looking for cheap places for me to stay. As I was sipping my coffee she called over to ask me if I liked labradors. Eh? Well, yes, I'm a lover of all dogs really. "In that case, you can stay at ours tonight."

Her husband, Lou, was delighted to receive me, telling me that the royal family could bugger off and leave Australia to become a republic. Wendy chimed in that perhaps I was a royalist, which I conceded was the case. To avoid a diplomatic incident, I opined that the Aussies should be free to decide their own future and if they didn't like the monarchy then they too could bugger off and leave us to enjoy it. Ah, what laughs we had as the labrador tried to work out who to bite in the ensuing discussion.

The next couple of days involved similar walking along the Olympic Highway and then a diversion along the 94 Highway, through the towns of Harden and Binalong. On leaving Binalong I was now heading back to rejoin the Hume Highway for the final approach into Sydney.

The 94 Highway was even narrower than the Olympic, and I struggled to find much room at the side of the road for walking and pushing the stroller. Fortunately, by downgrading the walking route still further, I encountered even less traffic. I had originally planned to make Bowning my stop for the night, but as the next target of Yass was only 12 more kilometres along the road I could easily make it through with a single day's walking and then give myself a day off. Yay!

I encountered nothing man-made for the 22-kilometre walk through to Bowning, which would have made for a very attractive day in the country except that all I could see around me was the yellow and brown scenery that with adequate rain should have been lush green. The farmers of Australia were suffering extensively as a result of the dry weather and any funds or methods used to water the land would have been - quite rightly - diverted to their needs first, so it seemed unlikely that this untenured, parched land would see any relief anytime soon. The conditions were equally detrimental for the wildlife; I had been walking through the Aussie countryside for more than three weeks and, despite the road signs, I had not seen a single kangaroo nor indeed any other animal along the way.

Rejoining the Hume Highway, I took the second exit into Yass, passing by a McDonald's before starting down the small slip road. As I did, I became aware of a figure approaching me. John, a 20-year-old native of Yass, introduced himself and offered to walk with me into town. He had seen me on the TV news and chatted away about my trek and then about himself and life in Yass in general. He recommended accommodation and places to get a drink and something to eat and told me a little about each. John had a great capacity to talk unaided for long periods and he helped pass the time walking into town nicely. As he made to leave me, he gave me one parting piece of information about his town: "By the way - Yass is really good for fights!" And then he was gone.

Armed with this nugget of information, I called into the tourist information office and asked if they could recommend any non-violent pubs where I could spend a couple of nights. Smiling an unspoken acknowledgement, the lady directed me to the imaginatively named Australian pub, where I comfortably settled in for $20 a night. There was nothing quite like that feeling of lying back on a bed and knowing that I didn't have to walk anywhere the next day. Looking back, I perhaps should have scheduled myself a day off whilst trekking through Oz but, by over-walking, this extra night in Yass sufficed and I had a couple of days in Sydney to look forward to anyway.

I spent Friday 10th June - my hard-earned day off - bombarding the media with e-mails and managed to schedule an interview with ABC National Radio (equivalent to the BBC) and a couple more local newspapers. The daytime weather was still warm enough to walk around in a t-shirt, although the steadily earlier descent of the sun brought a chill to the evenings. With 11 walking days to go to Sydney, though, nothing was a problem.

And then the rain came ... to much rejoicing all over the land. Lip firmly bitten and uttering not one word of complaint, I traipsed out of Yass and towards Gunning. On the day that the collective prayers of Eastern Australia had finally been answered, I had chosen to walk just under 40 kilometres.

Walking along the highways, I had noticed that Australia took the issue of tired drivers very seriously. At regular intervals there were road signs saying: 'Tired?' 'Sleepy?' 'Exhausted?' - yes to all three in my case. The remedy suggested by each one was 'Take a Power Nap', with the assertion that a 15-minute snooze would leave the driver refreshed and alert for whatever came along. Another initiative that had recently been launched was the 'Driver Reviver' stops, where a group of volunteers would stand in lay-bys at the side of the road, with a marquee giving out free tea, coffee and snacks. It was into one of these stops that I squelched an hour after setting off. Having abandoned my waterproofs for lighter cotton clothing on arriving in Australia, I was now thoroughly drenched, with the usual raindrops cascading from my hat, nose and fingers.

The volunteers were very keen that I should have the same comforts as the tired drivers and handed me a cup of hot coffee and a couple of biscuits. Next to the trestle tables was a large oil drum in which logs had been set alight to offer warmth from the accompanying chill. I went and stood next to the drum and watched in strange fascination as the steam rose from my rapidly drying trousers. Posted on the walls of the marquee were photographs of accident sites, showing mangled cars and the less bloodier images of victims of the crashes together with warnings about the consequences for fatigued drivers on long, uninterrupted car journeys. The drivers being revived switched between looking at these images and chatting with me, expressing sympathy for both.

I could happily have stayed there for hours throwing tea and coffee down my throat, but the day was progressing so I headed off again. Within half an hour I was drenched once more, but managed to think of the good that it was doing for the farmers as I continued on the ducks' paradise. The rain then halted and a keen wind blew me dry during the afternoon, but I knew that my porous backpack would have ensured that my spare clothes received a good soaking. As there was nowhere to sit down the entire day, all my rest breaks were spent standing up and it was with a good deal of relief that I finally saw the sign indicating I was entering Gunning. With a final flourish the rain came back again and I received my third drenching of the day as I staggered into the small town. Spotting the pub with rooms at $17 per night, I thought what a great bargain there was to be had but, mindful of the need to hang all my clothes up to dry, I instead decided to take a room at the nearby motel for $65.

That night, the news on all channels was dominated by the rainfall. Camera crews had been dispatched all across the state to interview farmers, wholesalers, community leaders, politicians and the folk dancing in the puddled streets. This was big news, and as I draped my boxer shorts, t-shirts and socks all round the room I reflected that my minor affliction was a small price to pay for this much-needed soaking. If only it could have fallen overnight ...

Providence handed me another challenge the next day. Conversations with all and sundry in Gunning had revealed that my next stop, the diminutive village of Breadlebane, had absolutely no accommodation at all. The village pub, which was the usual answer for travellers, had closed down in 1998, with the remaining residents resigning themselves to a trek elsewhere for a night out. I decided therefore to walk on to Breadlebane, then get a ride back to Gunning and spend another night there. Sorry, but you can't. It was the

Queen's birthday weekend (12th June) and all rooms in Gunning were fully booked. Grrrrrr ...

This is where being in an English-speaking country made all the difference. It was more in frustration than despair that I looked around for suggestions. Eventually the lady I chatted with in the gas station told me about the train service that ran through to the following day's target town of Goulburn. The next train was due to pass through at 4:30 that afternoon, giving me enough time to walk off to Breadlebane, get back to Gunning and catch the train to Goulburn. Tomorrow I'd have to figure out how to get back to Breadlebane to walk up the distance, but that could wait.

That short walk to Breadlebane allowed me to tick off one vital box. I saw a kangaroo! Whilst walking along the highways I had seen a few 'roos lying lifeless on the side of the road, but as I turned a corner down a quieter stretch of the highway I saw movement in the bushes to my left. Moments later a small, brown, furry kangaroo bounced onto the shoulder in front of me and, with a brief twitch of its nose, it started springing across the highway. I was so excited! I stood beaming away as the little fellow bounced across the road and into the undergrowth on the other side. "See ya, Skippy!" I shouted out, and laughed at this wonderful moment. It was one of those rare occasions where I really felt pangs of the solitary nature of what I was doing. It was a daft little moment, but a special one, and I just wished I had somebody to share it with. I even considered pulling out my mobile phone to call home to tell them "I've just seen a kangaroo!" but decided to save it for emergencies. I did get a chance to share the experience with a couple who gave me a ride back to Gunning, who I think were more amused by my getting excited about something they saw every day.

The train arrived bang on time and I took a seat next to a lady who introduced herself as Helen. She was travelling to Goulburn herself to visit her family and felt sure there would be a hotel room for me. In no time, the train arrived and we disembarked. Helen's son, Rowan, was waiting for her together with his wife, Caroline, and their three children. I was introduced as a new friend and Rowan was dispatched to help me find a hotel room. After two aborted attempts, he floated the idea that I might like to stay with them for the night. I was by now fast losing all sense of embarrassment over generous offers and readily agreed, although I did have the decency to wait until the ladies had also consented.

Following two breakfast interviews with 2GN Radio and the Goulburn local newspaper, I powered my way along to the next town, Marulan. It was from there the next morning that I spoke 'live' to the nation on ABC Radio

Breakfast News. This had the twin effect of more honks along the road and also bringing me to the attention of the nation's premier newspaper, the *Sydney Morning Herald*, which sent a photographer out to snap me walking along the highway.

I had now been back on the road for more than three months. It was the middle of June, winter time in the Southern Hemisphere, but apart from the soaking I had received on the road to Gunning the weather had continued to be kind, to the extent that I had started applying suncream.

I had a real treat the next day whilst walking on to Moss Vale. Covering most of the distance on my favourite Hume Highway, I was told by a lady in McDonald's to take the Mittagong exit along the Tourist Route through to the town. Turning off the highway, I walked with rising wonder at the gorgeous countryside leading eastwards. Whether it was smart local irrigation I don't know, but the rolling fields were sumptuously carpeted in the richest green grass I had seen so far. Trees of all hues provided elegant punctuation of the landscape, whilst beautifully maintained country houses, some now clubs or hotels, stood keeping watch at the side of the winding road. The village of Sutton Forest blinked into view, enhancing the journey rather than interrupting it, with antique shops sporting English, Scottish and Welsh flags paying me their compliments as I glided past. On passing a red brick school whose fees I didn't want to contemplate, a little triangular village green insisted that I sit and rest for a while and I didn't argue. This two-hour sojourn through New South Wales' finest brought a wistful sigh as I contemplated the last few kilometres.

Coming down to urban earth with a bang, I rounded into Moss Vale. The view of the town was smart enough, but the noise levels rose sharply. I popped into the local hair salon to make enquiries and was directed to two pubs offering rooms for the night. I chose the Jeremy Moss hotel and hoisted self and stroller up the concrete steps and in. The main entrance was the door into a long, spacious bar, populated by the local lads. I had half my mind on a repeat performance of the Dover pub affair as I shuffled up to the bar and was told that a modest room would cost me $20 for the night. A boisterous shout went up to the effect that we had the World Walker in the bar and I sensed bodies moving up closer behind me. All was well, however, as the lads congratulated me on my performance so far and bought me a drink. To cap another great stay in Oz, when I went downstairs the next day the manager, who had just been told about this crazy Pommie, handed me a coffee and gave me my $20 back. Brilliant!

~ 21 ~
Harbouring Lights

I was now coming to the end of my Australian adventure. Apart from the abscess, everything had gone according to plan and more. My faith in the goodness of people and the kindness of strangers had been richly rewarded in this land and they hadn't finished with me yet. I already had accommodation promised in Sydney, now less than a week away, but I was harbouring hopes that I might enjoy further hospitality and a couple more freebies along the way. My budget had taken quite a battering in Europe and the support in Australia had been not only very heartening, but also vital to financial recovery. Even so, I faced the prospect of trying to make my way across America with less than $50 per day to cover accommodation, food and all other expenses.

Arriving in Mittagong the next day, I found the tourist information office and slipped inside. Before I had reached the desk, one of the ladies gasped, "We've been waiting for you!" Eh? Yes it was true. One of the enterprising young reporters on the local paper had followed up the TV story and gleaned from my website that I would be passing through Mittagong on that day and had alerted the tourist office to look out for me. A quick phone call confirmed that the reporter would be with me presently, which was grand. And now on to a cheap place to stay, please!

With a knowing grin, the officer behind the desk told me she was going to phone Peter at the Mittagong Motel, who was a trouper and she was certain he'd be able and willing to help out. Before I'd had a chance to express my thanks to the officer she was on the phone again to a motel in the following day's target town of Belgo, chatting with Jeanette the owner, who also agreed to give me a free room for the night. By now I was gulping down my gratitude for the lady in the office, both motel owners and, well just about the whole damned country! I really wanted to hug someone, but the kind officer didn't look the hugging type …

I did the interview for the newspaper and woke early the next morning to do a radio interview for 2ST's breakfast show. I was becoming quite the media darling, but it did help that I was doing essentially the same interview each time. Packing up, I headed to the office to bid Peter farewell, and he told me that I had received a phone call following the radio interview. Louise, who lived in the area, had heard me and called the motel immediately to say that her great-grandmother had emigrated from England to Australia many years ago and that her name was Victoria Cundy. She and her husband had done extensive family research and she would be delighted to meet up with me to tell me the whole story. We agreed to meet later in Belgo.

The road turned a little gravelled and rickety as I made my way out of town, but soon smoothed out again as I rejoined the Hume Highway. The rest of the walk was a mere 15 kilometres, so I strolled with ease into Belgo, spotting the motel as soon as I hit the main street. At that moment, Louise and her husband, Bryan, stepped out of their car parked at the roadside to meet me. Louise and I hugged and I shook hands warmly with Bryan. They had brought with them a file full of photocopied historic documents, which certainly bore out that they had done some serious homework. Back in nineteenth-century England, Victoria Cundy had thrown her lot in with a Mr Samuel Spicer, who was by the evidence of his own convictions a petty criminal, guilty of stealing rabbits, larceny and housebreaking. For these crimes he was cumulatively sentenced to solitary confinement in jail and 'private whippings'. He was eventually sent to Australia under the convicts' cloud. The scenario was fascinating, though I claim no shadiness to our family, as it was Spicer not Cundy who dunnit!

The next day comprised a pretty spectacular stroll along to Campbelltown. This was really it. Despite the fantastic scenery I had witnessed to date, these were the sights reminiscent of the Crocodile Dundee movies that I had wanted to see. Ignoring the warning signs about high winds, I stepped onto a series of three bridges spanning spectacular ravines cutting across the land. The mountain peaks arched up and the valley floors plunged deep down to the still-flowing river below. Hundreds of metres separated me from the valley floor, with the bridges providing narrow passage across. The walls of the ravines were completely covered in trees, nature's wallpaper on the dramatic backdrop. As I walked, the traffic rushing past shook the bridge and I experienced some decidedly wobbly moments, adding to the sense of being a very small speck on the landscape. It was truly awesome.

I was now on the final approach into Sydney. The Hume Highway became very busy and I encountered once again the rush and turbulence of high-volume traffic the next day as I wound my way along towards Liverpool. This was a very short day, with just 16 kilometres to cover. Despite growing concerns about the abscess, I managed to relax and made my smiling way along, with regular stops at the side of the road. One particular stop I made was as I passed underneath a huge bridge, accommodating another highway crossing the Hume. Sitting on the crash barrier, as was my custom, I glugged down more water and wiped the ever-present sweat from my face and neck. Ready to roll once again, I turned to face away from the traffic and bent over to settle the bottled water back in the stroller, When I turned back to resume my journey, I almost had a heart attack - two feet away from my face was the quizzical face of a police officer. I literally jumped and almost fell with the surprise, which brought one of those instant grins to my face and colour to the cheeks.

There were two officers actually, in a patrol car which had managed to sneak up next to me without my hearing. The window rolled down and I launched into what would become my signature tune when speaking with the authorities, "Hello, I'm Mark Cundy - British as you may be able to tell. I'm walking around the world etc., etc." This brought a suitable series of compliments on my efforts from the very friendly officers, who confided that they had received a series of reports of a woman pushing a baby along the highway. A woman? I really must try to walk in a more butch manner …

Coming into Liverpool, I took the local F1 motel up on their offer of a free room and, with few alternatives in the immediate vicinity, took a McDonald's supper. Sitting back in the motel room later, I looked in affectionate admiration at the boots that had carried me from Berlin to Moscow and now from Melbourne to Sydney. The soles were wearing pretty thin, the inserts had crumbled away and they didn't smell as sweet as they might, but they would get me through to the end of Oz and probably last for the plane journey; I'd need replacements on arriving in America. After doing two newspaper interviews I spoke with host Lynne to confirm my 2:00 arrival the following day at Sydney Opera House, together with the New South Wales Cancer Council.

The next morning the excitement was too much for me to lie dozing in bed and I found myself up, showered, dressed and breakfasted by 8:00. Not wanting to be late, I started off shortly afterwards, walking along an annoying stretch of grass verge before the route became entirely urbanised with nice wide pavements all the way. As I came along to the end of the Hume Highway, I nodded a silent thanks to the road that had brought me almost all the way along the 550 miles from Melbourne and turned right into the artery streets heading for Darling Harbour. Immediately I saw a sign telling me that the Opera House was eight kilometres away; as it was still only 11:30, I stopped off for a long whisky and Coke.

Walking along Broadway and then into George Street, I became engulfed in the usual big city hustle and bustle happening all around me. Sydney itself is a splendid modern cosmopolitan city and everything one would expect, but what really sets it apart becomes evident as soon as you pass the end of George Street and step onto Darling Harbour. Passing through the huge quayside structures of the train station, you are hit by the view of the incredibly wide arched bay, with both modern and historic buildings lining the sides. Your eyes are drawn to the lively, shimmering water of truest blue, with crafts of all sizes cutting gentle swathes or fizzing the air with great elan. Cast your eyes to the left for the incredible Sydney Harbour Bridge, scene of every spectacular New Year's Eve fireworks extravaganza and famously subject to continuous painting (as soon as you've reached the other side, it's time to start again). But for me the biggest prize lay to my right: the stunning, bizarre, unmistakable Sydney Opera House. It is easily one of the most recognisable buildings on the planet, with its multiple curved arch shells clustering an enigmatic charm of world-class acoustics within and a unique marine majesty without. I had visited the Opera House back in 1993, but marvelled anew as I approached it again, arrested once more by its quirky beauty. It is curious to consider that it opened as recently as 1973 - it seems like one of those buildings that has been there for ever.

Padding along around the harbour, I ran - yes ran - up the steps of the Opera House and did my best to hug one of the edges of the nearest shell. Two reps from the New South Wales Cancer Council hugged me and took photos of their new poster boy for the next quarterly newsletter. Shortly afterwards I met up with host Lynne and we repaired back to the family home just outside the heart of the city. We, together with husband Kevin, friend Maureen and the rest of the family, settled in for an excellent evening of good food, wine and chat.

The next day was my allocated day off for tourist duties in Sydney. I caught the train into the city with Maureen and we spent a happy hour or two mooching around Darling Harbour before taking tea in the shadow of the Harbour Bridge. Lynne then joined us and we did a very enjoyable tour of the beaches in the area, starting obviously with Bondi Beach and working our way around the coast. All too quickly the day passed, leading on to an appointment I had made earlier to see a doctor at a walk-in clinic back in town.

As I lay there, the doctor, talking to my rear end, expressed modest admiration for my exploits and moderate concern for my well-being, intending as I was to walk for another six months with the abscess in its early stages. We agreed that anything that could be done in Australia was preferable to trying to negotiate the astronomical costs of American healthcare. He prescribed antibiotics, which would hopefully zap the abscess before it could manifest fully. I concurred, as this had been the successful approach of my doctor back in the UK the last time it happened.

Lynne, Maureen and I took a last, valedictory walk around Darling Harbour as the sun was setting. In case anyone has not yet realised it, I had a wonderful time in Australia - a grand sporting nation with exceptional landscapes, great infrastructure, an astute sense of environmental concerns and a population that in my experience were warm, funny and very welcoming to a stranger passing through. I was told early on that the Aussies love someone who is 'having a go' at something. To their great credit and my benefit, this was spot on.

So I spent my last night in Australia with my new friends once again, thinking about the 8:30 flight the following morning, which would take me to California to start Part Three - the biggest part - across the United States of America.

~ 22 ~
Good Morning America

California! The dazzling, glamorous sunshine state with Hollywood, Disneyland, San Francisco, golden surfing beaches and billionaires by the score. Here was the American Dream writ grand, where the aching dreams of so many crash and die, but the chance-in-a-million success keeps 'em coming.

My arrival in the States was a modest American dream itself. I got off the plane at LAX on Tuesday 23rd June and my host, Andrew, collected me and drove me in his convertible along the immaculate highway, back to his ten-minutes-from-the-beach apartment in Santa Monica. Not bad!

Andrew was a screenwriter by trade. He carried with him an easy Californian charm, together with a sharp sense of what it took to scale the greasy pole of the entertainment world. He told me that my story was a great one and added, "That accent won't do you any harm either." I enjoyed one drunken night out with him on my arrival and a quieter barbeque evening the next night with the other resident of the small apartment block. This was a welcome to be cherished for sure, but I felt that I was somehow just delaying the inevitable.

Ahead of me lay 2,800 miles from the Pacific coastline to the Atlantic; 155 days to complete the American leg of the walk, with an unmissable deadline of 26th November for my flight back to Heathrow. In between were the uncertainties of the wilderness states of Arizona and New Mexico with ghost towns dotted along my chosen route. The flatlands of Texas would soon give way to Oklahoma's spiralling highways leading into Missouri's hills. After the pretty states of Indiana and Ohio would come the undulating valleys of Pennsylvania before I could finally step onto the asphalt and concrete of New Jersey and New York.

I felt depressed. Incongruous though it was in the signature state of California, I was laden with doubts and fears both real and imagined about the trek eastward. Moreover, I felt cheated about the achievement of the 2,400 miles I had already crossed. Where was my reward? Where was the glory? After the euphoria of reaching Sydney a mere 48 hours earlier, I wanted praise beyond the fond messages from family and friends. I wanted someone to notice me and what I had done and say, "Hey buddy - Well done! Congratulations! That's something special you've done." I slowly came around to the knowledge that here it all counted for nothing and any accolades would now have to be earned all over again across this vast land. Back to square one. With a little effort, I turned my mind over to the immediate practicalities of this new situation.

June in California meant that the afternoon highs in the 60s in Australia were replaced with the high 80s here. I dumped the sweatshirt straight away and consigned the Gore Tex jacket to the stroller indefinitely. Light cotton trousers (sorry, pants), white trainers, the ever-present white t-shirts and a white long-sleeved shirt supplied by Andrew completed my ghostly wardrobe. This would offer the best protection against the sun - walking through California, Arizona, New Mexico and Texas in June/July/August with temperatures well in excess of 100 degrees was bonkers enough without inviting skin damage. I also bought a pair of thin white cotton gloves in consideration of my naturally freckled complexion. Best of all, I spotted a cart selling baseball caps, including a selection with ear and neck flaps. I rather hoped this would make me look heroic in a Foreign Legion kind of way, but I ended up looking like '70s cartoon star Deputy Dawg. A pair of fetching sunglasses were added and my new look was complete.

Bidding farewell to Andrew, I headed out of Santa Monica towards Los Angeles on a modest 17-mile stroll for the first day. I quickly picked up Pico Boulevard, the most direct way into the City of Angels. It was clear from the beginning that this would be an entirely urbanised walk, with neighbourhoods and shops dotted all the way along the route. From the very start, the warm air filled my lungs and sent searching waves of heat fanning all over me, and I settled into a determined stride along the stretching road towards LA.

Apart from the heat, that first day of walking passed quite easily, punctuated mostly by the majority Hispanic population all along Pico Boulevard. Guatemalan, Bolivian, Costa Rican, but most of all Mexican people were everywhere and I became aware that mine was one of the few Caucasian faces to be seen. The issue of alien settlers and particularly illegal aliens took up a great deal of airtime and column inches in the news, with lawmakers expressing grave concerns over the levels of immigration and 'porous borders' as they put it, whilst businesses discreetly appreciated the supply of cheap labour to increase profits. The Mexican immigrants enjoyed referring to this mass influx as the 'reconquisto' (re-conquest), remembering the annexing of their land by the United States centuries before. As I came closer to Los Angeles I noticed increasing numbers of Oriental residents also, with shops and restaurants catering for their tastes too.

My host in LA, Aira, was from Finland. Why not? Everyone else seemed to be represented in this United Nations city. I stayed for two nights so that I could then walk unencumbered through LA and on to West Covina before doubling back by bus.

When it actually came to doing the walk the next day, the upbeat sunny disposition of California was shattered as I made my way across town. Walking along one of the major streets, San Pedro, I witnessed the utterly obscene sight of the city's homeless. I had started off early, so some of them were still emerging from the cardboard box shelters and cheap tents to look in the garbage cans for food or anything else of use. I couldn't avoid walking along as I was too far down the street to go back and around, so I weaved in between these forlorn figures, for whom there were no rungs on any social ladder to climb. I didn't allow my gaze to linger on anyone, but occasionally caught their eyes which seemed to look straight through me. What really appalled me was that this scene was played out a handful of blocks away from the glittering skyscrapers dominating the skyline. There was a depressing inevitability about sights such as these, but I can never remain unmoved by the plight of the homeless, no matter how many times I see it.

I turned right at the top of the street and walked past Little Tokyo, which looked quite charming, and then the eastern reaches of LA once again took on a very Hispanic flavour. As the morning turned to afternoon, I felt I should ask for some professional guidance and so walked into the Hollenbeck police station.

I was received with great interest by Officer Lopez who, after an abortive attempt to print out an Internet-based map for me, instead did a hand-drawn map of the route I needed to take. As I thanked him, he leant over the desk to shake my hand, looked me very earnestly in the eye and said, "Be careful." As one confronting real danger every day, he faced this high spirited and apparently naive Brit planning to walk the mean streets of LA, and he was clearly concerned for my well-being. Little did he know I had a cunning plan …

In a very short space of time my bright clothing became soiled by sweat, dust and both urban and natural grubbing. After stopping to wash my clothes they never really looked white again and the repeated laundering thinned the materials nicely. As a consequence, walking through towns, cities and deserts pushing the secondhand stroller with my battered backpack inside, I looked like a bum. Anybody glancing at me would conclude that life had chewed me up and spat me out and that I wasn't worth mugging. With my restricted finances, this wasn't too far from the truth, but I cultivated this image willingly.

I left Aira the next day and took the bus back to West Covina. Public transportation in America is a rare thing indeed. I would be fine for short shuttles to and from starting points in the big cities, but once outside there was nothing. The train services, such as they are, exist primarily for business freight and I was told that passenger services often stack up behind the business rail traffic and always come second. The Greyhound bus line is still in service and for long-haul journeys remains a relatively cheap option, but single stops can cover more than a hundred miles.

However, during the first week in California I was still in a permanent suburban state. Getting out at West Covina, I walked eastwards and was told by a chap working on the road that my next stop, Ontario, was not more than ten miles away. Encouraged by this, I walked down a long boulevard past a high school and then into a very exclusive-looking neighbourhood. Enormous houses lined the road, with carefully manicured lawns out front and indeed all along the pavement (sorry, sidewalk). With the exception of several gas-guzzling people carriers ambling past, I was quite alone. The sun was providing an abundance of light and heat, and the 90 degree temperatures ensured that my clothing clung skin tight with sweat. Suburbia ended and a steep incline led around a mountainous bend with some rather delinquent-looking trees occasionally blocking my path. I scaled the hill, came down the other side and flopped into a 7-Eleven store for more water. Another hour of walking left me in the middle of a road-widening project, with single-file traffic splaying in all directions, and I faced up to the fact that I was completely lost.

I walked into an Applebees restaurant and explained my plight. The staff were curious about why I was taking such an elongated route to reach such an easy target. With no adequate answer, I simply smiled weakly and asked for suggestions, the summary of which was that I should take the 484 bus back the way I had come, which would then veer north back to the road I should have taken on leaving West Covina. I followed her instructions and on leaving the bus spent another two-and-a-half hours getting to where I should have arrived ages ago. Never mind. I was in Ontario and called host Mary to let her know the eagle had landed.

She arrived a few minutes later and soon I was once again at home in the company of a new friend. We chatted for hours about the walk, Mary's progress to ending up in Fontana, music and mountain lions. Apparently I was heading into the area where mountain lions were most prevalent - great! Something else to worry about ...

I stayed for two more nights with Mary and the family, walking on through Redlands and then Beaumont. At the police station in Redlands I asked the desk sergeant about the best route through to Beaumont and was told that as walking along the Interstate was forbidden I would need to take an alternative route through the mountains. After consulting their maps, they came up with a route that would stretch over 40 miles. Slightly stunned, I asked if there were any other options. Jackie on the front desk was very sympathetic to my cause and called out to John from Homicide. He was equally supportive, but told me that the issue of Interstates was the exclusive domain of the Highway Patrol. He told me that he could give me a ride to the California Highway Patrol offices to discuss the matter with them.

And so it was that I found myself in the passenger seat of a police vehicle with a Homicide detective driving through to the California Highway Patrol offices. John dropped me off and I slipped inside and asked to speak with the Watch Commander. He looked at me and said with a wink, "You know, I can't tell you it's okay to walk along the Interstates ... but it happens ..." I therefore took my life in my hands several times over during the coming months and walked along the Interstates of the western United States.

A motel stop in Beaumont later, and I set off for Cabazon. Walking through Beaumont and its close neighbour Banning, the scenery began to thin out somewhat. I was now most definitely in mountain and valley territory with wider stretches of scrubland in between the towns. In less than a week, I had gone from the big city into the big country.

Passing along Banning before cutting across the highway towards Cabazon, I spotted a Christian Centre and dropped in to see if the good people of Christian California could offer any support. I met with Pastor Alce, who had undoubtedly the deepest voice I had heard in a good while. When I rang the reception bell, he emerged shimmering from behind a screen and filled the passageway with his strong, silent gait. His towering frame and reverberating voice made me want to kneel on the spot, but he beckoned me forth as a mortal equal. The support he could offer was by way of prayer. Now I'm not the world's most committed disciple, but when the pastor took my hand in his and offered up a prayer for my divine mission, asking God to watch over me, it was an electric moment. The strength of this man's belief and his own considerable charisma charged the moment and I felt moved, not so much by any divine insurgence but more by the pastor's extraordinary presence and conviction. Thus blessed, I moved on.

Getting to Cabazon was less than straightforward. After crossing the highway to the south side, the road ended at the advent of an airport. I faffed around for a good 20 minutes before coming to rest outside an industrial area. The workers welcomed me in and gave me a much needed large cup of water and suggested that I walk alongside the railway line into town. I now added railway shingle to the list of surfaces used to straddle the world.

The south side became particularly gravelled, so I hopped across the tracks and continued along the north side. As the stroller and I made further rumbling progress, I saw a car driving down the dirt track towards me. Although I stepped aside to let it pass, the car slowed and the window rolled down. A state trooper said to me sharply: "We need you to expedite this area immediately." It was a curious way of putting it, but I got the point that I had to get off the line as soon as possible. I was given an added incentive to hurry along when he went on, "There is an armed suspect in this vicinity." The stroller's rumblings became somewhat more insistent as I found from somewhere a burst of energy to get to the nearby bridge to exit the track. There was another half a mile for me to cover, past several empty trains, and I felt rather exposed whilst walking along in the knowledge that somewhere close by someone was wielding a gun.

There were no motels in Cabazon, so I asked for suggestions at the local gas station - their best idea was for me to return to Beaumont and Banning, where the nearest and certainly cheapest motels could be found. Grrrrrrrr ... I spent another achy hour waiting at the bus stop to go all the way back to the start of my walk that day. I settled for a $60 night at the very basic Sunset Motel and sat back to consider the big issue I was left with: how to cross the Interstate and get onto the road leading down towards Palm Springs. It was one of those crazy situations where I wanted to progress about 100 yards with no discernible way to do so. A large intersection decorated with roundabouts on both sides stood between me and the road leading off to Palm Springs.

The solution came from, of all sources, Greyhound. They had a bus service running out of Banning, which ran the short distance across the tracks into Palm Springs. I would therefore buy a ticket and travel across on the bus, then get a taxi back up to the intersection roundabout and walk back into Palm Springs properly.

~ 23 ~
The Heat is On

I took the Greyhound bus into Palm Springs and promptly took a taxi back up to the intersection to walk back in. Back at the top of the highway, I started heading along the road I had just seen twice by bus and car. It was completely wild. The dusty highway stretched out and weaved a little around the valley floor and I was walking through a desert scrubland area, along a tarmac strip of road within the shadow of mountains. Although still relatively early in the day, the sun was already beating down on the harsh, dry land with a little relief provided by the wind, sending dust spiralling across the lanes and bending the cacti slightly.

Some way further along, I saw a pretty amazing man-made sight. Hundreds and hundreds of windmills stretched across the valley floor, resembling an alien invasion fleet intent on setting up a colony on Earth. The desert land, barren in the extreme, eschewed all but the hardiest forms of life, and the immense windmills appeared as residents tough enough to withstand the trials of this life. I was later told that the valley approach to Palms Springs was a constant wind tunnel, which is why it had been selected as a site for the wind farm. Nice to see an American investment in clean energy sources.

As I rounded another mountain, I could see in the farthest distance a faint trace of green as the lush lawns announcing Palm Springs came into view. It was here that I made my first appearance on American TV. A Channel 3 News reporter drove up, complete with camera and boom microphone. No doubt in line with company cutbacks, he was alone and asked if I could hold the microphone myself whilst he operated the camera. No problem. He asked the usual questions and I gave the usual answers, although his manner was more dramatic than previous reporters. I realised that for the American press I would need either to match their frenzied style or amplify my clipped BBC-type tones. Remembering Andrew's wise words in LA - "that accent won't do you any harm" - I chose the latter.

135

Coming into Palms Springs I eased myself down gratefully to sit on the first green lawn at the city limit sign. Host Jack arrived soon afterwards and took me back to his house. We stepped through the door at just the right moment, as the afternoon sun was hitting its peak.

Unlike in Europe, where the advice is always to avoid the midday sun, the crazy days of the western American summer are characterised by warm mornings, sweltering lunchtimes and then blistering afternoons, culminating in 5:00 being the hottest part of the day. Jack took me out for dinner in downtown Palms Springs, with its very attractive uptown area. Thousands of people milled along the immaculate streets, in and out of the mostly forbiddingly expensive shops and into the restaurants offering a variety of culinary delights. I took Tex-Mex with lashings of guacamole.

After learning I was due to walk on to Indio the next day, Jack offered to drive out there and bring me back to stay another night at his place, which I readily accepted. The route was only around 15 miles and with this arrangement I could leave the stroller and backpack behind to walk through the suburban valley to Indio. Bearing in mind my new knowledge of the day's temperatures, I set off at 7:30 the next morning, hoping to be done by 12:00.

The yellow workman's vest I was wearing frequently led to misinterpretations from people I met along the way, resulting in enquiries as to when the roadworks were due to be finished or which was the best route to take to get to a certain town. However, my walk through Palm Springs that morning also featured the most useful instance of 'the power of the vest'. A road accident had left a car wrapped around a tree, although thankfully it didn't seem that there were any major injuries. An official-looking car was parked at the head of the street, bearing the title 'Citizens Patrol', and had spilled out a couple of said citizens who with great importance diverted all traffic including pedestrians away from the main road. This would have thrown me off course badly, so I boldly continued walking into the street and, vest gleaming, passed them by unchallenged.

Pounding along the streets as the little districts passed me by, I began to feel a little light-headed and could not seem to guzzle enough water to ward off the feeling. I stopped at a café for a cup of tea and a gentleman behind the counter advised me that if I took a left turn it would provide a marginal shortcut to get through to Rancho Mirage and Indian Wells, the last districts before Indio itself. Thanking him, I set off at an angle to the main highway I had been following and found myself strolling along Frank Sinatra Drive. Whilst a little amusing to be walking down this illustriously named street, I soon realised what a mistake it had been. The tree-lined road stretched way out into the distance, the sidewalk edged by the walled gardens of several impossibly rich people. Walking along, I could not see over the walls and was only mildly aware of some far-off activity of keeping the gardens spotless. The only other human being I saw all along the road was the security guard in a little booth guarding the entrance to the gilt-edged, oyster-like communities.

On and on I walked, feeling more bedraggled by the minute as the heat climbed, the water I kept throwing down my throat seeming to have less and less effect. I finally came upon a car dealership, thankfully announcing Indio. I collapsed on the side of the road, on the manicured angled lawn and tried to assess my state.

I was conscious - good. I was hot and itchy - not good. I was light-headed, but not about to throw up or lose that consciousness - fair. I called Jack and tried my best to describe my location. He said he'd be along presently. I nestled myself in the partial shade of a bush on the lawn, away from the eyes of the dealership staff, but still only four feet from the side of the road. As I half-sat, half-squatted there, a thought ran through my mind: I don't think I can get up again ... I knew that those were my feet and legs because they were undeniably attached to my body, but summoning the energy to make them move resulted in nothing more than a pathetic twitch. Just across the street an electronic information board was telling the date, time and temperature. My weary eyes were greeted with the message: '113 degrees'. That'll be the reason then ... Jack collected me and shovelled me into the passenger seat of his pick-up truck and, whilst maintaining his laconic, amiable air, I could detect a little understandable concern.

This was my first, worst and last incident of serious heat exhaustion. Accordingly I made a couple of switches in my behaviour after that. Getting up before sunrise was key, but also was ditching my reliance on water to keep me going. I had always been a little sceptical of the heavily marketed isotonic drinks, believing they were fancy presentations of little more than water. However, after adding Gatorade to my daily routine I found out they were much more than that. Replenishing the body with sodium, potassium and other minerals worked like a treat to ensure that I was properly rehydrated and to keep me going.

Jack told me he wanted to show me something and headed off further east. Passing Coachella, the district attached to Indio at the end of the valley conurbation, we drove out onto Interstate 10. With the Cottonwood Mountains on one side and the Mecca Hills on the other, we headed into the spectacularly desolate desert land of lower eastern California. The road rose

137

and fell in line with the landscape, punctuated by the wild scrub flora, the only living things hardy enough to withstand the climate. Hundreds of square miles stretched out as far as human sight allowed. Half an hour later we arrived at the General Patton Memorial Museum, right in the middle of the desert. Its location was sealed by the barren landscape all around, which had provided such an effective training ground for America's toughest soldiers. Jack informed me that we were one-third of the way across to Blythe, the last real town in California before Arizona. In total, the distance to cover between Coachella and Blythe would be 75 miles of the same. He didn't need to say any more - it was impossible.

Even if I had a backup crew to shuttle me back and forth each day, the terrain, conditions, heat and perilous nature of the road would have been suicide to contemplate. I felt another sinking feeling as I had in Lithuania when confronted with an impassable road, but this time my mind was eased a little by the fact that the only people who would be considered for such a trek would be the US Marines. Back at Jack's house later, I looked for alternatives. Northwards the first populous area was everyone's favourite good-time centre of Las Vegas, Nevada. The same problem persisted, with deserts all around. Looking south, there was the sprawling area around El Centro along the Mexican border, but this too brought long stretches of wilderness. My mind ached with the mental contortions of trying to piece together some way to make it across to Arizona on foot and being brought back always to the same conclusion. In the end, I had to accept it. With no backup I could not make it. I would have to take a ride to Blythe and pick up the trail from there.

The decision, once made, brought a curious relief. Although 'disappointed' does not really capture the mood I had, knowing I'd exhausted all the options meant I could live with it. My spirits were brightened by an invitation from Jack's friends to a 4th July dinner party, and so a very relaxed, enjoyable Independence Day ensued, with a swim in the pool and a delicious barbeque dinner, accompanied by drinks and good conversation. The night was topped off by watching the various firework displays into the night.

The next day I took the Greyhound bus across to Blythe and prepared to walk into Arizona.

~ 24 ~

Snow Birds and Red Rock

Arizona. If I had thought that California had turned stark and arid, it was nothing compared to what awaited me next door. I had dropped in to the Chamber of Commerce in Blythe to ask for a map to help me cross the state line and any tips on finding accommodation once I got there. As I made my way towards Quartzsite, the first stop in the new state, my cellphone rang. It was a lady from the Quartzsite Chamber of Commerce saying her colleague across the state line had notified them of my impending arrival and I should go to see them as soon as I arrived in town.

Quartzsite set the pattern of many days in Arizona. The town is one long strip along the valley floor of La Posa Plain, between the Dome Rock Mountains and the Plomosa mountain range. The town's normal population is between 3,000 and 5,000, but during the winter months it rises to almost 100,000 due to the influx of the 'snow birds'. These are the people who are fortunate enough to be able to leave behind the freezing temperatures of the north to spend those winter months down in Arizona. Every winter, a mass exodus from the north results in an invasion of 'Winnebago' and recreational vehicles (RVs) swelling the city limits. I, of course, had picked the scorching summer to make my way across the state …

Cate and Tiny at the Chamber of Commerce had already set in place the arrangements for my well-being: Cate would do an interview and photos for the local newspaper, then Tiny would take me down to the Veterans of Foreign Wars (VFW) club for lunch. I would then be dropped off at the local motel, which had agreed to offer me free accommodation. Tiny and her husband, Cecil, would then collect me later for dinner and make arrangements for shuttling me back and forth to my start/end walking points. Welcome to

Arizona!

The following morning I woke up at 4:00 and was picked up by another VFW member, Mary-Ann, who drove me out to start walking at 5:30. She then collected me at just before 11:00 as arranged. This pattern continued as I made my way through Brenda, Hope and Wenden, walking along Highway 60 all the way. Each day I plastered my face, neck and ears with SPF 45 sunblock, put on my white outfit, hoisted the stroller onto the hard shoulder and rattled off down the highway.

The scenery held its wonder all the way: awesome plains of desert, tailing off each side at the feet on the vast mountains, ready to be roasted on a daily basis by the relentless furnace of the sun, unimpeded in impossibly blue skies. The advent of Interstate 10, as with all the other superhighways across the United States, had choked the life out of the smaller towns, turning the previous major highways into little more than back roads. It was along this lonely back road of Highway 60 that I found myself trudging, passing miles and miles of nothing.

And then I saw it. And I froze. Lying under an age-worn shelf on the side of a rock face, I could see one paw and a lazy tail of a bloody mountain lion, 50 feet ahead of me and on my side of the road. "Don't worry, it's too hot for them to be hanging around here," one local had assured me the previous day - well so much for taking bloody local advice! I had been edging around a bend in the road, following the contours of the land, and it was on finally looking up as the road began to sway back into a straight line that I had the ultimate pants-filling moment.

I couldn't move. The tail flicked momentarily. I felt a chill of fear run through me, breaking a fresh sweat all over me. Hardly daring to move, I slowly turned my head to see if any convenient car was about to appear. No such luck. The oppressive heat of the day evaporated as I suddenly felt very cold and started to shiver involuntarily. I moved slowly to the opposite side of the road, cursing the grating rattle of the stroller on the road surface. I looked back - no point in trying to retrace my steps. I looked ahead and could see a flag waving slightly above a wooden building, maybe half a mile ahead. Standing on the dust-laden road, knowing that one step after another would rack up the volume of the stroller wheels, I felt so alone and very vulnerable. Mouth dry as the desert around me, I took the first steps and walked, oh so slowly towards the flag.

That half-mile was the longest of the entire walk. Every pop and cracking sound brought a new thrill of fear shooting through me. Each step was taken with increasingly heavy boots. My nose started to run. I felt like doing the same. At length I reached the drive-in to the wooden building (café closed, grocery store open) and slumped down on the bench outside. One of the customers asked if I had managed to get a photo of the beast. Oh yes, I used up a whole roll of film and waved some barbequed ribs to try to get a closer shot … what do you think?

Convinced that lightning could not strike twice (or did I just have a death wish?) I headed on towards Wenden, where I met the next two angels, Milly and Earl, who had themselves encountered a mountain lion or two in their time. I slept in their caravan in the backyard and they shuttled me strategically around to my start/end points for the rest of the week. Those baking-hot days along Highway 60 and then Highway 71 would have been extremely difficult if I hadn't known that help was a phone call away. The landscape was as before, wild and forbidding, and the shoulder at the side of the road had steadily become overgrown and churned up. The only other people I saw walking were the ever-present immigrant workers dressed in dusty clothes making their weary way back to the coach pick-up points after working all day in the scorching heat. I would see them from time to time out in the fields, their berry brown faces sweating their way through another day's hard grind for a minimum wage; and later in the day crowded around the phone booths waiting their turn to call home and speak to the family, hundreds maybe thousands of miles away.

Three weeks into the coast-to-coast American marathon I was surviving. And that's about as good as I could have hoped for. The daily walks were scheduled to start before the sun rose and then it was a dash for the line before the worst of the heat took over. Arizona's state capital of Phoenix was regularly registering temperatures in excess of 120 degrees. I often found myself completely alone out on those desolate highways trudging alongside the decrepit roadway, my feet brushing against the yellow, withered desert scrub. On reflection I was taking quite a risk each day setting off across those barren stretches, but at the time I simply accepted that this was what I had signed up for. Those long, hot, dusty days gave me more time - and indeed a need - to daydream, and I found myself replaying the scripts of *Fawlty Towers*, *Blackadder* and even *The Two Ronnies* in my mind, to divert it from the strains. It also made me smile doubly to be a Brit in the middle of all the forbiddingly American wilds, defying the odds to walk on regardless.

Climbing out of Congress, I finally left the valley floor behind me and began rising up to Yarnell, a pretty little town a couple of thousand feet above sea level. The effect of this rise was immediate, as the scenery started to incorporate some greenery. The trail along Highway 89 through Kirkland

141

Junction and Wilholt continued this effect and I reflected that I had probably survived the worst of it now, with the considerable help of the senior citizens. The final approach into the major city of Prescott, however, did not spare me any thrills, as it weaved in and out of the forested mountain passages.

The walk on from Prescott to Jerome was approximately 26 miles, but the next day to Cottonwood only eight miles. I planned to start early and get to the glamorously named Potato Patch, five miles short of Jerome, then get a ride into town. That would leave five miles to make up the next day plus eight miles into Cottonwood. I was musing over my options with the chap on reception at the St Michael hotel when Roger came over to introduce himself. Roger had resided in the area for 30 years and was very familiar with the route I was planning to take. His considered verdict was that I should walk from Prescott to Potato Patch and then let him and his driver give me a ride up to Jerome. I was grateful for his interest, but not keen on taking a ride if it could be avoided. We agreed that I would head off for Potato Patch, then give him a call when I arrived and he could show me what I was up against.

I set off and in a surprisingly short two-and-a-half hours made up the distance to Prescott Valley, roughly ten miles down the road. Encouraged by this, I stopped off to ask a police patrol officer the best route through to Potato Patch. He advised me to make for the appropriately named 'Walker Road' and turn right. Progress became a little more laboured as the temperature was by now rising into the 90s and I sweated my way along the highway, coming at last to a small shopping mall etched into the side of the valley.

Dripping with sweat by this time, I sauntered into a gas station and just stood for a minute or two, enjoying the icy blast of the air conditioning. None of the staff had heard of Potato Patch, so I lurched outside once again to survey the drivers filling their tanks on the forecourt. I consulted a greasy-haired biker who looked as if he were used to roughing it in the hills. He gave me what turned out to be very precise directions to Potato Patch, which involved the old favourite routine of retracing steps, then cutting across to the left to join up with the 'alternative' Highway 89. Loading up with Gatorade, I made a determined stride to get back in line, which involved a very long sideways trudge across a desolate area, with the bridge adjoining the highway in the far, far distance. At length I made it to the slip road and walked up to join the highway. From there, another hour was spent heading finally in the right direction. With the Black Hills now getting nearer, I finally caught sight of what turned out to be Potato Patch in the distance, although I was still a good five miles short. I had had enough. I could walk no further. I consoled myself that the miles covered by the wrong directions given would account for the distance required, although panged a little not to have set foot on Potato Patch. I came off the highway, found a gas station with a café and bench attached and called Roger.

True to his word, he appeared shortly afterwards and concluded with sympathy that I looked like someone who had bitten off more than he could chew. We climbed into his car and sat in the back chatting, whilst his driver, Danny, headed towards the base of the Black Hills, gliding past Potato Patch on our right. As soon as the road started climbing into the hills, it became clear that Roger had been spot on in his analysis of my chances of successfully scaling to Jerome on foot. Right from the moment that the road starts to climb from the base, there is no shoulder. Absolutely nothing. There are two narrow lanes for traffic to negotiate, at the side of which you see the solid white line with a crash barrier on the outside and a sheer drop. On the other side is the white line and a sheer rock face. If I'd tried, I would have been dead or very badly injured and, equally important, I would have been the cause of injury to unsuspecting drivers. This mountain represented five miles I could not walk.

The little town of Jerome was improbably founded two-thirds of the way up Cleopatra Mountain in 1876. The reason was the vast store of copper found inside, with a booming 15,000 population making the most of the natural resource. Following the depression in the '30s, the town received a brief boost in the demand for copper during the Second World War, but then shrank again to become what is now described as the "biggest ghost town in America". The population now stands at less than 500, doing a reasonable trade in tourism.

The 25 days I had spent walking from the beaches of Santa Monica would have ticked off an entire country in Europe but had only made a small dent in the overall distance in America. I was fast falling into the grip of obsessional behaviour, my mind continually processing figures relating to the daily targets. If I woke up at 5:30, I could shower, take breakfast and be on the road at 7:00, then spend seven hours walking, then an hour finding a place to stay and having a shower, then another hour having something to eat and two hours watching TV then eight hours' sleep, to wake up in time to have breakfast, etc. These incessant calculations, recalculations and extrapolations made me jittery, especially as I wandered from motel to motel with no hosts to distract my frantic mind. All the time I had the budget, the flight dates and the abscess to add to the considerations.

The next day took me into the Verde Valley, stopping off at Cottonwood, a mere ten miles down the road. I paid for a room at the View motel on the far side of town but, after loudly discussing my story, the guests gathered around reception made sure that when the owner arrived I was refunded the cost. The next day was a considerably greater challenge as I set off to walk across the Red Rock State Park to Sedona.

To gear myself up for this trek into the wilderness, I called into a bar across the street from my hotel. Sitting on a bar stool, I attracted the interest of a grizzled old Arizonian wearing a yellow bandana to match his teeth. His face resembled some of the topography maps I'd studied when planning my route. I had the impression that his ex-wife had contributed to most of the lines on his face, whilst his fierce eyes reminded me of Lemmy from metal rockers Motorhead, and he screwed his face up (adding a few more contours) as I shared my plans with him. He was only too keen to give me his opinions: "You're walking across the f****** desert? Are you f****** crazy? I heard about this one f****** guy who went out across the f****** desert - after one f****** hour he was f****** dead! You know what I'm saying?" I confirmed I had the gist of it.

Well, I walked off along the f****** highway at 4:30 the next morning just as the sky was adjusting the inky blue to a lighter hue. There was virtually no traffic on the road as I strolled beyond the last building and once again into the vast wilderness. Glancing back, I saw Cottonwood disappearing behind a rise in the road and I was now firmly out of the comfort zone of having buildings in sight. The ever-lightening blue sky gave space for some pink shafts to straddle the horizon as the sun announced its impending arrival. I had managed to cover several miles before the first rim of its fiery face peeked into view. From then, I knew I had maybe another hour or so before the temperature began seriously to rack up. I was by now approaching the Red Rock Country and once again marvelled at Mother Nature's offerings. As I walked along, the red rock mountains began to close around me, pulling me into the narrow formations surrounding the wondrous town that is Sedona.

Taking its name in 1902 from the wife of one of its principal landowners, Sedona has grown up into quite the most elegant and bohemian settlement in the west. Once regaling in the ever-elusive status of the 'best kept secret', Sedona is now an established must-see tourist and traveller destination. The majesty of its surrounding red rock hills and mountains would make it worth a stopover of anyone's time, but those very elements have proved an irresistible draw for artists, writers, naturalists and new-age healers - the kind of new residents that arrive to enhance such a place rather than simply exploit it. The range of eclectic shopping, healing, culinary and artistic experiences make it the kind of place that a long weekend wouldn't do justice. Sadly, I had even less time.

The Moestlywood Bed & Breakfast provided me with free food and accommodation and, better still, uninterrupted views of dry lightning striking the red rocks all around Sedona. Along with owners Roger and Carol, I took coffee in the darkness of their veranda as the night sky sparkled with jagged bolts exploding across the desert floor. The air filled with angry rumbles of nature's finest orchestra, while Roger sagely advised me if I ever got caught in a thunder storm to make sure I had a copper rod to wave around. I'm sure the Yanks loved me really ...

~ 25 ~
Sweating It Out

Leaving Sedona, I was climbing once again to the highland town of Flagstaff. The immediate effect was the sudden drop in temperature. Being at 7,000 feet above sea level does that and I was appreciative of the cooler climate, now back down into the 80s, as I made my way along.

Flagstaff is another historical stop along the westward route. Downtown shows off clean streets with an old theatre, hundred-year-old hotels, all kinds of eateries and a main square in which hot dogs and burgers were being sold at kiosks whilst live musical entertainment was happening as I arrived. The charm of the town wore a little thin as the night progressed, however. The freight trains rolling through town insisted on blasting their signals at all hours, and by the time the midnight train whistled through shaking the ground and piercing the peace I had had enough. Having not drunk any alcohol for weeks, I ventured that one whisky and Coke would send me off. As I lay still awake at 2:07 after the latest earth-shattering train rumbled by, I prised a valium out of my backpack and did not see 2:15.

Although not walking the next day, I had lined up my one treat in America - a visit to the Grand Canyon. Even though money was tight, I reckoned that I couldn't come all this way and not see this wonder of the world. My round-trip ticket on a coach would cost me $50, but having been granted two free nights in Flagstaff I figured I could lash out on the price of a ticket. Due to a late start (damn those trains) my coach was leaving for the Grand Canyon at 3:30 that afternoon, arriving at 5:00. The return coach would be leaving at 5:30, giving me 20 minutes max to enjoy the view. I ruminated about paying $50 for 20 minutes but quickly decided that it was better than nothing and booked my seat.

What can I say about the Grand Canyon? It is quite simply the most-visited hole in the ground in the world. I raced down from the coach to find the lightly fenced pathway running along the rim and much-worn pathways leading around the nearest downward track. As I gazed across, I had a feeling that I later found out was common to most first-time visitors: it doesn't look real. It looks like an oil painting or a jazzed-up photograph. Anxious not to waste my 20 minutes, I had a quick round of obligatory photographs with my World Walker vest on full display and then stepped onto the winding path leading downwards. Finding a suitable rock, I sat down to emblazon the view on my brain.

"Exuuse mee - yew arrr walkeeng?" came a voice.

"Oui," I replied, and looking round to see a stick-thin chap with a splendidly understated moustache, "Vous êtes français monsieur?"

"Non, non. Canadian," replied the chap.

I then entered into a brief chat about the walk and how I came to be there. Now I was always very flattered and delighted that people should be interested in what I was doing, but as we chatted away I couldn't help thinking to myself, not now ... I've got 20 lousy minutes to enjoy the Grand Canyon - bugger off. I rushed back to the coach and was transported back to Flagstaff. On arriving, I dropped into the theatre to meet up with Tina and thanked her for her efforts in securing my accommodation in town. She then added that she had arranged for me to stay with her friend, Fred, in Winona the next day. Excellent! Also, he was planning a 'sweat'. Eh?

I arrived a little after 2:00 the next day and Fred made me feel at home in an instant; together with visiting friend, Rory, we sat down to tea and toast, followed by a strumming and singing jam session, always my favourite way to unwind. Fred went on to explain what was happening that evening, specifically the 'sweat'. It was in fact a sweat lodge, a tradition of the Native Americans. This had been used for centuries by Indian tribes as a ritualistic way to offer homage to the great spirits and declare aspirations for family, children and their societies and, as a by-product, it also provided a healthy sweat session for their own well-being. I was invited to attend by Fred and couldn't refuse this unique opportunity.

The sweat lodge is an igloo-shaped frame made up of tree branches woven together, which is then covered with blankets to make it light-proof and airtight. Inside the lodge, a small circle of rocks is arranged in the middle of the bare floor, with room for those attending to form a seated circle around it. Into the small circle are placed lava rocks that have been heated in a fire for several hours ahead of the ceremony.

By the time all the guests had assembled we were nine strong, and as the sun bade farewell we made our way out of the house and across Fred's considerable backyard to the lodge. Stripped to underwear (attendees are

147

often naked, but we had only just met that night), we stepped up one by one and spread our arms wide to the side. A flaming wooden torch was waved up and down front and back, the flames licking the air inches from the body, as a cleansing procedure prior to entering the lodge. I crouched down and crawled into a spot at the back, facing the 'door'. Once we were all in, the heated rocks glowing delicately in the centre gave the only light as the blanket door-flap was closed behind us. We sat, nine people in a very enclosed blanket-laden structure with no light and the steady consciousness of a rising warmth given out by the heat-infused rocks. Fred welcomed everyone and explained the procedure: there would be four 'rounds' during which each person would offer homage to the great spirit and then say a few words or take a moment for silent thoughts on the subjects of children, self, family and the wider world. Each person's contribution would be punctuated by the phrase, "I pass it on ...," which indicated the next person could take over. In between rounds, we had the option to stay put or pop outside for a couple of minutes.

I was just thinking to myself that, whilst mildly oppressive in the extreme warmth, this didn't seem too bad, when Fred introduced the final vital element of the proceedings - water. Ptsssshhhh! A ladleful of water was thrown over the rocks and the temperature jumped about 30 degrees in 3 seconds flat. I recoiled immediately with hot air rushing up my nose, quickly opening my mouth to accommodate the heat but finding that too was burning my throat. I let out an involuntary squeal and leant back to try to get away from the wall of heat. Instantly I felt sweat dripping off my head and rolling all over my body. After a few seconds I gradually managed to control my breathing, albeit very shallow by now, and paid attention to what was happening.

Fred was opening the ceremony and rounded off by saying he 'passed it on' to the next person. Ptssshhhhh! Another slosh of the water and the steam raced from the rocks to assault my sinuses once again. Gulping down air, I gave myself terrible wind pains. Something told me I wasn't cut out to be a Red Indian. Ptssshhhhh! The flow of sweat became constant from every inch of my body. It came to my turn to say a few words and I was gasping to breathe, let alone offer a suitably coherent, respectful message, so I babbled something about my wishes for the children of the world. As the speaking duties passed around the lodge and more water was applied after each speech, I felt myself sinking fast. The complete darkness meant that was it was impossible to see what each other was doing and so, taking advantage of this, I leant back into a recumbent position and spotted a chink of light at the rear. I leant virtually horizontal and pursed my lips to suck in some air from the outside and remained in that position until the end of the round. I was convinced that somewhere was a hidden infra-red camera capturing every dignity-shredding moment - I mean, hadn't I sweated enough lately? Fred thanked us all and opened the flap. I darted out and gasped in the night air, sweat dripping from nose, chin, hands, knees, everywhere.

A few others joined me out by the fire and we briefly swapped notes about the experience. Regrettably, when it came to the subsequent rounds I excused myself, partly as I had no desire to be back in there again for my own sanity, but also because I didn't want to ruin the experience for the others. I sat as a solitary but contented figure, towel around me, watching the flickering flames of the dying fire and listening to the ongoing ceremony. At the end, everyone hugged and we repaired inside for showers, food and relaxation.

The next few days comprised strenuous 22- to 25-mile stretches through the ghost town of Two Guns and the larger towns of Winslow and Joseph City before a quiet nine-mile stroll through to Holbrook. This was high desert walking, with similar landscape to the west side of Arizona, but this time at a higher elevation. Nevertheless, I was getting pretty saturated and the thought never left me that I really was in the middle of nowhere out there. Now 35 days into walking America, I was relying on blind optimism, and bloody-mindedness carried me through and didn't allow me to dwell on the prospects of a sprained ankle, wheels falling off the stroller or total collapse. I got several looks of horror from drivers wondering what that guy was doing pushing a baby along the Interstate, but the state troopers did not stop to chat - I did wonder if word had been passed down the line to turn a blind eye.

Arriving in Holbrook, I took a $22 room at the Sahara motel and, with the best of the day still ahead of me, walked into town. As I passed under the bridge holding up the Interstate, I was approached by several Native Americans asking for money. Being mindful of the history of disenfranchise-ment of the Indians over so many years, I was sympathetic to their plight and would have loved to have handed a fistful of dollars to all of them. However, I was on such a tight budget myself it wasn't an option.

I walked on easily to Sun Valley, found Adamana challenging, and then skipped neatly along the shorter days through Navajo, Chambers and Sanders. These days were characterised by one aspect I didn't feel able to discuss with people I met - the boredom.

Most people I met and had the chance to talk with were very enthused about the walk and spoke with great animation and interest. They would look at me with expectant eyes as they remarked on how interesting and exciting it must be for me to go to all those places and see so much of the world. Well, yes, it was exciting seeing all those places and how the people lived, but in between were the long, arduous daily grinds of walking up to nine hours per day. Left, right, left, right, and repeat ad infinitum. Some days I would wake in the morning, aching and barely refreshed from sleep, knowing I had to go out and walk another 20 miles. But where discussions with the people along the way were concerned, I had to save any feelings of ennui or hardship for my own reflection.

All the time the sun was beating incessantly down on me and I was passing through some of the remotest parts of the state, with several hundreds of square miles given over to Indian reservations. I had enjoyed the Arizonian experience and felt pretty chuffed to have come through in one piece and smiling. Next stop was New Mexico.

~ 26 ~
Galluping Through

The final straight into New Mexico brought back into view those glorious mountains with Interstate 40 (I-40) threading its way across the state line. After the flattened monotony of the last few days, it was a great welcome into the new state. It was also the link-up with historic Route 66 on which I had based the main part of my walk.

I puffed my way across the state line early in the day on Tuesday 2nd August, 40 days after starting out from Santa Monica. From there it was another 20-mile slog through to Gallup, although the mountains did make for a great backdrop. I knew little of New Mexico before actually arriving, but it became clear very quickly that I was passing through areas in which the remaining populations of Native Americans were most prevalent. My first stop, Gallup, announced itself as being the nation's centre for Native American art and artefacts, which was no idle boast. On entering town, the extensive line of cheap motels gave way to a downtown area full of stores selling rugs, statues, clothing and, above all, jewellery typical of the Indian tribes. By happy coincidence I had arrived in town just as the annual Indian Festival was happening, where tribal representatives from all across the country gathered to celebrate their culture with parades, dances, markets and a big 'concert' performance on the Saturday night. It was also in Gallup that another angel appeared to make sure I saw the best of it all.

Deb Misra was an Indian gentleman (from India) and with his wife, Rachel, had offered me a place to stay for the night. I was collected by their daughter, Sheila, from the Chamber of Commerce and, after doing two interviews for the *Independent* and *Gallup Herald* newspapers, she took me back to the family home. As it turned out, I stayed with them for five nights, with Deb shuttling me to and from my start/finishing points. On my first night they took me down to see a show in the small open-air auditorium next to the railway station. Groups of young members of each tribe danced in full tribal dress

151

with drum accompaniment, to the delight of the local community and visitors.

Coolidge was the next designated target town and I was dropped off in that town to walk back into Gallup, covering the distance in reverse. After negotiating a large exit bridge from the Interstate, I turned down onto the smaller, less busy Route 66.

The day was dusty. I think that's the best way to describe it, as the very dry weather and inevitably beating sun meant that the road running along in the shadow of the red rock mountains was devoid of any moisture. I sucked in the air hanging in the valley in a somewhat laboured manner, leaving my mouth dry except for the trickle of salty sweat permanently riding on my lips. Traffic was very light, but the shoulder along the neglected road had been long overgrown with the desert weeds and I skipped on and off the road as each vehicle approached. A couple of times drivers stopped to ask if I was okay and if I needed a ride. Very kind of them, but I waved a gracious 'no' each time. As the land became more urban on the approach to Gallup, the wind started to pick up considerably. It was blowing north to south, so not in my face, but nevertheless scooping up the dust to blow crossways in my path. Bunches of tumbleweed frolicked across the road, playing dare with the drivers and usually winning; nobody wanted their wheel axles clogged up with that stuff. Eventually I came gratefully alongside a McDonald's and stopped to test my throat muscles with a strawberry shake. As I sat with all the veins in my neck standing to attention, I became aware of a moderately painful throbbing you-know-where. I had made it through more than a month in America without being too concerned about the abscess, but it was now making itself known to me again, having grown a little, no doubt encouraged by the continual walking motion.

I confided in Deb about the condition and he whisked me along to the local hospital. I always approach any kind of American health facility with trepidation, checking if there is a price tag attached before I even take a sip from a water fountain. I sat in the reception area and was called to go into the Emergency Room. I have to say that it was quite impressive. The place appeared to be kitted out with every conceivable gadget, both large and small, and the whole place sparkled and hummed with the efficiency of a facility that really knew how to make money out of illness. My temperature was taken and a brief conversation with the triage nurse established my need and a doctor was called. I went back into reception to await his arrival. Whilst there, I broached the subject of the cost with the reception clerk. On being told it would cost me $300 just to walk through the ER door again, I decided to continue with my policy of grin and bear it.

The next day, Deb drove me back out to Coolidge at 6:15 in the morning to carry on walking, meaning that he could then go off to work as I walked. The arrangement for later was that I would call him when I arrived and he would come and pick me up, unless I managed to get a ride in the meantime. I walked off once again along the I-40. Two state trooper cars passed, but neither stopped for a chat, so I once again figured that word had been passed along.

A while afterwards, I came to an exit from the I-40 which led up to a large Native American store with café attached. To the side of the café was a parking area, with a fenced-off ridge overlooking the mountains. I had reached the Continental Divide. I found this an extraordinary site, as it designated the spot where rainfall literally divided itself along the two lines of flow between the Atlantic and Pacific oceans. I could well understand the rain flowing into the Pacific from here, as it was only travelling the 800 miles I had just covered. However, just across the Divide, the remaining water would flow 2,000 miles east into the Atlantic, which seemed bizarre. Maybe a tad optimistic, but I reasoned that this would mean that the rest of the journey across the States would be generally in a descending direction. It is truly wonderful what adapted logic will do for morale.

My ride back to Gallup was secured with a cheery family with a dilapidated pick-up truck. Pick-up trucks are great vehicles. They offer a reasonably spacious cab up front for the driver and passengers and then a completely open space in the back that could easily accommodate an entire set of furniture if need be. However, the rear section can be a little draughty when you are sprawled over the floor with the driver going along in a breezy mood. I crouched down, holding on for dear life, with one hand on the stroller and another on a winching hole on the side of the truck. As my new friend decided to switch from the small road onto the Interstate, I began to ruminate about the laws of gravity and how much of the swirling wind would be required to elevate me up and out of the truck to be dumped on the side of the highway. He was clearly not in the mood to be slowed by the juggernaut trucks and began a series of darting manoeuvres, weaving in and out of the traffic. More than that I cannot impart, as I spent the rest of the journey with my eyes firmly closed, thinking hard about childhood Christmases and other comforting distractions.

After walking to Thoreau, I headed off towards Bluewater and saw evidence of how the new Interstate had choked the life out of the small towns and villages dotted along the old highway. In its heyday Route 66 had been the first highway to criss-cross the nation from Chicago, Illinois, to LA. The advent of the 'Mother Road' had led the way to the establishment of motels, diners and all kinds of weird and wonderful side-of-road visitor attractions, illuminated by the characteristic neon signage synonymous with the golden age of individual freedom of travel. The country had been opened up for nationwide driving vacations and each area responded with local businesses springing up to cater for the increasingly mobile population in the grand American Way. Now, rusted-over motels, dilapidated gas stations and derelict houses characterised the scenery.

I came to within a few miles of Bluewater and stopped at the side of the road for a break. A car pulled up on the opposite side of the road and a lady called out, asking if I needed any help. The stroller had struck again, with another concerned citizen wondering about the welfare of the supposed baby. She introduced herself as Sunshine and she was a witch specialising in stones. Hearing about my trek, she asked if I wanted to have a reading on the likelihood of my success. I had enough to worry about without the occult forces passing judgement, so I gratefully declined. Unperturbed, she recommended that on approaching Bluewater I should call in at the Dairy Queen and not venture further into town as the people there were 'strange'. So, with the guiding words of a stone witch, I headed towards town, minding to avoid 'strange' people.

Inside the Dairy Queen restaurant, I sat guzzling a strawberry shake unaware of the fact that I was being watched. At length a lady came over and, after her careful, surreptitious study of me, introduced herself as Nancy from Oklahoma. She had been primed by one of her family that there was a guy on TV who was walking across the country and would be passing through New Mexico at the same time as her. We chatted away about my quest and she invited me to stay when I arrived in Oklahoma City. What a country! Meet someone in a Dairy Queen, chat for five minutes, and they invite you into their home! Deb arrived soon afterwards and ran me home again.

I finally bade farewell to Deb and Rachel the next day as they dropped me back at the Dairy Queen restaurant. I continued along Route 66 towards the next town of Grants and enjoyed a really touching moment as I walked through the main part of town. As it was Sunday the place was deserted and I saw from a distance one of those electronic message boards set up outside the closed Chamber of Commerce. Along with the time, date and weather prospects were messages to local sports teams and civil associations. Then one rather different message floated onto the screen: 'Good Luck World Walker Mark C ... Good Luck World Walker Mark C ...' It was a lovely moment. I stood fixed to the spot and waited for the message to come around again, with a broad grin and teary eyes, but of course nobody to share the moment with.

New Mexico was turning into a very pleasurable state for me, as I progressed over the following days through San Fidel and Laguna. Next up was the first big city since Los Angeles: the sprawling state capital of Albuquerque. I was being hosted there by Jeremy, another contact made through the hospitality club website, and as I crossed over a bridge leading onto Central Avenue I glowed in the warm knowledge that I would no doubt soon be in his lounge enjoying a cool drink. What a mug. There was another ten miles to be walked until I was actually in the heart of the town and it was with a very weary frame that I finally sat down outside a Starbucks and called Jeremy to come to collect me.

I had a day off scheduled and so a very pleasant evening ensued, with several friends calling round, food in the garden and a few drinks along the way. Very happily, there were two other students from France and Germany at the party, so I could finally talk about football for a while. Unbeknown to me, Jeremy had done some separate research and told me that the next two towns I had earmarked (Tijeras and Edgewood) had no motels, so if I could get back I would be welcome to stay with him for a further two nights. Great!

My day off was spent doing nothing of a strenuous nature: I made some calls to the media (securing a couple more newspaper interviews and a slot on Channel 7 TV News in Texas) as well as washing my clothes, getting camera films developed and having coffee with a couple of the party guests in town.

The next day I walked through the rest of Albuquerque and out the other side. At the large junction on the edge of town, Highway 333 continued alongside the I-40 and so did I. It was quite an impressive walk all told, weaving in and out of the mountains on a fairly level road. My reward was a charming little coffee shop just inside Tijeras, which unfortunately did not come with matching staff. They did have the goodness, however, to supply me with another cardboard box, from which I made a sign 'Need Ride To Albuquerque' so I could get back to Jeremy's.

I got lucky within ten minutes. A woman pulled up and offered me a ride and, glancing at the two sleeping babies in the back seat, I hopped in. After establishing I was European, she asked me slyly if I 'smoked' and pulled out a spliff. I replied in the negative, to which she was a little disappointed but restored her good humour by lighting up. Pedantic I may occasionally be, but I'm not of the opinion that it's the best idea to be riding along a busy Interstate, with two young kids in the back whilst smoking a joint. "This is fine," I said as soon as we hit the city limits, and I jumped out and caught a bus the rest of the way back into town.

That night I was invited to a farewell party for one of Jeremy's friends from university. Lyn was heading home after several years of hard studying and a party was in order. I bought a bottle of Southern Comfort and some Coke so I could party on with the no doubt lively 20-somethings. After about an hour I wanted to enquire who had died. Pizza was distributed and each guest sat down to sip their beer delicately. I was waiting for someone to start knocking the stuff back, raise a raucous laugh, have some good, clean, bawdy fun, but they were having none of it. Mildly anxious conversation followed revolving around next career/life options. They were so bloody earnest. To enliven my own evening I made a few waspish remarks, but as with many Americans I was operating in an irony-free zone so my sparkling wit squibbed out.

Words formed in my head: I know there's nothing especially big and clever about getting pissed and being loud, but if you don't do it when you're of graduation age, when will you? You've got your whole adult life to be sober, reflective and respectable. You're all friends together here. What's the matter with you? To keep my mouth in check, I poured another drink and fixed a benign smile to my face.

After the next day's walk to Edgewood, Jeremy came to collect me and brought me back to the house for the last time. We spent the evening chatting, playing music and having a few drinks. In one of the most surreal moments of the walk, we tuned in to BBC Radio 2 via the Internet and listened to the Ed Stewart show. Margaret, my aunt, had e-mailed the show asking for a dedication to be played for me, and Ed - bless him - had obliged. So I found myself in the midst of Albuquerque drinking brandy with my student friends listening to Ed Stewart on Radio 2 playing Dire Straits' 'Walk of Life'. Nice.

After we'd all gone to bed for the night I sat looking at the Excel spreadsheet with the dates and towns carefully listed in order. It was by now rather grubby and creased, but served as a reminder of what lay ahead and what had already been achieved. When preparing it I had shrunk the font size so the whole journey fitted onto three double-sided pages and I was now working my way across page 2. I was thus able to say, "This time last month I was in Hope, Arizona. Two months ago I was in Yass, Australia." Memories still fresh in my mind convinced me that the way ahead would pass just as quickly - in two months' time I would be in St Louis heading for the east coast.

I said goodbye to Jeremy and headed once again eastwards. The walk into Moriarty was languid; only nine miles and mostly downhill, which was bliss.

Route 66 again was pretty much parallel to the I-40, and without too much fuss Moriarty drifted into view and held its place as another of those long, thin towns straddling both highways. I took a room in the Lariat motel just as the afternoon temperature was soaring into the 90s once again. Ahead of me lay ten more days roaming across New Mexico before entering the fourth state of Texas.

~ 27 ~
Santa Claws

Moriarty was the last real town prior to another stretch of wilderness, with the I-40 heading straight as an arrow eastwards into Santa Rosa before climbing slightly to Tucumcari, just short of the state line to Texas. A Herculean effort through slightly more undulating scenery got me to the less than useful spot of Clines Corners and I found myself getting a ride back to Moriarty once again to plan a more effective campaign east.

I spoke with the Chamber of Commerce, the local police and the churches, trying to get a ride forward to Clines Corners to continue walking, but nobody was able to help. This was another example of how without the almighty Car you are pretty lost in most of America. Standing with another cardboard cut-out sign at the side of the road pleading for a ride in the general direction, I spotted another pair of travellers with a sign of their own. The couple - let's call then Bryan and Jean - were standing with a sign requesting a little gas money from passers-by to help them continue on their way across country. They were the owners of a medium-sized van, which had their entire worldly possessions haphazardly strewn across its interior. Bryan explained to me that they were heading back east after trying their luck and failing to settle in the west coast states, ruefully reflecting that he was just another army veteran for whom the country did not have any answers. We wished each other well.

Half an hour later, having secured their gas money, they drove up and offered me a ride through to Santa Rosa. Given the hour and the sparse offers I had received, I agreed and we loaded up the stroller and my backpack with a little difficulty and headed off eastwards. The windows on the van did not close entirely so there followed a shouted conversation as we passed along, with Bryan doing most of the shouting and singing. He eventually pulled up outside the Budget 10 motel in Santa Rosa, which looked like my kind of place, and suggested that we could probably all crash there for the night - then things started to go a little weird.

Bryan had got out of the van, but immediately jumped - literally jumped - back into his seat and looked as though he was about to start up the van and scoot us all off. Jean asked, "Did he see you?", to which Bryan nodded darkly. The sun was still hovering for its last dance before final descent, but the heat it was still giving out played no part in the sudden rise of the temperature inside that van at that moment. Moments later, a police officer appeared next to Bryan and tapped on his window. He wound the glass down.

The conversation started badly and went downhill after that. No, Bryan did not have any insurance on the vehicle; no he did not have a driver's licence but was sure that Jean had her own licence. I sat rather awkwardly wishing that I could just get out of the van and check into the motel, but felt that rather than complicate the situation I was better staying put for the time being.

The officer remarked to Bryan that he seemed rather nervous and, as soon as he said it, I did notice that his fingers were working overtime twisting around each other. Bryan mumbled something unconvincing in reply and the officer then asked if he had any arrest warrants outstanding in any other states. In a weak voice, Bryan admitted that there were three warrants outstanding, but that they should have been cancelled by now due to administrative errors. I now had a real compulsion to just say, "Okay - I'm just a guest here, thanks for the ride but I'm getting out now ...," but due to the intensity of the exchanges I couldn't find an apt moment to butt in. I didn't know what the arrest warrants related to and I didn't want to know - I would have been happy to thank another stranger for helping me out and quit the scene, but the chance did not arrive.

Slowly but surely, the officer's persistence in demanding the reason for Bryan's state of mind emerged. He said, "Officer, I want to tell you now. I'm a registered sex offender. It's not what you think. I fell in love with a girl - she was a teenager and I thought she felt the same way ..." And the whole sorry story came out. Bryan spoke in breathless tones, words tumbling out, sometimes in contradiction, sometimes in nonsensical ramblings.

Internally I tried to switch off and started replaying the European Cup final in my mind, but nevertheless the toe-curling tragedy played itself out next to me and I also wondered about Jean's silent presence behind us. When Bryan had finished, the officer said he was going to check a few things and disappeared back to his car, reappeared, disappeared and then finally came back to the window. He would give Bryan three citations for the motoring offences, for which he would need to appear before the local court the following morning, beyond which there did not seem to be any further action planned. As an afterthought, the officer enquired about the guy in the passenger seat. A brief explanation and I was finally out of the van. Stroller and backpack in hand, I rather awkwardly thanked Bryan and Jean for the ride and went inside quickly to get a room booked for a couple of nights.

This inauspicious arrival in Santa Rosa marked the beginning of the most frustrating few days of my time in America. I managed to get a ride back to Flying C Ranch the next day to make up some distance, but was stranded miles from anywhere on the I-40. I thought I had really blown it that time. After walking 22 miles in the heat, I was standing at the intersection with Highway 84 with very little left to drink, vainly trying to get a ride. As the temperature rose and the scrubland view offered no signs of civilisation, I crouched at the side of the highway, fearful that I had ridden my luck once too often this time. A state trooper came to my aid but was not happy with my exploits and I couldn't blame him. The authorities had been wonderful to me so far and I really did not want to antagonise them, let alone leave myself in a potentially dangerous spot. Accordingly, the next day I walked out to the Colonias exit and back into Santa Rosa to cover the required distance at least.

I checked into a cheaper independent motel on the far side of town the next day as the base for the next few days walking east. Cuervo and Montoya were more or less ghost towns with no motels, so I had to come back to Santa Rosa each night.

Highway 156 reached high into the hills surrounding Santa Rosa and then plateaued for some while on what felt like the top of the world. After a strenuous climb up the hill, following which I needed oxygen, I found myself walking along an elevated plain with slightly scrubbed landscape and wafted by that gentle breeze that accompanies high grounds everywhere. Livestock glanced occasionally at me as I trundled past, my sunblock mixing nicely with my sweat following the climb and the salty, gooey mess slunk into my eyes, glazing my contact lenses and leaving me blinking hard for clear vision. The plateau gently sank into a dip and rose again, leading onto a dirt track on which I made the final few miles up to Cuervo. A nagging thought that had started beating subtly in my mind earlier in the day grew to a crescendo as I approached the ghost town - how am I going to get back? I had seen just three cars passing me all day and, whilst I was sure I probably had the reserves of energy to make it back to Santa Rosa, if I had to walk back again it would bring the day's total distance to 35 miles. With no prospect presenting itself, I started back with that little buzz of tense adrenalin putting a drop of urgency in my stride.

Fortunately I'd only been back on the 156 for a couple of miles when a local chap pulled up in his truck and remarked that he had seen me earlier and what the hell was I doing ...? I explained briefly and he agreed to give me a ride back to Santa Rosa. He informed me, however, that I may not be so lucky in the future as there was a correctional facility (prison) nearby and there were signs all over the surrounding roads not to pick up strangers due to the risk of jailbreakers taking advantage. That was a useful thing to know. Sure enough, at the T/A Travel Centre at the foot of the hill was a road sign warning drivers not to give rides to anyone. Oh, great. At that point, I made the executive decision that if I did not get a ride to Cuervo within 20 minutes of starting the next day, I would simply walk there again to cover at least the mileage due for the day even if I couldn't do the intended walk from Cuervo to Montoya.

At 5:30 the next morning my cellphone alarm buzzed and squealed, cutting a vibrating dash across the bedside table. Resisting the urge to send it flying against the wall, I dragged myself out of bed and into the shower. Coffee and doughnuts (sorry, donuts) sent my sugar levels spiralling and I made my way to the foot of the hill once again. I didn't actually wait 20 minutes. It was 7:00 in the morning, I was in a bad mood and I had no desire to waste time waiting for a ride that had less than a 1 per cent chance of materialising. Cuervo, here I come ... again.

I had now been in Santa Rosa for five days, traipsing first back to the west and now with patchy success to the east. Knowing now how unlikely it was that I would get a ride onwards, I was facing something of a dilemma. I had used Vyliki-Luki and Rhzev in Russia as base towns to walk to and fro along the highway, but, unlike poor, decrepit, underfunded, structurally starved Russia, America did not have any kind of public transportation between towns. Say what you like about the grim and drab conditions in Eastern Europe, but at least they care enough about their poorer people to supply them with a means to get around.

Saturday 20th August was far and away the worst day I had in America. I had a cunning plan to circumnavigate the issues about people giving rides - my latest cardboard sign read: 'British Charity Walker Needs Ride - Direction Tucumcari'. I thought this combination of words would a) alleviate initial fears about my worthiness, and b) at least engage conversation that may lead to a ride. After seven hours, I had had enough. It was 4:00 in the afternoon and I was resigned to spending yet another night in Santa Rosa, without having walked a step. I stopped off at the local liquor store, bought a small bottle of vodka and a carton of orange juice, and then shuffled back to check in once again at the motel. The air conditioning was set to a chilly 60 and the vodka was history by 10:00.

Sunday 21st August was heading the same way, as I found myself in desperation sitting outside the Love service station. Also in attendance was PJ, a chap heading home to Arkansas, who had spread a selection of goods over the bonnet (sorry, hood) of his car, which he was trying to sell to pay for gasoline for the next leg of his journey. The manager of the Love station came out and said it was fine for us guys to hang around for a little while, but no more than half an hour please. PJ headed off and, after another fruitless period, so did I.

I arrived back outside the T/A Centre and sat once again outside the entrance to the restaurant with my cardboard sign, now unconcerned about whatever expression was on my face. I had by now resigned myself to growing old and living in modest retirement in Santa Rosa. It was then, from across the forecourt of the gas station, that I heard a call: "Hey - you going to Tucumcari? I can give you a ride ..." It was PJ. I fairly skipped across to his car, shook his hand and beamed in gratitude. I have never been so appreciative of a ride in all my life as PJ steered the car onto the I-40 and Santa Rosa disappeared behind us as we chugged purposefully along the highway. Passing Cuervo again and then motoring along past Montoya, the whole world felt brighter and I delighted in the happy chatter with my new friend now that I could see my way was clearing.

PJ dropped me off at a gas station just off the Interstate and I fished out $9 change that I had in my pockets and handed it over for him to get some more gasoline. I walked on, deliriously happy, Bruce Springsteen on my Walkman and my own singing voice found at last, walking rhythmically to the strains of 'Born In The USA', playing air guitar and generally grinning like a loon. On arrival at the Holiday Inn, I was greeted by a reception signboard reading: 'Holiday Inn Tucumcari Welcomes Our Guest Of The Day - Mark Cundy'. I took the key to my free room, thanking the staff for agreeing to host me at the request of the local Chamber of Commerce, and took a long, leisurely shower.

The following day would be my last full day in New Mexico before heading into Texas. On balance, I had enjoyed such an amazing experience from Gallup to Albuquerque and beyond, soured only by the temporary nightmare of Santa Rosa. That didn't matter. New Mexico had become and remains one of my firm favourite states in America - now what would Texas bring ...?

~ 28 ~
On the Way to Amarillo

Walking out of Tucumcari into San Jon, I was able to see some of the 'historical buildings' dotted alongside Route 66, much trumpeted by the enthusiasts' magazine. I concluded that only the really diehard fans of the Mother Road could have been excited to see the derelict shells of old motels and the rusted-out gas station forecourts. The iron bridges were still intact, but the idea of travelling long distances to see them was a little too specialised for me. During that walk and the next section towards Glenrio, Route 66 actually diverted away from the I-40, leaving me wandering along a dirt track in real 'middle of nowhere' territory. A local sheriff's officer drove along to check up on me, one of only three cars that passed during that day, and he looked rather doubtful as I explained my mission.

I was a little doubtful myself during those days, as the spectre of American teen horror movies kept flashing through my mind, in particular the tale of isolated slaughter, *Jeepers Creepers*. On hearing the distant engines of infrequent cars ahead or behind me, I turned to face them and saw a dust storm being blown up by the churning wheels of the car and stepped back onto the dry, heavily sanded land until they passed. On the rare occasions that people did actually live on these lands, it was in large farmhouses set way back and up in the hills, the only clue being wisps of smoke emerging from the nested chimney pots on the roof. Road signs were very few and far between, until I was finally given a clue that Glenrio, my first target town in Texas, was approaching. This was just as well, since I was feeling very, very hot and thirsty - the dusty conditions of the road had meant I was supping my drinks at a higher rate than normal and I was ready to finish.

As I walked the last mile, inching gratefully ever closer to the I-40, I felt a strange comfort from the increasing volume of traffic noise. Just along from the junction, I sensed a vehicle approaching me from behind and stood aside to let it pass. Another pick-up truck, driven by a young man who introduced himself as Hayes, gave me a brief dusty dousing.

"Where you headed?" he asked with a cheery smile. I told him and he confirmed that Glenrio was less than a mile down the road. He asked if I wanted a ride and as usual I declined with thanks, but Hayes wasn't going to leave it at that. He asked what I was planning to do in Glenrio, so I told him about the walk and my intention to make this my first stop in Texas before walking on to Adrian the next day. He said it might be better if I climbed in and let him show me Glenrio by car, and then if I changed my mind about staying there the night he could maybe give me a longer ride.

Americans do often get a bad press as being loud, insensitive and generally full of themselves when travelling abroad. Some are guilty of this, but meeting Americans in their own country gives a different perspective, as the vast majority reveal themselves as warm, friendly and very interested and welcoming to foreigners. And so it was that with Hayes' gentle suggestion I got into the pick-up truck and within a minute I received the grand tour of Glenrio. Population: one eccentric old lady with about 100 cats. I was so relieved that he had persuaded me to get in, as I would have been heartbroken at the end of the long day's trek to find this ghost town and risk a moggie mauling from Cat Woman's grandma.

Hayes wasn't content with that one good deed. He drove me on into Adrian, set me down in front of the town's local motel and paid for the night's accommodation for me. I protested, but seeing as I had only $10 in my wallet I accepted his $34 with thanks. The motel was owned by a middle-aged lady who occasionally employed her 88-year-old mother to act as stand-in on reception. I rapped on the window for service and gazed around the area and, when my eyes returned to the window, I got the shock of seeing the ghostly image of a frail old lady looking directly into my eyes. I shouted my requirements and she directed me to her daughter who was busy cleaning the rooms. Within half an hour I was showered, cooled and recumbent on the bed, watching the local news and sipping a Coke. Welcome to Texas!

I was elated. The first three states had all showed foreboding stretches of isolation with very few towns interrupting the landscape. Hiccups, getting caught short of target towns, wilderness, heat exhaustion and 101 other problems receded from view as I stepped across into the pan-handle of Texas, safe in the knowledge that the I-40 would deliver me into well-distanced towns. My AAA road maps showed a number of towns in pink, which indicated I would find accommodation. I took a small bottle of Southern Comfort and, Walkman on, had a little party in my motel room to celebrate. America ... America ... It was starting to look possible ...

I stopped in the Mid-Point café next door for breakfast the next morning and saw immediately a sign on the opposite side of the road telling all and sundry that this was the official halfway point of Route 66 between Chicago and LA, hence the name of the café. I was interviewed by Channel 7 News and hammed it up nicely for the camera, including a quick burst into song with 'Is This the Way to Amarillo?'. The American Association for Cancer Research later told me that the media coverage was causing ripples all the way across to the east coast, which was terrific. I took my lunch and headed back into the motel room for several hours of TV viewing.

One of the biggest headaches for me was the lack of reported news outside of America. There were innumerable choices of which news bulletins to choose from - ABC, CBS, MSNBC, Fox, CNN et al. - but each channel was exclusively devoted to 100 per cent American news. The only instances of foreign news were reports about the ongoing wars in Afghanistan and to a greater extent in Iraq. No wonder there's a degree of ignorance about the wider world among the good folk of America.

In contrast I loved the adverts, in particular those selling the zillions of pills, potions and powders designed to alleviate every and any kind of illness. Nothing was taboo. An attractive woman, with flowing dress fluttering in a slightly revealing manner, would sweep across the screen and bend alluringly to smell a bouquet of flowers. Looking seductively into the camera, she uttered those immortal words, "Do you know what I do when I get haemorrhoids ...?" Following in quick succession were ads warning viewers about their blood pressure, cholesterol level, circulation problems, digestive tract disorders, mental deterioration and the more mundane headaches. Each product would then be hard sold as the answer, with winsome pictures of a former sufferer now undertaking marathons, parachute jumps and generally turning out ten times the person they were before. However, there was now a new aspect to these ads that I had not seen on previous visits to America: the disclaimer.

Fears of legal action had prompted the manufacturer of each drug to insert a series of warnings as part of the commercial blurb, informing the viewers of potential side effects. So in the middle of the hard sell would come a serious voice, speaking as quickly as possible to get the bad news out of the way, saying, "Using Splott can impair your vision/you may experience joint or muscular pain/you may become dizzy or disorientated/some people have reported severe vomiting and incontinence/sexual side effects have been reported/in rare cases liver failure has been reported/thoughts of suicide may increase/severe reactions have caused death in a few cases ..." Would you take these products …?

Walking on from Adrian across the blissfully flat land of Texas, I headed for the little town of Vega. There is a red traffic light in the centre of a small crossroads in town, which I was told was the only traffic light in a 200-mile radius. You can see I was passing through real small town America by this stage. I stayed in the local Vega Motel - a superbly maintained motel in the style of the glory days of Route 66. Outside was a vintage open-top motor car with a very fetching arrangement of flowers growing over the side of the main body and inside was a central garden with chairs and parking spaces adjacent to each room's front door. The room inside was of entirely wooden structure with a high-sheen finish, with linoleum flooring and a bijou bathroom with a shower compartment, beautifully reflecting a bygone era. I desperately hope that they continue to do business and avoid either falling into disrepair, or worse get snapped up and made over by the chains.

Continuing along Route 66, I passed by Wildorado and through Bushland, heading for the next big city in my path, Amarillo. Reaching the final approach into Amarillo, I spotted one of the sights I had really been looking forward to: Stanley Marsh's Cadillac Ranch. Constructed back in the sixties, this was one of those roadside attractions that has actually endured and continued to bring visitors in from around the world. Marsh arranged 12 Cadillacs in a field just outside Amarillo and sliced them in half. The rear sections were then stacked up in a row at a 75 degree angle. Over the years they have been resprayed and dubbed with graffiti and they were all sprayed black when Marsh died. When I arrived they had most recently been sprayed pink, but were resplendent once again with graffiti, to which I added 'MJC' as a souvenir of my visit. Trudging back across the mud to the road, I glanced back over my shoulder and grinned. Brilliantly batty and strongly recommended.

I negotiated the final approach into Amarillo and crossed the city limit at Exit 64. Stopping off at the On The Border Cantina, I called my host Tommy to let him know of my impending arrival. We agreed I would carry on as far as my legs would take me and he would then come and pick me up. As I walked on further into town, I heard a shout of "Hey! Hey!" which I correctly guessed to be in my direction. Then three young lads, maybe 16 years old, rushed over, telling me all at once that they had seen me on TV, and did I know I was famous? "I do now," I replied with a smile and they insisted that I pose for them whilst they took pictures on their cellphones.

I managed another couple of hours of walking across Amarillo, until I arrived at the Wellington Shopping Centre and I could walk no more. Tommy came and collected me shortly afterwards and drove me back to his apartment, which was adorned with a huge Pearl Jam poster and various bottles of alcohol for a little home entertaining. Excellent! His buddy, Dallas, came along a while later and we three went out for supper at Hooters - a bright, brash and cheerful fast-food restaurant that gets its name from the exclusively female waiting staff and the - ahem - stylishly short cuts of their staff outfits. It was an eye-opening experience in a country that is often perceived as being gripped by political correctness at all levels. After drinks later, Tommy and Dallas dropped me off back at the apartment for a night's sleep whilst they went on to enjoy the rest of their Saturday night.

The next couple of days' walking through Conway and Groom were unremarkable, except for seeing the 'Biggest Cross in the Western Hemisphere' just to the north of downtown Groom. Some avid group of Christians had been bitten by a particular bout of religious fervour and had constructed a huge, white crucifix on the side of the road. It was a pretty amazing sight, with the huge trucks roaring down the highway looking like small toys rolling past.

After that, I was really walking through barren landscapes, with a 23-mile hike taking me on to the tiny town of Alanreed. I started off at 7:40 and in the much cooler morning temperatures covered eight miles in the first two hours. I managed to maintain a good pace, but found that with increasing frequency Route 66 would disappear, having been built over by the I-40. On several occasions I had to hoist the stroller up onto a grass verge and cross over to walk alongside the Interstate, and then scurry down again as soon as 66 reappeared. Crossing the road really shouldn't be such an adventure, but, with the speed and volumes of the traffic and the requirement to get self and stroller and contents across two busy lanes within a few seconds, it was always a thrilling moment as I stood poised on the side of the road ready to push off and run.

Seven hours after starting, I finally arrived in Alanreed and was delighted to see that the first building in view was Crocketts motel, gas station and store. In the shop window they had thoughtfully placed details of the town's inhabitants: 'Alanreed Population: 52 people, 104 dogs, 88 cats, 2 skunks and a few snakes ...' Yep, I was in the right place ...

~ 29 ~
Oklahoma!

After avoiding the skunks and snakes I set off eastwards towards the state line with Oklahoma. The original plan had called for a long day out of Alanreed along to Lela, followed by a comparatively short hop to Shamrock the next day. However, after consultation with the local police it turned out there was nowhere to stay in Lela, so I walked a mere eight miles along to McLean and took a night at the Cactus motel, leaving myself a mighty hike through to Shamrock the next day.

Although it was now September, the weather showed no signs of letting up, with temperatures still gliding effortlessly into the mid-90s most days. Combined with this were signs that I was coming to the end of the glorious flatlands of Texas as the roads leading towards the state line started to add some dips and falls into the equation. For the first three hours between 7:30 and 10:30 I had made great progress, covering 11 miles, but as the day started to heat up and the road began to resemble a roller coaster my pace suffered accordingly. More worrying was the fact that the abscess was now taking a grip and making itself felt significantly.

My thoughts each day consisted of one potential disaster tumbling into another. Would the abscess now finally manifest itself and require me to check into a hospital and be laid up for two or three weeks in recovery? That would blow my schedule completely and require a lot of trans-Atlantic form-filling and claims on insurance. Would my money last me all the way to New York? Despite the frequent freebies received, it was still a daily struggle to try to locate the cheapest place to stay, the cheapest food and, where possible, people who might consider donating a room or a meal to help me out. This all came after I had completed each exhausting daily walk. Then there were the warnings of coming difficulties, with Missouri identified as one long series of hills and valleys to be negotiated. If I had given in for a moment to the pressures of these multiple concerns, I would probably have been reaching for the phone through to British Airways to get me out of there! But I stuck with it doggedly, figuring that I'd managed to get through everything that had been thrown at me so far, and held out the hope that perhaps Oklahoma City and host Nancy might offer a temporary solution to the abscess.

Shamrock appeared finally, although it was yet another long strip of a town, with the Econo Lodge motel to which I was heading being, naturally, the last building in town. The Chamber of Commerce had arranged a free room for me and I took a long, hot bath after checking in, as a pharmacist had advised that this was one way to stave off the development of the abscess in the short term.

The next day I slipped quietly across the state line into Oklahoma. Despite everything, I felt quite a psychological boost on setting foot in the fifth state on my journey across America. The sprawling map of the United States on the Weather Channel each day ceased to depress me, as my arrival in Oklahoma showed I was reaching the halfway point on my route across the country. Nevertheless, the pressure still came through, evidenced by the fact that I found myself getting moist-eyed whilst watching an episode of *Little House on the Prairie*. I decided to keep quiet about that one.

The days that followed were more of the same, hopping on and off the I-40 as Route 66 became quite fragmented, with Sayre and Elk City providing relatively cheap accommodation along the way. The biggest difference I noticed between the two states was that as soon as I entered Oklahoma there was suddenly a great preponderance of greenery. Whereas Texas had been predominantly brown and yellow along its flatlands, Oklahoma was awash with trees, whether little clusters or much greater forested areas. It was a pleasant change. Clinton, Weatherford and Hinton came in quick succession before heading into 'historical' El Reno. I was by now used to the idea that in America anything over 100 years old constituted a heritage site, but El Reno's 'historical' broken pavements and filthy municipal buildings really took my breath away. My consolation was that the next day would be a 12-mile amble to Yukon, followed by a similar stroll the day after into Oklahoma City. Deep joy.

After Yukon, the country views faded, the concrete took over and I finally came along into the city itself, cutting down to join up with 23rd Street, which would lead me all the way through to the State Capitol building. As I tried to whistle along at pace, the domed roof and statue atop the Capitol building did not seem to be getting any nearer and I found myself getting more weary as the minutes ticked by. It was big city walking once again and a quick glance at the map revealed that the building was in fact three-quarters of the way through the city.

Oklahoma City repeated the pattern of many of the big cities I came across in America. The outskirts were unofficially designated to the poorer sections of society, mainly but not exclusively the ethnic minority population. As the more affluent streets emerged, the lighter-skinned and well-heeled took over, either in residence or as the smarter districts' workforce.

I finally came off the road and walked along to the entrance steps to the State Capitol after five-and-a-half hours of strenuous walking with few breaks. And there was Nancy, the lady I'd met in the Dairy Queen restaurant six weeks earlier in New Mexico - and the latest of my angels - waiting, as promised, to welcome me to town. We hugged and went inside to take a coffee. Nancy drove me back home (around 20 miles south of OK City); a house on a plot of land on a gloriously underdeveloped area with one solitary neighbour so far. There I met up with husband Jon and young Joshua once again. I also met Nancy's daughter Stephanie, plus boxer dogs Rocky and Adrienne, the cats, the chickens, the snakes and a promise to meet the family horse too.

The next day was my day off, the morning of which was spent paying a visit to the memorial to the Oklahoma City bombing. On the site of the original building that was destroyed, an oasis of calm has been created with a still, shallow stone-clad rectangular pool with two huge tablets at each end bearing the date and time of the fateful explosion. Alongside the water stand 185 wooden-structure chairs - one for each of the victims - arranged in rows denoting the floors occupied by the dead at the time of the blast. It is a simple, elegant design offering a dignified memorial to the worst day in the city's history, still raw in the memories of many who lived through it back in 1995.

The most important call of the day was to a medical clinic just a few miles down the road from Jon and Nancy's place. I had confided in Nancy about my condition and the fact that the abscess seemed to be getting worse and I was fearful about my ability to complete the remainder of the journey. Nancy understood my concerns about the cost of any treatment (I think most Americans have the same concerns), so she suggested we visit a clinic rather than a hospital to see what could be done. I sat a little apprehensively waiting my turn with the doctor. I passed the time beforehand explaining my mission to the lady on reception who made the right approving noises. The message of the adventurous Brit was actually passed around the clinic following this, with the result that, by the time I had been called to go through, everyone knew who I was and what I was doing.

The doctor came in to see me and took a look at the affected area. You certainly leave your dignity at the door when suffering from an anal complaint. We chatted for a while about the walk and she left for a moment, coming back into the room a few minutes later. She gave me a hug, told me what I was doing for cancer charities was wonderful and said that they would only charge me for a nurse's visit ($35) rather than a doctor's consultation ($80) and that she would give me some free sample antibiotics, so I had my drugs also. Tears came quickly as I thanked her and all the staff profusely, with the medical clouds hovering over me being blown away by the great kindness shown by this little clinic just outside Newcastle, Oklahoma.

My chosen route out of Oklahoma City was looking a little uncertain, as neither my chosen next target of Arcadia nor the alternative of Luther seemed to offer any accommodation. After a conference with Nancy and Jon, they suggested I stay another night and walk out to get myself within striking distance for the next day of Chandler, where I definitely would find accommodation. We settled on the chirpily named town of Harrah for my revised target, with Nancy coming to collect me once I was done.

I went berserk that next day, completing the walk of 18½ miles in four-and-a-half hours. The combination of a much lighter stroller and Nancy's secret recipe muffins definitely made the difference. As I waited inside a gas station for Nancy and Jon to collect me, a lady sidled up to me by the coffee machine and whispered, "I'm a cancer survivor. Thank you." We hugged and I had another of those moments that told me it was all worthwhile.

Spirits greatly boosted, I thundered along Route 66 north-eastwards, heading towards the town of Chandler. I passed under the mighty Turner Turnpike, the main toll road leading all the way through to Missouri, and stopped off for a daring whisky and Coke at the town of Warwick. As the day was not so hot and with only eight miles remaining, I felt decadent enough to try reintroducing the midday swifty after two virtually alcohol-free months.

The small town of Stroud came and went and I headed on towards the larger town of Bristow for my next stop. For the first time since California I strangely suffered a mild bout of heat exhaustion. As the journey to Bristow was only 17 miles, I had rashly taken only two Gatorades and a bottle of water for the day. I was okay for most of the day, but the last seven miles from Depew to Bristow turned into a nightmare. Those old familiar feelings of incredible dryness in my mouth and throat, slight dizziness and very heavy limbs came back to haunt me. Coming past the 'Welcome To' sign, I stumbled along a row of suburban houses until I found myself in front of the Trinity Baptist Church, with another hill ahead and no sign of the town centre.

I pressed the church buzzer, but although this was a Sunday nobody was around. I sank down on the mat beside the door and actually laid down on my back. I was so exhausted I could not summon the energy even to prop myself up on my haunches. I carried a forlorn hope that anyone gazing across to see this recumbent figure clearly in need outside the church might dash over to offer assistance, but no such luck. What I didn't know was that on the other side of the hill - maybe 150 yards down the street - was a Shell gas station with all manner of food, drink and gorgeous air conditioning.

The only motel in town was, of course, right on the other side. I hauled myself along for another hour and finally checked in for $42 for the night. A Pizza Hut dinner followed, but there would be no breakfast provided, so I faced a stroll back into town to Wal-Mart the next morning ahead of launching myself on a 25-mile slog through to Sapulpa.

One very positive result during this week was the immediate effect of the antibiotics on the abscess - from the beginning the four-pills-a-day regime had begun to attack the infection, with the result that the lump was shrinking nicely. I would have liked a ten-day course rather than just seven, but considering the drugs had been free I had no complaints. I still had just over eight weeks to go before New York, but lived in hope that this course would give me breathing space until I was back home and in the arms of the National Health Service to patch me up for the last month through southern England.

I woke at 5:00 the next day and walked down to the town's Wal-Mart to load up with supplies for the mammoth walk to Sapulpa. Not surprisingly, I was one of only a handful of customers wandering around the supermarket and I emerged with Gatorade, orange juice and a pack of allegedly healthy Quaker bars. I set off at 7:00 and walked furiously along Route 66, chewing up mile after mile with the benefit of early morning cooler temperatures. The road weaved around a little but was relatively flat and by 11:15 I had made it to Kerryville where I stopped for a coffee at the Phillips gas station in a slightly giddy state, which owed more to the high octane pace and good feeling about progress than to dehydration. After my dizzy spell the previous day I was trying to make things a little easier on myself, whilst realising that I had 25 miles to cover. My primary motivation these days was to get the walk done, then get a shower and food out of the way so that I could be sat down by 7:00 for the three nightly episodes of *Law & Order*. As motivators go, it was pretty modest, but it worked for me.

These were long, solitary days in which my only contact with other people was during coffee stops at gas stations and pleadings for cheap rooms in motels. Loneliness has never been part of my make-up and, despite the daily demands on my ever-slimmer frame, I was quietly being infused with a belief in the coming success of my mission. Barring injury, I began to become confident of my ability to just keep walking towards the dream of my triumphant entry into Manhattan.

Leaving Kerryville, I passed a sign telling me I had another eight miles to cover to get to Sapulpa, enabling me to slip down a couple of gears and concentrate on smiling a little. The rest of the walk was very easy going, and it seemed that the previous day's physical meltdown was a one-off as I strode with firm legs and a bit of a swagger into town, finding the Chamber of Commerce quite easily.

I chatted with the Chamber staff for a while about the walk, whilst they phoned around to try to get me a complementary room for the night. Once again the Days Inn came up trumps and an hour later I was ensconced in my room in time for my favourite cop drama. Oklahoma was being very good to me, and with another host waiting for me eight miles down the road in Tulsa, I slept easily.

~ 30 ~
The Longest Day

Eight miles. That's what the map officially told me I had to make up in order to get into downtown Tulsa. This, of course, was for the benefit of motorists rather than those of us relying on strictly human propulsion, for whom the spaghetti-like road system leading in, through and out of the city was a death trap at every turn.

Setting foot outside the Days Inn, I could see the skyscrapers just over the heads of the trees clear enough that each window was discernible, so it was with a breezy air and a happy humming of tunes that I started off along the joining road. This mood did not last very long. Almost immediately 66 ran out and was superseded by the I-44, spoiling for a fight with the Turnpike into whose path it was heading. As I stood gazing down on the mighty road complete with thundering traffic from a raised grassy bank, I knew that it would probably not be a good idea to try to join the Interstate just as it was about to become the main connecting road across a bridge spanning the river on the west side of town.

Three hours later I finally crossed a pedestrian bridge over the river on 71st Street, 20 blocks due south of where I needed to be. I decided to head for Harvard Street first and then make my weary, wheezing way up to 51st Street to meet with my host Mary.

All of this was quickly forgotten as I sat in the bar of Mary's restaurant and her brother Jimmy cheerfully came along to collect me. Mary's house became my latest base for operations for the next few days, as she readily offered to help out if I came into difficulties finding accommodation over the coming days. She also engaged the help of a friend with contacts in the medical world to get me another set of antibiotics 'just in case' to combat the onset of further abscess problems.

The next day I was dropped off on the north-east side of town and walked on to the moderately sized town of Claremore. After that it was a 20-mile slog through to Chelsea. I set off at 7:30 the next morning with the still neutral hues of the early morning sky not yet broken up by the coming sun. By 10:00 I was in Sequoyah and drenched in sweat.

Coming into the little town of Foyil I did have a treat. This was the hometown of Andy Payne, who won the legendary coast-to-coast 'Bunion Race' in 1928. Andy Payne had been one of thousands of entrants who had taken up the challenge to run from LA to New York for the enormous sum of $20,000. The town is rightly proud of their most famous son and as you enter the city limits a bronze statue stands on a little village green with Andy shown in full running mode. I flattered myself slightly that I was following in his footsteps, but at a more relaxed pace, 77 years later.

Shortly after Foyil came the small town of Bushyhead and then the final straight into Chelsea. I could now feel the sun hacking through my white cotton protective layers to singe my arms, so I stopped at the side of the road and crouched under a winery sign to call Mary and ask if she wouldn't mind coming to get me as there was no place to stay in Chelsea. She kindly obliged and after staggering on for another half an hour I made it into Chelsea and awaited the blessed Mary to arrive. Another happy evening was spent moving beyond talk of the walk and their history and on to contemporary life and global issues.

During the whole period of the walk I studiously avoided bringing up the subjects of politics and religion, but was happy to chat in neutral mode if others wanted to. From almost the very first day in America I experienced every kind of political view imaginable. Some told me that they were ashamed to be an American because of the administration of President Bush, whilst others said they thanked God that they had a President like George W. Bush at this time in history. If nothing else, the increasingly polarised nature of politics in the United States had served to make people think about it, and I did find myself trying to merge with the furniture when discussions heated up between friends and family.

Walking through to Vinita and then Miami (bizarrely pronounced 'Miama') brought me to the edge of Oklahoma and a final farewell to Mary and Jimmy who turned out one last time to wish me well.

It was Saturday 24th September and I sat in my hotel room, musing over the three maps laid out before me. I was leaving Oklahoma the next day and heading along Route 66 into Kansas, with the next stop listed as Joplin, and then Missouri the following day. The road journey to Baxter Springs was coming in at 16 miles, so I inevitably thought of extending the day to get me further along. Galena, another nine miles down the road, presented itself as the obvious option, thus making a total of 25 for the day. It was tantalisingly close to the state line, and would leave just another seven miles for the next day into Joplin. As I lay there watching TV in an abstracted manner, I then mused about extending the journey even further and trying to walk all the way through to Joplin the following day, which would actually mean passing through three states in the same day. Madness, I thought, and switched off the light to sleep.

My taste for the grand gesture meant that the following morning I still harboured the dream of completing a walk through three states in one day, so I set off at 7:45 and headed east along Highway 10. Consultations with the locals had given me a cunning plan to circumvent the Turnpike and find an easy passage through to Baxter Springs. One hour later, I arrived at the intersection with Highway 137 and set off due north towards the state line. The surrounding area was very tree laden and gave me quite a pretty send-off for my last hours of walking through Oklahoma. Joining up with the 'alternative' Highway 69, I stopped off briefly at Quapaw for a coffee and continued steaming north.

With a superlative effort, I powered across the Kansas state line and immediately came into the town of Baxter Springs. As my watch had only just conceded the morning over to 12:00 p.m., I decided to carry on and headed off once again northwards on the alternative Highway 69 in the knowledge that at some point I would have to cross over and take a right. Fortunately the signposting was refreshingly clear and I rejoined Route 66 for the final stretch into Galena; I had by that time decided that the additional nine miles into Galena would provide an entirely respectable 25 miles for the day and I could stroll along into Joplin the next day at my leisure.

The day warmed up considerably as I walked along 66 amid some still fetching green country lanes until a large hill swept the road up before me. And another. This rolling feast of back-breaking undulation finally yielded as Galena blinked its way into view and I managed to extract a final spurt to get me into town and through the doors of a gas station, which appeared to be the only thing open in town on that Sunday. The lady behind the counter told me there was one motel in town located at the far end, on top of the rising main street. I huffed and puffed the final mile and came to rest on a deckchair thoughtfully placed by the motel owners next to the Coke machine. On the door of the reception office was posted a handwritten sign: 'Call this number - we can be there in 5 minutes'.

I called the number and left a message announcing my arrival and my wish to check into one of their no doubt excellent rooms for the night. I smiled at other guests coming and going, but only received one smile in return. So I waited. And I waited. And I waited. After 15 minutes I left another voicemail message. After 3:00 had become 3:35, I realised a decision had to be made. I could either stick it out and wait for the owners of the Galena motel to call me back - OR - go wild and return to the dream of hitting three states in one day and just kick out at another seven miles to get me to Joplin. I was still a little weary, but better for the Cokes and the half-hour rest. Daylight was still with me. That old devil-may-care attitude that caused me to leave Buckingham Palace in the first place gripped me once again and I headed off down Route 66.

Walkman on, legs in motion, the immediate result was a steady descent, a twist to the right and then a fairly levelled road. Passing the 'Welcome to Missouri' sign, I raised a defiant smirk to all who would deny me and strutted along with the entirely appropriate Rolling Stones booming in my ears. That attitude carried me along at an unbelievably storming pace as I felt myself finally growing into the shoes of the person I had claimed to be all year. I was the World Walker and was going to smash through the 30-mile barrier and do it with a smile on my face.

The road was long and straight and from an early distance I spotted a Ferris wheel adorning the horizon, which became the beacon guiding me into Joplin. Green became grey once again as the urban sprawl ushered away nature's shades to welcome me in. I passed a handful of cheap motels on the outskirts of town but rejected these directly, leaving as they would a further distance into and out of town the next day. Onwards I strode until my internal dials finally told me that I was almost out of gas and needed to call it a day. And so I came into a Wendy's restaurant to a large cup of water and a free call to a local taxi firm to take me to the cheapest motel in town.

With a hazy sun gently heating the back of my neck in the taxi, I lazily watched the passing streets of Joplin, reflecting on the biggest single walking day so far - at least 32 miles completed. I celebrated with three hot dogs from the gas station next door to the motel and sat down to review my campaign across the seventh state of Missouri.

~ 31 ~
End of the West

The phone calls to the media were paying off now, as both Channel 10 (CBS) and Channel 12 (ABC) caught up with me that first morning in Joplin for interviews, which were broadcast on the lunchtime, 6:00 and 10:00 bulletins. I was a little doleful about my prospects of raising huge sums for the American Association for Cancer Research and/or the Pediatric Cancer Foundation, as the aftermath of Hurricane Katrina had (quite rightly) resulted in mass donations from every corner of the United States.

It was a long, awkward walk along 66 after leaving Joplin, as the sidewalk disappeared to be replaced by a part grass/part shingle surface with thousands of spiky pebbles, sending the wheels of the stroller rattling in all directions. Not only that, but the traffic along the now minor highway seemed excessive; I soon found out that an accident on the I-44 meant that all traffic had been diverted off the Interstate. Just past the junction it cleared and I was soon walking along a pretty deserted road, with houses every couple of miles or so, but still echoing with the near-distant sounds of the bumper-to-bumper Interstate.

I had been warned several weeks earlier to expect very hilly conditions across the whole state of Missouri and the road out of Joplin towards Sarcoxie was certainly giving me a good taster. The road rose and fell dutifully, but did at least have the goodness to show me extended areas of greenery. I had one dicey moment when Route 66 disappeared and the parallel Interstate rose to become an impassable elevated bridge across the adjacent Highway 71. Confused? So was I. I'll leave it that I scrambled down a steep grassy verge, dashed across four lanes of traffic and scaled the bank on the other side to join the now walkable I-44. Having avoided loss of limbs and the clutches of the law, I carried on with an improved air of invincibility.

I had a shock the next day as I walked out into a fog. What happened there? After waiting so long for a change in temperature and climate, Mother Nature

178

had drawn a dramatic cloak over proceedings and for the first time in months I felt cold air filtering into my lungs. Fortunately I had a full set of frontage roads running alongside the I-44 all day, seeing me safely through to the next town of Mount Vernon. Watching the TV national weather picture, it was clear that here at the end of September changes were finally afoot, with torrential downpours predicted for the next day.

With the dire rain warnings in mind, I stepped out in a rather lively fashion the next day, kicking off at 8:00 and arriving in Republic just after 2:00. I was directed to the newly built Americ Inn hotel, which looked worryingly posh, but with no other options in town and the storm clouds gathering I stepped into reception to bite the bullet. Shelly, the owner, took my mission to heart and gave me a room for half price. Twenty minutes later I heard a familiar noise. Outside a rain storm of biblical proportions was in full cry, creating streams of water across the car park. Millions of huge raindrops on a relentless kamikaze mission raced each other to hit the ground first and the afternoon sky dulled to a very dirty grey hue, suggesting the sun had been given the rest of the day off. I watched, thankful that my timing had been spot on for this trek, and checked the Weather Channel to see if there was more to come.

Fortunately the torrent had been a mere reminder of what the Fall can bring rather than the overture to a symphony of meteorological misery. Ducking neatly under the bridge at the end of town the next morning, I crossed over to Highway 60 and then back to the 174 the next day, to enjoy a very straight-forward walk into Springfield.

Missouri certainly didn't disappoint as far as the beautiful countryside was concerned. As I would later recall, it was stunning to look at but murder to walk through. As I weaved my way along the I-44, I passed Lebanon, Rolla and Sullivan without ever really seeing the towns themselves. A pity it may have been to miss out on the sights and sounds of these outposts of the Midwest, but I was now dead set on making sterling progress and the Interstate's habit of bypassing the towns whilst providing motels just off the main road suited me fine. Despite the welcome drop in temperatures into the 80s, the landscapes of Missouri continued to lend themselves more to coach travel and watercolour painting than strenuous walking. This was a state to be conquered before I could enjoy the flatter courses of Illinois, Indiana and Ohio next.

Just south of Sullivan I stopped in a gas station for a reviving coffee and found myself chatting with a lady waiting in line behind me. Kristin had read the back of my jacket and, despite having two toddlers with her, was happy to chat about my mission. She asked where I stayed each night, and after I had explained my daily quest for the cheapest room in each town she invited me to stay with her and the family at her home, just short of St Louis.

Walking through to Eureka that same week, I came across one of several correctional facilities (prisons) that had sprung up over the years in the mid-states. The main building was set way back from the highway, but the open grounds in front stretched all the way to the sidewalk I was walking along. Perimeter fencing topped off with barbed wire lined the street and in the mid-distance I could see the observation towers manned by armed guards surveying the scene in the exercise yards and football fields below. The extreme irony was not lost on me as I strolled freely along the highway whilst hundreds of men drifted around the fields wearing their blue prison garb, stretching their legs in the only free space they would see for some time. The rest of the afternoon turned out very well, as I arrived in Eureka and managed to hijack a Fox News TV team, covering another story, to interview me. My next break came in the local Days Inn after the reception staff had told me they couldn't go lower than $63 for the night. I met the manager, who had spent some time in England and was a Manchester United fan. A free room followed, helped by the fact that I didn't mention I was a Liverpool fan …

The next day I was interviewed by Channel 5 for CBS News and finally came to rest with Kristin, husband Tom and their three girls just outside St Louis. My first hour in Kristin's company was spent driving around the area to meet up with her old friends, who luckily ran sports clothing and footwear stores. They had agreed to resupply my wardrobe, which by now was seriously in need, and I emerged a short while later with new shoes, socks, trousers, sweater and t-shirts for free. Brilliant! Back at their home later, Tom became the latest American gent to try to explain the rules and intricacies of American Football to me, but I was once again beyond all hope. I'll stick to proper football.

Walking into St Louis the next day was a pretty monumental moment for me. I had now made substantial progress across the United States since leaving Santa Monica three-and-a-half months earlier, with roughly 1,800 miles covered and now just 1,000 more to go. I was a mere six weeks away from the big finish in New York, and three more days after that would see me flying back to England.

I had enjoyed my time walking through America and had met some wonderful people. I had seen the country from a perspective that few others have; whilst crossing the country is not unusual for travellers, the view from the road is substantially different when you have your feet on it rather than

180

wheels. And yet …

I was beginning to feel more and more British as the days went by. That strange enhancement of patriotism and sense of identity tends to become most acute when one is far away from home. In truth it was only seven months since I had left England for the second time, but I was feeling every one of those miles that separated me from friends, family, big red buses, my Saturday crossword, football, seaside strolls and BBC Radio. Adaptability was the key to success on this mission and I had passed all the tests that had been thrown at me. However welcome I had been made to feel, I was feeling more and more like an outsider as I passed from town to town and I looked forward to setting foot back in my homeland once again. As I walked triumphantly up to the spectacular Gateway Arch next to the Mississippi River flowing through St Louis, it did not denote for me the gateway to the west but the entrance to the final eastward stretch towards the end of my American adventure.

~ 32 ~
Corns and Beans

I felt a few chilly blasts as I passed over into Illinois, only one of which was provided by the finally turning weather. Kristin dropped me off on the other side of the river, thereby enabling me to avoid a hair-raising attempt at playing dodge-the-traffic across the bridge.

From Troy I picked up the old Highway 40, which appeared to cover most of the journey scheduled for Illinois and Indiana next door. It was my use of the roadways that brought the second icy blast. Old Highway 40 was doing its job well, but then disappeared under the newer Interstate 70 for six miles between Pierron and Pocahontas. As usual, I stepped out and walked along the Interstate until I reached the exit indicating that Highway 40 was back in service. After wandering around for a while I still couldn't see the entrance to Highway 40, so with only five more miles to the Greenville exit I rolled myself and stroller back onto the Interstate. A state police car appeared in front of me almost immediately. I got ready with my "Hello, I'm Mark Cundy, British and walking" speech but didn't get the chance to voice it, as the window of the police car came down and a ferocious voice spat angrily at me:

"You canNOT walk on the Interstate! It's illegal and against the law! [Not only is it illegal but it's also against the law ...] You will be arrested! Get your ass back up and OFF the Interstate! You canNOT walk along the Interstate! It is illegal. It is against the law! Get back up there! It is illegal!"

I tried to see if there was a 'pause' button, but no, this officer, clearly in love with his job, uniform and position, did not delay for breath as he bellowed out the same message three times. I asked about Highway 40 and with the same volume and delivery style he pointed out a half-mile walk to the south that I needed to take before rejoining the 40. He reminded me once more of the illegality of pedestrian traffic on the Interstate and then roared off. Clearly things were different here and that was the end of my adventures on America's superhighways.

That was, in fact, the second time I had been barked at that day. Earlier I had stopped for a coffee break at a gas station just before the first sojourn on to the Interstate, and whilst quietly munching a Payday bar and sipping my coffee a lady came along to chat after seeing me on TV. A man hovering in the background, whom I presumed was with her, finally stepped forward to chip in to the conversation. He had long, grease-shined hair and unblinking blue eyes.

His opening line was: "Do you know they make televisions with radiation deliberately racked up to higher levels and then sit babies in front of them so they get cancer?"

There really is no answer to that, so I sat with a sad smile on my face to indicate my distaste for the practice by 'them' and awaited his next bon mot. I didn't have to wait long.

"You British?" (I nodded). "Me too," he drawled in a now familiar eastern American accent. "In fact I'm more British than you are."

I've been familiar with American people keen to discuss their heritage involving earlier generations who emigrated from various parts of the UK, but he was taking more of an accusatory, derogatory line. He pointed to the Union Jack on his t-shirt by way of proof and then to his pick-up truck, which was festooned with several British flags across the body.

"My name's Berkley. You heard of the famous British family called Berkley? Well I'm one of them," he sneered.

They must be so proud, I thought. Then came the enquiry I had been dreading.

"Do you read the scriptures?" (No). "Do you know that the name of Jesus was first used in the fifteenth century in Europe?"

This was my cue to insert the "I respect your views but ..." phrase, but he cut me off by saying, "Good - you should respect my views and I'm going to give them to you."

Fortunately the lady who had originally come over to talk to me interceded to ask me if this kind of thing happened often. I replied that it was actually the first time, deliberately ignoring the increasingly unhinged, self-proclaimed preacher. Chided by losing his audience, he proceeded to tell me that I would be better off going back home and reading the scriptures than doing what I was doing and, furthermore, that he hoped we both got cancer. My lady friend called him a sinner and he left us. I had often wondered if people like that only existed in the movies and TV, but here, today, I had found a 'live one'.

The rest of my time crossing Illinois passed without any repeats of those incidents and, to be honest, without very much happening at all. As I chatted for some time with a young motel owner in Marshall, he told me sagely that, "All people care about round here is corns and beans," which to this day remains the most succinct, accurate description of a population I have heard.

This was reinforced as I left the state five days after entering, via the border town of Weaver. In the fields all around was the unmistakable aroma of manure fertilising the land. After 20 solid minutes breathing in as much crap as I could ever want, I scuttled inside a gas station café. There I was met by a career manageress who said to me brightly, "You smell that? It's money - or so they tell me. Just smells like a pile of pig poo to me."

Quite. I crossed over into Indiana.

Highway 40 became a glorious new friend as it hummed flatly and directly across Indiana with equal efficiency to the I-70. The big town of Terre Haute was easily found, but a room for the night was less easily located, as a 'covered bridge' festival was taking place. I didn't want to know any more … Star Trek conventions I can understand, but a party celebrating bridges just stretches it a bit for me.

Indiana did turn out to be a good deal more handsome than Illinois, with excellent forested and thoughtfully developed stretches of road all along the route of the 40. The knock-on effect of having two large cities (Terre Haute and Indianapolis) in relatively close proximity, however, was that the smaller towns and villages in the intervening 70-plus miles had had some of the life squeezed out of them and places to stay were intermittent.

Walking on from Brazil on day three, I came along to the tiny village of Putnamville with no place to stay and called in to the local post office for a chat. Jackie, who worked behind quite a security screen, saw quite easily that I was no homicidal maniac and stepped outside her booth to tell me that I could get a place in either Greencastle or Cloverdale, both of which were 4 to five miles north or south of the main road. Getting there was another matter. Of course there was no public transport, so Jackie telephoned her husband Jerry and he gave me a ride down to Cloverdale. The same problem in reverse in the morning led me to calling the police for their opinion of how I could get back up onto the main road. Luckily I had picked a good day - the very kind officer on duty said his father came from Essex and so he gladly gave me a ride and set me on my way again.

A couple of days later I emerged from the pleasant country roads to arrive in the state capital, Indianapolis. Walking in from the west, you are afforded an engaging view of the skyscrapers whilst passing the city zoo and the downtown area fulfils everything that one would expect from a major American city. Unfortunately the welcome was not the warmest from the bar owners, the tourist information office or the bus station. The library staff were friendly enough, but, after hearing that my host in town was now unable to get away from work to let me stay, the early evening turned into a struggle to get a cheap room for the night. I ended up drinking a vodka and orange in Charley & Barney's bar, whilst flipping through the *Yellow Pages* and phoning several motels in town. I finally got lucky at the Indy East motel and headed off eastwards out of town, bringing my brief visit to Indianapolis to a close.

The remaining days across the east side of Indiana were unremarkable, passing through Greenfield, Spiceland and Dublin before arriving at the last post, Richmond. I was quite moved by the enthusiasm shown by the staff at the Chamber of Commerce in Richmond, who were determined to look after this 'man of great inspiration' as I passed through their town. Several conversations ensued in regard to finding me a cheap place to stay - limited budget, anywhere will do, no fancy frills, etc. - and they came up with the suggestion of Hope House and called through to confirm I could stay there that night. Something in the name should have given me a clue ...

A taxi arrived to take me out to Hope House, doubling back westwards and dropping me off along a country lane far from downtown. I walked around to the main entrance of what looked like an aristocratic country home that had been going to seed for several decades. A young man called Brad opened the door and invited me inside, helping me to shift my backpack and stroller through the reception area and into the main hall. Behind a glass-fronted desk sat a watchful, brawny man with a mountain of paperwork, with a large message board fixed to the wall behind him. To the right was the main hall area, housing half a dozen chewed-up leather sofas and a single bed with a pile of assorted blankets and pillows. It was explained to me that this was a halfway house for recovering alcoholics and former drug addicts, who were allowed to check in at 4:00 each day, have a communal supper and then bed down for the night, rising at 6:00 sharp the next morning to be back outside again by 7:00 a.m. The service was provided free by the local authority.

As I sat listening to all this, some of the regulars came in and word of my mission soon got around. On first impressions, the men were almost exclusively white, tattooed and looking not surprisingly rumpled by their life experiences to date. They were friendly in a rough-house kind of way, joking with me that they would join me down at the bar for a celebratory drink on my progress so far. This brought admonishing looks and words from the chap behind the glass and they immediately responded that they were 'just kidding', although more than one had a grimly wistful look in their eyes at the thought. You'd need a granite heart not to feel compassion for these men, for

185

whom the prospects in life would never look rosy again. For the rest of their days they would be facing the daily battle to resist their ruining addictions, unlikely to engender sufficient trust from those who could give them work with a good salary and more likely than not having the company of fellow sufferers for friends.

I couldn't stay there. I was due to take a day off and the idea of waking at 6:00 and then fighting (metaphorically!) for a shower followed by a hurried breakfast before heading off to another place to stay was not feasible. I mentioned my desire to find another place for those reasons and Brad told me about a motel in town with rooms for $25 per night. This sounded good, but I didn't really want to shell out for another taxi to take me back into town, so he went to the guy in charge and asked for his permission to drive me there. With a pronounced eyebrow telling him to be safe, the boss agreed. As Brad dropped me off, we shook hands and I wished him well.

~ 33 ~
Heading for the Fall

Thirty-one days. That's how much longer it would take to walk through to New York as I stepped into Ohio. I had studiously avoided thinking more than a few days in advance during the entire walk, as thoughts of the mammoth distances ahead had previously plunged me into rather uncharacteristic black moods. Now, though, I was close enough to start dreaming about landing at Heathrow Airport to be greeted by my family and be back on home soil once again.

The day that I took off in Richmond had an immediate effect, as I walked across the state line with greater energy and drive than I had felt for a long time. Covering 16 miles in the first three-and-a-half hours, I powered onwards through the autumn rain for the remaining 13 miles to arrive in Clayton in time for tea. A young guy called Levi in the local gas station said that as it was a slow day he would give me a ride to the local cluster of hotels in Englewood, just due north. With 29 miles behind me, I gleefully accepted a sideways ride.

Monday 24th October was my mum's birthday and I called home to sing 'Happy Birthday' across the ocean to her. As it turned out, this was the highlight of both our days, as my new trousers turned out to be emphatically not waterproof. The light, teasing showers of the previous day had been replaced by a much more determined deluge, and the soggy material wrapped itself tightly around my knees, cold and wet. Undeterred, I marched relentlessly on towards Springfield. Just short of the city limits the rain turned absolutely hellacious, with a cold wind sweeping sheet after sheet of water into my face, inside my jacket, down my trousers and invading my socks. Dropping into the Crawdaddy huntin' shootin' an' fishin' store, I checked the remaining distance and, happy with progress, I asked the chuckling owner how I might get a ride to the nearest motel. In the end the Sheriff's Department came to my aid, inserting me into the rear of one of their squad cars and shuttling me the short distance to the Knights Inn. They were sadly unable to grant my request for the lights and sirens to be switched on.

I hit something of a purple patch with my hosts in Ohio; whilst financially very helpful, it also gave me the comfort level of support to enjoy the state proper. With Halloween just around the corner, the already beautiful countryside that I was passing through took on a gorgeous autumnal hue, with reddening leaves still clinging on in the ever burgeoning forestry. Small villages were dressed up for the season. Local churches were organising harvest festivals and the porches of the family homes were resplendent with pumpkins and, of course, ghosts and ghouls strewn across the windows and front lawns. Halloween is big in America and, as one village turned over the road to another, each was determined not to be outdone by its neighbour's decorations. The weather also turned, with cold, clear skies succeeding the grey and wet introduction I had 'enjoyed'.

I had been very busy bombarding the media about my impending arrival in Columbus and my host Steve had also been on the case. Channel 4 dropped out of the running, but Channel 10 did me proud with a breakfast show 'live' interview on the road at 7:30 in the morning. Steve, bless him, rose early that day to drive me down to the appointed spot on the side of Highway 40 and I stood there trying not to look too bleary-eyed whilst chatting away with the presenter back in the nice, warm studio.

Puffing ever eastwards, I enjoyed a great night with Cliff and Erika at their home, located out in the sticks beyond the big cities but close enough to get a monster pizza and enjoy it, still warm, back at home. They gave me a tour of the surrounding area, including the ancient symbolic mounds and burial sites, but the biggest treat was a visit to the 'basket' building.

The Longaberger Basket Company decided back in the 1990s that its new headquarters should go the extra mile in engendering a sense of the company's worth, values and identity. As a result of this resolution it constructed the building along the lines of its best-selling medium hand-woven basket. The building opened in 1997 and now stands as a testimony to the brilliance and glorious eccentricity of what can be achieved when the rule book is not so much thrown out as shredded with contempt. Driving along the street you cannot fail to see from a distance the seven-storey, 200ft x 140ft monster basket dominating the urban skyline. The depth and width of the building shrink down towards ground level to maintain the proportions of the basket and the roof is topped off with huge metal handles to complete the picture. It's totally bonkers and I loved it.

I turned in another marathon the next day, busting through 26 miles to arrive in Zanesville, where I was collected by Becky and headed back home to spend the night with her and husband, Dick. Becky worked with the local health authority and when I confided in her about the nature of my abscess complaint she offered to see what my options were for a 'quick fix' without laying myself up for a long recovery period. The abscess was now the size of an almond and getting quite painful when sitting. After about half an hour umming and ahhing on the morning of my departure, I decided just to press on. It was four months since the abscess had raised its ugly head and I had managed to hold it at bay so far - I would see it through to whatever painful end may come my way.

Leaving Zanesville, I squeezed in one more TV interview with WHIZ (ABC) News as I made my way on towards Cambridge. This was another day of walking through the wonderful scenes of the Fall, with splendid views of the country assuming its autumn garb. Walking along Highway 40, I passed a farmhouse with shop attached, with a pyramid of pumpkins stretching maybe 30 feet into the air whilst hundreds of other hopefuls scattered around the shop frontage grinned an orange greeting to all.

That day is emblazoned on my mind for ever. I felt free. Truly free. Of course, I had the ever-present concerns about the abscess, money and an unmissable deadline in New York, but none of those were going to spoil my mood on that day, as I sensed I would never again experience that level of absolute freedom. The long, hard road stretched onwards for hundreds of miles in front of me, but a much longer, harder road lay behind me, already conquered. Every petty annoyance, frustration and obstacle faded from view as I made my way along that road. The day was topped off by an encounter with a retired couple who drove up and called out to me. They had seen me on the TV earlier and had driven for over an hour in the hope of catching up with me to wish me every success for the rest of the walk. It was long out of their way, but they just felt moved to come out and spend a few moments chatting before heading back home again. Nice.

My last 'hosted' stop before crossing the state line was with Janet and Wade, owner of a large country house located once again well off the main road. My invitation to stay with them also included an evening in the open, with the whole family and their neighbours invited to a 'wiener roast'. All the local families from grandparents to toddlers assembled down at the largest house within the tree-lined village. We sat on bales of hay and tree stumps in the darkened night around a huge bonfire, taking it in turns to spike a couple of wiener sausages on long-handled prods and hold them mid-air over the fire until cooked to a crispy finish, the into the dog rolls and splattered with ketchup and mustard. That was a real rural American evening and I loved it.

Wade was also running the annual 'hayrides', using his tractor to pull a hay truck full of passengers way off into the night, crawling around the local country roads and slowing strategically alongside graveyards before chugging away once more into the labyrinth of high-hedged trails, illuminated only by the moonlight. These were scenes as far removed from the skyscraper images of America as you could imagine, reminding any who cared to drop by what 'community' really means.

I continued along the next day, reaching St Clairesville at the edge of Ohio and catching my last glimpses of the state's rolling autumnal vistas, each new rustic view demanding my attention and crying out to be made into a fiendish jigsaw puzzle. The road began to rise and fall again, in anticipation of the last great hilly challenge I had to face in America - the splendour of Pennsylvania beckoned.

First of all, however, was the small matter of my one day in West Virginia. I don't know what settlement was made between the states when the final borders were agreed, but there is a weird spike of land flaring up between Ohio and Pennsylvania which remains attached to the state of West Virginia and through which I was due to pass. I assumed that the strategically placed town of Wheeling must have been what the Virginians were unwilling to concede, sitting as it does on the crucial Ohio River gateway. After the walk, my day in West Virginia was spent doing an interview for the *Intelligencer* newspaper, checking e-mails at the library and getting stung by the Super 8 motel for a $65 room.

Pennsylvania welcomed me with continuing dry weather, but immediately threw down the gauntlet at my impertinence in assuming that I could just stroll in and easily conquer its majesty. Hundreds of square miles of nature's finest gave me the workout of my life and still managed to catch what breath I had left with its stunning views as the fields, hills, forests and intermittent towns collided into a mosaic of all that was great about America.

Coming out of Washington on my second day in Pennsylvania, I scaled the appropriately named Scenery Hill and halfway down the other side dropped into Jan's Tea Room, which was every bit as quaint as it sounds. Here in the genteel village sitting in between the rolling hills was tea shop and rooms that could have been lifted out of dear old England and placed here just for me. The lady in attendance gave me a free coffee, but warned me that in my target town for the day - Brownsville - I would not find any accommodation. My new friend was on the case straight away. She called up the offices of Mayor Ryan in Brownsville to elicit help for this brave/idiotic traveller who had walked over 2,000 miles from California to see them. "Don't forget Europe and Australia," I wanted to pipe up, but I left my efforts in the States as my sole reference. The mayor's office swung into action and three hours later I was in a car being driven by Sandy from City Hall due south, to Uniontown where Super 8 mugged me for $66 this time.

This did form part of the approach to Pennsylvania. There was no single highway burrowing its way in a convenient straight line, so I hopped from one to another, getting strategic rides to put me back on course on three further occasions. Some days I gained and others I ended up walking further than planned, so on balance I was happy with the distance covered. The weather had cooled further to hit daily highs in the 70s, but the very undulating landscape still left me sweating profusely and aching. I was heartened by the knowledge that in a matter of days Pennsylvania would level out for the last stretch towards Philadelphia. After that, the next hills I would be facing would be in Cornwall.

Connellsville was passed, as was Breezewood, and as I headed up the hills away from Breezewood I gazed enviously at the flat, wide Turnpike with a generous shoulder running flat around the side of the mountain I was heading straight up. Highway 30 was a fine road, but built in the pioneering days when the style of the day was necessarily to follow the contours of the land, unlike the modern approach of ironing out the dips. Two hours of steady uphill walking left me a little puffed and legs jellied, so I took a good 15-minute rest, sitting on a bench surrounded by woods. Another 20 yards or so brought me to the very summit and, once atop the mountain, I was presented with the downward track, which warned drivers of 'dangerous curves' and what to do about 'runaway trucks'. Gulp. I headed bravely on and came gratefully to rest in McConnellsburg.

These buccaneering exploits led me inexorably towards one of the towns I had been looking forward to seeing more than most others in America. I had previously been guilty of chuckling inwardly at some of the locals in other states who told me of the historical buildings in their town ("There's one house that's more than 100 years old!"), but I knew there was one place waiting for me that would provide a genuine historical landmark, quite apart from the centuries-old Native American sights I had enjoyed; a place that symbolised the struggles that had been fought and won to define the nature of the new republic as it emerged from the yolk of colonial rule and its own convulsions towards a national identity; and a town that continued to provide focus to the changing nature of the nation's proclaimed aims of liberty and justice, cherished for so long in this land.

I walked on towards Gettysburg.

~ 34 ~
Birth of a Nation

All roads into Gettysburg are steeped in the history of the most decisive battle of the American Civil War, which took place at the beginning of July 1863, and the town's iconic status was sealed later that year with President Lincoln's visit, during which he delivered the famous Gettysburg Address to thousands of his attending countrymen. On that day, 19th November 1863, Edward Everett of Massachusetts delivered an address to the vast crowd which lasted more than two hours. After he resumed his seat, President Lincoln stood and delivered his address in just over two minutes. Although puzzling at the time, the President's words grew in stature as the years went by and have passed into the vernacular, both political and social, to this day. One rather jaded gentleman remarked to me as we sat together on a bench in town that "they ought to drag Bush and his cronies down here to be reminded what this country's about".

The entire town of Gettysburg has been declared a site of national historical importance, with the result that the town can never expand - new housing developments will never spring up to cover the historic fields. As you walk into the town itself, statues and historical markers tell the stories, and the downtown area has kept pace with certain aspects of development, whilst retaining its heritable air. As I strolled through the town the next day, I gazed at the converted yet preserved buildings and dropped into Abe's Antiques, resisting the urge to buy some period hats. I dearly wanted to go into the Lincoln Museum but, as with all the stops on the walk, my time was up all too quickly. Before I could become irresolute, I bent my steps towards Abbotstown, passing through the heart of the Pennsylvanian Dutch Country.

The Pennsylvanian Dutch are in fact descendants of German settlers with the self-descriptive 'Deutsch' becoming 'Dutch' as time went by. The Amish people try to remain faithful to their traditional way of life, eschewing modern conveniences such as electricity and motor cars. I saw a few of the characteristic horse-drawn carriages passing on adjacent roads and a number of Amish stores selling traditional handcrafted goods and furniture, but again I had little time to investigate further. I passed through the larger cities of York and Lancaster, including a thrilling walk across the Susquehanna River on Highway 462, but my karma was out of synch for the time being and my mood was one of dissatisfaction.

To discover why, I went through what had become something of an on-the-road ritual of weighing up the good and the bad of the current situation. On the positive side, firstly, I was pleased that the abscess seemed to have just decided to hold its relatively small state. Secondly, I was now just three days away from my arrival in Philadelphia on 16th November.

On the negative side, I was just so tired. In my logbook I wrote:

"My legs, back, feet feel awful at the moment. Don't know why. Seems like I may have had the best of my long-distance, long-duration power walking. The weather is great, the roads are now generous with minimal hills and the PA [abscess] seems contained for now. Why is this walking so hard?"

I never did figure out why those days were so hard, but carried on regardless. The other most prominent negative factor was money. My remaining funds were now running very low and I was entering the pleading stage each time I went into a hotel/motel to try to eke out the money further. The food I was eating was of the cheapest variety and the only area where I didn't compromise was with the water and Gatorade. Everything else could go. I now held on to my camera films, not wanting to spend money on getting them developed, I thought twice about getting a coffee from gas stations midday and I took several rolls of toilet paper from the motel bathrooms so I didn't have to buy packs of tissues - this was life on the cheap!

But ... it felt good. The lifestyle I'd had back in England was full of all the accoutrements of modern living and as a result it was fairly easy to be contented. But that same lifestyle, which had left me drifting through life from one birthday to the next, had left me unsatisfied. In Dickens' *Life and Adventures of Martin Chuzzlewit*, Mark Tapley had opined that "there was no credit in being jolly" when surrounded by comforts, insisting that you could only derive credit from being jolly in miserable circumstances. Whilst I was far from miserable, my much-reduced circumstances and the need to be resilient throughout did leave me emerging with some credit. I wouldn't go so far to say I was enjoying the pain, isolation and money worries, but I was enjoying the daily triumphs of completing each walk and the vindication that each of the 5,000 miles I had now completed gave me.

That said, money worries were eased by the fact that my friend Gaye back in London had been contacting her international colleagues to rally to my cause, with the result that hosts had been arranged for me in West Chester and Newton Square.

At length, I finally began the walk from Upper Darby towards the city that confirmed I had made it to the east coast of America. I walked on with the skyscrapers of Philadelphia in my vision from the first minute. It was a long, long road leading into the city. Passing the huge '69' denoting 69th Street, I wandered further along into Market Street and then switched to Chestnut Avenue to take me all the way in. The poor neighbourhoods gave way to slightly nicer neighbourhoods, until I walked across the Schulykill River and into downtown Philadelphia. I'd made it! Four-and-a-half months after starting out in the blazing sunshine of California, my passage along the chilly Philly streets marked my arrival on the east coast. The sun was still shining that November morning, but without its withering intensity. I was given a hero's reception by the American Association for Cancer Research and was promptly whisked off to their annual conference to meet and greet delegates from around the world.

Within two hours of arriving I had also secured myself a spot on the sofa of Fox News' flagship 'Good Day Philadelphia' for a live interview in the studio on the Friday morning. I met up with my hosts, Farrell and Claire, who spirited me back to their house on the west side of town, and settled in for some more tourist duties.

The next day Farrell ran me all over Philadelphia. Translated from the Greek, the city's name means 'City of Brotherly Love', a fact that is reinforced by the 'Brotherly Love' statue in Kennedy Square. Its greatest day came when the Declaration of Independence was written, signed and publicly read in the auspicious year of 1776, followed ten years later by the US Constitution.

We visited the Art Museum, where I ran up the steps to get some fists clenched, 'Rocky' style photos taken. I didn't feel too bad mixing the low with high culture, since the museum itself had added two booted footprints of the legend Rocky at the very spot where Sylvester Stallone had stood 30 years earlier. The long avenue stretching away from the museum and towards the south side was festooned with flags of all nations, and as I eyed the Union Jack shimmering at the roadside I felt a thrill of joy knowing that ten more short days were between me and my return home. Farrell took me over to the south side, where we sampled the famous Philly Cheese Steak from both Pat's and Geno's restaurants.

Later in the afternoon Claire took over tourist guide duties and we visited the City Hall for some truly epic views across the whole city. We then visited the Constitution Centre, which was holding an exhibition dedicated to the War of Independence and I promised not to cheer for the British. That night I attended a meeting of Claire and Farrell's local community association and gave a short talk, answering questions from the audience afterwards.

I woke at 5:00 the next day and showered myself into something hopefully presentable to the Fox TV viewers. The early morning darkness and whistling wind gave a wintery backdrop to the short walk across to the studios, where I was set up with coffee and snacks. Presently I was ushered downstairs and onto the set. Unlike the numerous pre-recorded 'on the road' interviews, I was now going to be interviewed 'live' on the Fox studio sofa by Kirsty, beaming out across two states. Weather, traffic and sports news were going on all around me until the great moment came. The signal light twinkled and Kirsty faced the camera to tell the viewers, "Now have we got a story for you," before introducing me to the spotlight in front of hundreds of thousands of viewers. The interview was a great success - except for the point where I trod on my microphone (!), but this was laughed off. I left the set, shaking hands with all and ready to walk on.

I took a ride to the north side of town and headed off, with just 100 miles now separating me from the big finish in New York City.

~ 35 ~
East Side Story

Philadelphia proved to be just as much of a pain to leave as every other big city, as I wandered in a vague northward direction for hours. The people from whom I asked directions were utterly bemused that anyone should want to walk such a distance as 20 miles and urged me to take a bus or at least a taxi. I eventually made it onto Highway 13 and yanked myself out of the city through Cornwells Heights, Croydon and Bristol.

The day ended with me finally circling round to Levittown, a strip of a town with suburban developments attached. I took a room at the inappropriately named Ace motel, which won the award for the worst motel in the States at a canter. The block of rooms set back off the highway were filthy, with several-times-turned bedlinen just about managing still to cover the beds. My room was a dark, dank affair, with mouldy walls and patchy carpet finished off by the cheap, broken furniture haphazardly scattered around the marshmallow soft bed. Most troubling was the front door, which sported a swivel lock that was clearly for decorative purposes only as the wood of the door frame had rotted away and been stuffed with tissue paper to prop up the illusion of a safety feature. As I settled in for the night, I took the precaution of ramming the bedside table against the door.

I woke in the night at 3:23. That time will for ever be emblazoned on my mind as it was the moment I started awake, suddenly conscious that both light and a chill were invading the room. The front door was wide open! In one movement, I twisted myself off the bed and threw my arms at the door, slamming it shut, and then sat down with my back against it to prevent further breach. Outside the door I heard footsteps crunching on the gravel, inches away from where I crouched. I reached across deftly to the displaced bedside table and manoeuvred it once again into place. With my heart beating loudly and a curious sensation of feeling suddenly hot then cold, I grabbed the bed and pulled it against the door frame. I leapt around to the far side and sat on the floor next to the bed. I then did something I have never done in my life before and called the emergency services. I dialled 911 and asked for the police. I told my story to the operator who seemed a little too used to the whole routine and asked me why I hadn't switched rooms earlier when I saw the state of the lock. Probably a valid question, but not whilst I was crouching next to the bed at 3:30 in the morning! They sent a car around and one of Levittown's finest had a brief doorstep chat with me and assured me that this motel was hardly ever the subject of breaking and entering. "I mean - look at it," he said and meaningfully gazed at the shabby decor. I trusted that the appearance of the local boys in blue had put paid to any recurrence and managed to doze for another couple of hours before rising for coffee and doughnuts.

That experience put me on edge, especially as I was heading towards the heavily populated and crime-prone states of New Jersey and New York. Counting the days to go in single figures, I crossed over the state line into New Jersey over a small bridge into the state capital of Trenton. I had decided that due to the early hour I would press on and try to reach the vaunted town of Princeton, which lay a further 12 miles down the highway. I chatted with a couple of police officers who expressed grave concerns about my walking with a stroller through the streets of Trenton, as the area to the north of town had deteriorated to such an extent into a drug-infested pyre that most streets were 'no-go' areas at any time of day. I held out that I wanted to walk on and they finally advised me to head up towards the 'Circle' roundabout and then get onto Highway 206 heading north. I walked on warily.

The shabby main street turned into a downright nasty series of streets leading northwards. A mailman pointed me in the right direction to meet up with Highway 206 and I pushed the stroller onwards, looking and listening for any signs of trouble. I didn't have to wait too long.

Walking along a decrepit pavement, with wheels constantly getting chewed up, I heard a series of loud cracks echoing from a few blocks eastwards. The voices carried; unnaturally high-pitched male voices, urgent and desperate. A little rattled, I pushed on, disconcerted to see I was the only person walking along this particular street. Gunfire does not sound the same as in the movies, but screeching tyres do. A car swung wildly around the corner I was approaching and roared past me. Involuntarily my eyes darted to the windscreen and I saw the desperate face of the driver, eyes wide and mixing fury with fear and fortunately intent on the road ahead. The passenger was glancing over his shoulder, doubtless to see if anyone was following. I carried on walking as if nothing had happened and was relieved that no pursuing car came along. Moments later the sound of wailing sirens filled the distant air as I stepped up the pace to get the hell out of there.

Despite this, New Jersey fired up fond memories for me as such an avid fan of Bruce Springsteen as I walked on to New Brunswick to be met and collected by my host Ruth, whom I had not seen for 16 years.

My first trip to the States in 1989 at the tender age of 23 was ostensively so that I could attend the wedding of my school friend Paul and his American bride Lisa in New York. There was, however, a subplot in operation during my first week there - that of trying to meet Bruce Springsteen at his home in New Jersey. Ruth was a friend of the family who had been forewarned about me and she took me all around Freehold, Asbury Park and other places of significance. The climax of the visit was a trip to Bruce's house in Runsom, where I hopped out of Ruth's car and spotted the man himself sitting outside the house on a motorbike. Having come all that way I wasn't going to let a couple of hundred yards stop me now, so I started walking up the front drive, shaking as only the star-struck can.

A security van started driving around the side of the house, but Bruce raised his hand to halt it, then walked slowly towards me and said, "Hi - how you doing?" I had always been a fan of the music, but now I was such a fan of the man, who stood chatting happily, gave me an autograph, posed for photos with me and then waved me off genially.

All those memories of the summer of '89 came flooding back as Ruth and I met again outside a gas station in a dodgy part of town. We hugged and in the car chatted endlessly all the way home, where I met husband Ron and Ruth's son TJ, with whom I would be spending the last night of my brief passage through New Jersey.

Cutting over to East Brunswick and through Sayreville the next day, I had Raritan Bay, gateway to the Atlantic Ocean teasing itself into sight beyond the roofs of the houses and factories lining the highway. Two bridges spanned the bay, one being the traffic-only Edison Bridge and the other, to which I headed, the recently completed Victory Bridge.

And what a bridge! Usually one expects a bridge to glide levelly off the land and offer a horizontal passage to the other side, keeping a flat sense of proportion to the surrounding land. The Victory Bridge appeared to resemble the Gateway Arch in St Louis, rising up sharply to a peak, then falling back down again to meet the ground on the other side. As I stepped on, I was looking up at a good 45 degree angle to see the route ahead, with motorised metal whizzing past me all the way. Reaching the centre and therefore the summit of the bridge, I looked back down at the land I had just covered and switched to look down into the town below. It was a most peculiar experience, but at least I didn't get a nosebleed.

I crossed over into the district of Perth Amboy and conceded, as I stood at the foot of the Outerbridge Crossing, that I would need a vehicle to take me across the bridge to Staten Island. Pedestrians were very sensibly forbidden to walk on the bridge and a taxi driver, who had clearly seen me coming for days, stung me for $20 for the ride across, plus I had to pay the $6 toll for him. What else was I going to do? He dropped me off as soon as we hit Staten Island as requested and I continued walking on.

I was now in New York with the width of Staten Island and 48 blocks of Manhattan between me and the finish line at the Rockefeller Centre. I concluded the day by walking on to Oakwood, taking the train to St George's dock and making up the short distance the following day. I made several phone calls to the TV and radio stations and the newspapers, but despite my efforts and those of my hosts across the States it looked as though we were drawing a blank in terms of coverage.

Never mind. I was about to complete the biggest section of the walk and had the added bonus that my friend Beryl had just arrived in town from England to join me as I walked the final stretch through the city. As I settled in to sleep, I caught a glance of the world-famous New York City skyline through the mist and smiled knowingly at the docks where the Staten Island ferry was coming in to land. Tomorrow, that would take me through to set foot in Manhattan.

~ 36 ~
Start Spreading the News ...

I stood motionless, staring at the glass doors admitting all and sundry into the ferry terminal. The wind outside attacked the high-standing flag masts and frequently sent smaller divisions whistling down the corridors to try to breach the heavy doors guarding the entrance. Hundreds of souls washed over my eyes, scurrying to make the ferry before departure, all with their own stories, hopes, loves and fears. The clattering of footsteps all around, jostling baggage and the ever present pressure of time, time, weighing on the minds of the passengers flocking into their daily ritual, loving and hating their predictable, uncertain futures. The increasing rain crash-landed on long-worn surfaces, bringing no sign of immediate destruction but instead hinting at the slow, steady erosion of the certainties of concrete and tile. Each bit part built surely into the endlessly repeating grand drama known as 'normality' into which these souls willingly or not submitted themselves each day; constant, never-ending, where the small gains must be celebrated and the setbacks endured.

As I stood watching the scene unfold at the end of my five-month adventure in the United States, I came back to a question that had pricked my consciousness within days of my arrival - how was the American Dream faring in the twenty-first century?

The US Declaration of Independence had included in its 'self-evident truths' an inalienable right to the 'pursuit of happiness'. Now that may appear to lack gravitas alongside other nations' declarations, but for me it goes to the heart of the human psyche a good deal better than more contrived, worthy statements. Successive historical events such as the Gold Rush and pioneering industrial giants like General Electric and Ford brought an excitement and upsurge in living standards and perceived opportunities so that the American

Dream - the idea that anybody can 'make it' - became embedded in the hearts of the entire nation.

Americans that I had met - and I had met thousands of them in my time - had shown themselves to be warm, funny, generous and of a communal disposition that belied the oft-touted perception of self-interested oysters. So what of the American Dream for these generations?

The secret of the American Dream, if there is one, is that it bypasses politics. It belongs truly to the people who aspire to bring it to life if not for themselves then for their children. The degrees by which these aspirations affect those pursuing the Dream can be measured by whether their efforts are based on hope or expectation. Hope would always carry with it a second tier of pragmatism that endured the path towards the Dream and an ultimate acceptance of your lot if the Dream did not materialise. Expectation, however, imposes demands on the nature and to an extent the timetable involved for the Dream, with no 'Plan B', leaving the person devastated and bitter if the Dream remains unfulfilled. Certainly the cult of celebrity and the outrageous rewards afforded to those working in the entertainment and sporting worlds have upped the ante for what the Dream may represent in this new century. So would the encouragement of a more measured, sober pursuit of happiness and fulfilment lead to a more contented and accepting society? Perhaps, but I think this wholly logical thought process misses one vital aspect.

It is exactly the unrealistic, hopeless, outlandish dreaming that has propelled Americans through the ages to greatness. The collective will that brought independence rattled the apparently invincible and certainly complacent British Empire long before its twentieth-century disintegration. Set aside the political and business subplots of the two world wars for a moment and focus on the determined, courageous exploits of American troops who have fought and won unpopular battles far away from home. Remember the moon walk completed in 1969, following John F. Kennedy's improbable 1961 boast that it would be achieved before the end of the decade. I adored that spirit, which was often lent to me by appreciative new friends as I had made my strenuous walking way across the country. In the past I have myself been described as 'idealistic'. Guilty as charged, but look where it got me ...

I was rocked out of my reverie as Beryl came bouncing off the ferry and hugged me as if our lives depended on it. And it was so good to see her! Years before, when we shared a flat back in England, she had spent several hours in the pub listening to my plans to walk around the world and had been suitably encouraging. No stranger to travel herself, Beryl had bent her latest whistle-stop world tour to be able to arrive in NYC at the time I was passing through.

My old friend Pat in Brooklyn offered us both the use of his apartment whilst he was away for the Thanksgiving weekend, so we settled in for a couple of days after enjoying an evening with Pat and a large bottle of Southern Comfort.

Standing down at the ferry terminal next to Battery Park on the morning of Wednesday 23rd November, I thanked the weather for giving me a cool, clear day for the final trek through the dazzling island city of Manhatten. With Beryl at my side, I powered along Broadway, waving my regards to Wall Street as we slipped past. The huge skyscrapers lining the streets provided the stone and glass backdrop to the broad avenues guiding me towards the climax I had so often feared I would never see. The deserts, the red rock mountain passes, the flatlands and badlands, the cornfields and rolling valleys had finally given way to the concrete icon of the United States, New York City.

Yellow taxis weaved in and out of the traffic, honking their familiar impatience at the languid progress of others. I walked along block after block, pausing occasionally for Beryl to catch up, until I finally admitted we could stop for a break at Chinatown. We scuttled along the incredibly bustling streets, past the Chinese restaurants, supermarkets and general stores and slipped inside, of all places, McDonald's. Not exactly an inspired choice given that we were in one of the greatest cities in the world, but nevertheless totally American and the only place I knew we could legitimately take up table space with only a coffee.

Onwards we walked, with the Empire State Building drawing us further along the island towards the finishing point of the Rockefeller Centre on 49th Street. This was the day before Thanksgiving and, whilst the city wore its customary brash chic, there was a palpable air of pre-holiday bonhomie with the hot dog sellers bearing a genial countenance and the cops sporting an avuncular, indulgent air towards the moving millions. Racing for the finish line, I reflected that no press had promised any coverage of my final triumph, but given the fact that most of the journey had been completed on a wing and a prayer I was grateful just to be there.

We switched to Madison Avenue and I counted the streets as the final few blocks of the journey fell away before my eyes: 44th Street, 45th Street, 46th, 47th, 48th and finally 49th Street. I stood for a moment to draw breath and caught my reflection in the glass of a telephone booth on the side of the street. A thin, angular face with increasingly furrowed lines drawn onto my forehead, tufts of hair sweeping away from the side of my head and thinner tufts adorning my crown, hazel eyes with the slightest green twinkling through - all of which creased into a broad smile as the reality hit me that I was seconds away from completing the 2,800-mile trek across the country, bringing my total distance covered to 5,100 miles. My gaunt face told its own story of how I had lost 20 lbs during the whole trip, dropping down from 13 st to 11 st 6 lbs.

Camcorder running, Beryl filmed me walking oh so slowly along 49th Street until I came to rest by the Rockefeller Centre, dressed up for the holidays with Christmas Tree newly in place, a hundred flags flying and the ice rink full of delighted holiday skaters. I'd done it! Five months after setting foot on the Pacific coast I had made it to New York City and was ecstatic. Yesssss! Hugs, cheers and tears followed as I gazed skywards to the peak of the Rockefeller Centre tower, the delirium combined with the relief leading my sky-high spirits on to the realisation that in 72 hours I would be able to celebrate in the arms of family and friends back in England. What a day ... Beryl and I came to rest at a wine bar just across the street and enjoyed two glasses of white, compliments of the management. The chief executive of the Pediatric Cancer Foundation came out to meet me and joined Beryl and I for a celebratory drink. I apologised for the lack of coverage and attendant donations, but she beamed that I had 'done it' and they were very grateful. Despite bemoaning our failure to garnish press attention, that was soon to be rectified.

As this was my third visit to New York I had no first-timer pressure to rush around to the Statue of Liberty, Greenwich Village, Times Square, etc. I got a haircut from a Russian barber in Brooklyn who also repaired shoes and appeared to have another sideline in photography. I did my laundry and tried to chat with the locals, but unfortunately my Polish was still not that good ...

I took another sojourn into Manhatten and headed for the New York Central Library, making good use of their free Internet access, and I was generally enjoying a very relaxed and easy time of it, until one phone call and one e-mail thrust me back into mission mode. The e-mail was from my mum, asking if I could locate a Cinderella bicycle helmet for my three-year-old niece. The phone call was from the *Newsday* newspaper, asking if I could do an interview about my adventures. Now my niece is a very dear, sweet young lass, but I raced across town immediately to get to the coffee bar for my interview with reporter Lindsey. We met and chatted happily about the whole experience to date, and with an excellent photograph of me standing in the middle of the road just off 32nd Street *Newsday* did me proud with a full-page spread.

Mission one accomplished, now for the bicycle helmet. Fighting my way through the crowds (Thanksgiving had gone and the starting gun had been fired for Christmas shopping), I managed to insert myself into the flagship

Disney store on 56th Street. I had instantly ceased to be the heroic walker and was now just another frantic Christmas shopper, looking for the must-have item. Not wishing to join the melee of happy shoppers whirling en masse through the huge store, I swam across to the main cash register and waited my turn. A cashier smiled encouragingly at me to come forward. I leant across the counter in a conspiratorial manner and determined to play up a cosmopolitan status, and I uttered in my best polished British accent: "I've received a call from my sister in England. She heard I was in town and charged me with locating a Cinderella bicycle helmet for my niece." The only advantage I gained was from a very honest Disney worker who, joining my conspiratorial mood, told me that my best chance would be to go to Toys R Us on Times Square. An hour later I stood contemplating the heightened madness of Toys R Us in the middle of a heaving Times Square and threw myself into the ruck. Another half an hour later I escaped, helmet-less but having become very closely acquainted with several hundred fellow shoppers, and called it a day, heading back to Pat's place to finish off the Southern Comfort and get my backpack ready for the next day.

At 5:30 the next morning, a taxi pulled up outside the house and I hoisted myself, backpack and stroller out onto the bitterly cold street. The night sky lingered and I sat quietly in the back of the car as the driver nudged his way across to JFK Airport. The taxi came to a halt outside the terminal building and I handed over the $35 fare, saving my last few dollars for a drink in the bar. The plane was delayed by an hour, but I felt quite relaxed about everything - not to the extent that I skipped the valium, you understand, but nevertheless I was going home. America had been great to me, but I was ready to walk once again on the lands of my fathers. A crisp, clear voice announced that British Airways flight number 178 was now ready for boarding.

I walked through the departure lounge and onto the plane.

~ 37 ~
Back Home

Home! Great Britain! My very own land of hope and glory. Deep down, I'd never doubted I would return, but whether it would be with my tail between my legs or in triumph had been uncertain so many times that my elation to be back was tempered with a very real sense of relief.

I saw every minor thing (newspapers, driving on the left, pubs, phone boxes, chocolate bars, stone cottages) with new eyes; every sight, sound and smell playing a reassuringly familiar tune deeply embedded in my senses. There is no joy quite like coming back to a home you love after being away for an extended period of time. Add to that a mixture of exhaustion and great satisfaction following a good job well done and it was difficult to know whether to be hugely excited and hyper, or just wallow for a time in quiet contentment.

My arrival at Heathrow Airport at 9:40 in the evening of 26th November brought a moment of huge excitement (and not just about getting off a plane for the last time) to be greeted by Mum and Dad and my brother-in-law, Ian, our chauffeur for the night. Propelled home along the M25 and A13, I came to rest briefly in Southend for one day of quiet contentment, enjoying a long-awaited roast lamb Sunday lunch. On the Monday morning I called in to my doctor and got a prescription for the last course of antibiotics to keep the abscess at bay before jumping on a train to travel down to the West Country.

I now faced the last leg of the walk - a three-week stroll over 350 miles from Land's End back into London and to the gates of Buckingham Palace, last seen 14 months earlier. I knew the route would be far from easy, with the West Country's picturesque rolling hills presenting a stiff challenge during the first ten days. It was facing that awesome corner of our land that I presented myself for inspection on Tuesday 29th November 2005.

After doing an interview for BBC Cornwall radio, I took a bus from Penzance down to Land's End to kick off Part Four. To give myself a gentle reintroduction to walking mode, I had scheduled Land's End back to Penzance, a mere 11 miles, for the first day. Following interviews and photos for the newspapers, I pushed the stroller through the Land's End emporium and headed east. Almost immediately the pavement was cut, so I walked on the roadside along the A30. The West Country lanes are not well suited to walking; in fact they are not very conducive to two-way traffic at times. The sides of the little roads are lined with very high hedges sitting atop stone walls, which give the effect of almost travelling through a tunnel. That itself was restrictive, but the number of twists and turns meant that I was progressing extremely slowly, coming up to each curve at a snail's pace, trying to peer around the corner and listen hard for the sounds of approaching vehicles. Those that did swing around the corner were occasionally surprised to see a man pushing a stroller along the side of the road, but I didn't get any admonishing honks - perhaps they are used to locals making their way on foot between villages.

Despite being hours away from December, the weather was quite mild and the Cornish countryside was still wearing its beguiling green as I weaved my way through. A few hours along the way, a hilly aspect was added to the equation, so as well as going from side to side I was now also going up and down the rat run of the A30. As I approached Penzance, a delicate rain started to fall and I was actually quite happy to be stopping after the modest first day trek - and even happier to be ready for my first Cornish pasty.

Whilst many towns and cities in Britain have in recent years homogenised themselves into a series of largely indistinguishable high streets, my start in Cornwall afforded me the essence of the English countryside and village life that we are all so glad still exists. The fishing towns hugging the rocky coast and the small market towns and villages immortalised by the likes of Agatha Christie remain, although battered by the decimation of the fishing and farming industries in recent years.

Leaving Penzance the next morning, I continued along the A30, enjoying a modestly paved walkway amid the wide grass verge until the little town of Hayle. After that, it was a 2½ ft hard shoulder along the rest of the route, with traffic whizzing past in a fashion that was by now quite common to me. I walked past the large conurbation of Cambourne, before rising up to the exit for the day's target town of Redruth.

In each town, I spent a few minutes in the local library surfing the Internet for the cheapest bed and breakfast I could find and also trying to get contact details for the local television and radio stations and local newspapers. Phone calls and faxes followed to try to drum up interest for media coverage and the final push for donations to Cancer Research UK. For a time the actual walking became only one aspect of my mission. The good thing about trying to blag my way onto TV/radio or into the papers was that I didn't need to exaggerate the story. That I had walked more than 5,000 miles and was now coming into the home straight was usually good enough to engender great interest in me, and during those three weeks I featured on BBC TV News in five counties, ITV news in three and in several newspapers to boot. The honking from motorists started up again and people stopped me in the street to chat, all of which did wonders in keeping up my morale.

Dear old England did not make me wait too long for the traditional dousing with liquid sunshine. Coming out of Truro on the fourth day with the magnificent Cathedral still in my sights, the rain fell as only it can in this sceptred isle. Fortunately my Aunt Margaret had armed me with new trousers, which together with the boots and jacket still in place kept me dry. I tried for the first time to fasten up the toggles on my hood, which seemed to work a treat, keeping my head snugly protected whilst leaving my vision unimpaired. The toggles were a little tight but wrapped nicely under my chin. It was in this state that I meandered further along, receiving toots and waves from motorists who seemed inordinately amused to see me. As I approached a gas station and prepared to take a coffee break, I caught myself in a mirror. The closely wrapped hood holding the shape of my high forehead and diving chin made my head appear the shape of a oversized light bulb. Out of curiosity I opened my mouth as wide as it would go and my face resembled the mask in the *Scream* movies. I decided to save that look for when I really needed it ...

The wind continued to howl and the rain continued to fall as I made my way along the increasingly mulchy road to St Austell. From there, the A390 towards Liskeard dipped and rose quite dramatically, straining my calves and back like nothing since Pennsylvania. Stopping off in Lostwithiel, I called into the main pub in town for a cup of tea to sustain me. As I walked through the door, I became immediately aware that there was a bit of a 'do' happening. The local Cancer Research UK centre was holding a bring-and-buy raffle in the very best tradition of British fund-raising. The old pub, with oak beams intact and long-serving carpet, played host to a gathering of senior citizens with a large table propped up against the bar festooned with every imaginable knick-knack as well as locally produced cakes, sandwiches and, of course, huge pots of tea. The organisers immediately introduced me to the whole gathering, who applauded my efforts with great warmth and affection. Photos were taken and I delivered a little speech, and I was grateful for the cup of tea and the little bakery box of savoury treats thrust into the stroller for the rest of the day's journey. Wonderful.

The next day Cornwall became Devon as I edged one county closer to London, passing through the border town of Tavistock. Tavistock denoted not only the county change but also the outer limit of Dartmoor National Park. Dartmoor is home to forests, hills, reservoirs and age-old castles as well as historic sites of great significance to the ancient Druid faiths where many occult enthusiasts have gathered for centuries. I decided against dancing naked around the ancient runes in the moonlight, but did have the fulsome delight of skirting Dartmoor's borders as I made my way northwards to Okehampton and then across the top of the Park to Exeter. The newer stretch of the A30 ironed out many of the hills and I powered my way along the 22 miles feeling quite exuberant in the process, pausing only to have a chat with a police officer who stopped me after "getting reports ..." I could only smile as he approached with lights flashing, thinking it would be so bloody ironic if I'd made it across the highways of Europe, Australia and America to be denied the right to walk along the A-roads of England and finish the job. The police officer admitted, "I don't know what we do about you ...", before radioing back to HQ and getting the green light for me to continue, "as long as you are aware of the dangers". Thank goodness for police officers imbued with common sense.

My tenth day back on the road from Honiton to Ilminster tried my resolve once again, with narrow lanes and hills throwing unrelenting challenges. The Blackmore Hills outside Honiton led me way up to a higher level, offering stunning views of the Devonshire countryside sporadically lightened but never heated by the weak sunshine. More often the gathering, threatening clouds shaded the views.

Having scaled the hills, I wended my way downwards through an expansive area of grass-laden highways, until my mood was shattered by a signpost telling me that after three hours of walking Ilminster was still 15 miles away. Eh? It was only 17 when I started the day from Honiton! A roadside café confirmed the worst and I thundered off, breaking into the first serious sweat of the week, determined to make the target town by sundown. Within the hour I came to a blizzard of black and yellow tape and temporary signposts indicating extensive roadworks underway on the A30. All traffic was being diverted northwards towards Taunton, adding another eight miles to the journey.

Ignoring the diversion signs, I started walking slowly along the closed section of the A30 and could see in the distance the end of the roadworks. In between was an admittedly swooping road, in various states of disrepair, but if I could just sneak under the radar and carry on along my way I'd be in Ilminster in time for tea. I crept along, feeling oddly conspicuous with my yellow vest (blending nicely with the workers') and pushing the stroller (still bearing my backpack) until I finally attracted the attention of one of the staff. Dan from London had been seconded on contract to come down to Devon for this job and pulled up in his car to ask if I was local and how my baby was. I jerked the stroller to the side to show no baby and explained my mission. He was very sympathetic, but told me that somebody along the way would stop me for health and safety reasons and that I might as well jump in the car and he would drop me off on the other side of the works. Knowing that an English official with a badge and clipboard was a match any day for the Russian guards, I agreed. On the other side of the dip Dan let me out and I continued along.

The next day - my last in Devon - was the day I finally succumbed to gravity. The pavement ran out and the shoulder evaporated, leaving me yomping along the clumpy grass verge of a dual carriageway at around 1 mph. I finally loaded the backpack on my shoulders and scooped up the folded stroller in my arms. Stepping awkwardly from bare gravel onto slippery, uncut grass, I peered alternately to the road ahead and down to my feet for guidance. In one fell swoop I managed to drop the stroller, do a 45 degree twist and - splatt! - ended up face down on the grass. For a moment I just lay there. What was the point of jumping to my feet? Having remained upright throughout the worst excesses the world had thrown at me, I had finally ended up doing a bellyflop nine days outside of the big finish in London.

With a red face and slightly green hue on my trousers, I hauled myself up, crossed over to the central reservation and walked across the country line into Somerset and on to Yeovil.

~ 38 ~
Middle England

If not effortlessly, then certainly with confidence, I marched on through Somerset and crossed over into Wiltshire. Shaftsbury provided another small market town stop in the proceedings and the pub room I stayed in was reminiscent of those I enjoyed in Australia - basic and cheap, with guests sharing kettles between them for cups of tea.

As I left Shaftsbury on the morning of Sunday 11th December, I was heading towards the one day that had stood out for so many months as being a moment of unbridled celebration. Earlier in the year, when I was resting over in England and getting my Russian visa issues resolved, I had proposed that Mum, Dad and Aunt Margaret come down and accompany me for the final week. I suggested that my dad join me again for the final section of the walk and everyone else agreed, leaving the poor sod no chance at all. At the tender age of 77, he was to join me for another 85 miles from Salisbury back to Buckingham Palace.

Whilst the men of the family were puffing away, Mum and Margaret would take our stuff on to the next town, secure accommodation for the night and then go off to enjoy the sights of Middle England. Thus it was that with one week to go, and after all the trials, perils and hard slogs of the previous 14 months, I would finally have a walking companion and backup team.

The misty morning gave way to a dour midday, but as the afternoon wore on the sun finally managed to burn off the veil before announcing its imminent departure. BBC Dorset turned up with a TV crew and did an interview which was shown that night and subsequently syndicated to all surrounding counties, which was great. I was also interviewed 'live' on BBC Wiltshire Radio, causing a certain amount of consternation when I mentioned in passing the Polish prostitutes when asked for 'any funny stories'. I switched smartly to the wholesome subject of the Belgian monastery.

I had been offered a place to stay in Wilton that night with host June.

Wilton is three miles down the road from Salisbury, so I stopped off at June's house and was greeted by a reception committee including the local mayor. After slurping a restorative cup of tea, I left my stuff and carried on towards Salisbury itself.

The sun was descending fast as I motored wilfully along the leaf-strewn lane out of Wilton and into Salisbury. The spire of the Cathedral soon came into sight, but did not get closer very quickly. I called Mum to confirm that my arrival was imminent and she confirmed she, Dad and Margaret were waiting outside the Cathedral. The green fields gave way to the grey pavements and the twisting road lurched under a railway bridge and into the main shopping street of Salisbury. Amber street lighting fell across the moderately busy road as I hastened on. A huge Christmas tree outside the town hall gave a lustrous sheen to the ancient town's streets and I slowed my pace in appreciation. Finally, I turned a corner into the narrow street leading up to the Cathedral's park gates. A mist had descended to give the old building a magical cloak and three familiar figures motioned towards me, grinning and waving. "Hellooooooo!"

Everything was safe. All was now guaranteed. As we hugged outside the ancient church I knew that the end of the walk was now secure with no more scratching around for accommodation, no more threats of being stranded, no awkward manoeuvres with the stroller - all was now in hand with my fellow walker and backup team.

Tony from BBC Radio was on hand with congratulations and we all repaired inside the church for hot chocolate and an interview. The night had fallen completely now and it was a night that I concentrated hard on committing to memory. The walk out of the Cathedral grounds, the walk through the town centre, seeing the Christmas tree once again and the preserved older shop fronts giving way to more modern structures, crossing the road and threading through the backstreets to the car park and finally all seated in Margaret's car for the run back to Wilton. I was collected early the next morning by the family once again and headed off to the starting point for my 368th and Dad's first day on the road. Andover was the target with Middle Wallop the lunchtime stop. Off we went ...

The road out of Salisbury wound upwards into the hills. Dad and I made a sterling start along the flatlands spiralling around the town's ring road, but hit the first incline within half an hour. The pace was a little slower than I had been used to, but not too pedestrian. I had to account for the fact that I had been walking for a year whereas Dad hadn't put on his walking shoes for 18 months since Dover. At the peak of the hill we looked back on Salisbury and then turned to move on. After two hours we came to a roadside café and stopped in for a very civilised pot of tea for two.

The pavement had failed us early on, so we had been walking on the thin white line at the side of the road, bending into the grass verge as traffic approached. I took the lead and when any large trucks came hurtling down towards us I yelled "Grass!" in plenty of time for us to lurch hedgewards. After one particularly narrow stretch with trees providing more of a canopy that was necessary, we finally peaked and saw a long, gentle descent leading on towards the Wallops of Wiltshire. After 12 miles in four hours we came to the midday rest point of Middle Wallop and the family consensus was that Dad could do with sitting out the final six miles. Off they went and I romped home into Andover a couple of hours later.

Having the family with me transformed the whole experience for those last few days. The week took on the air of a family holiday, with various bed and breakfast stops through the mid-Shires and Home Counties and a nightly gathering after the day's efforts where we found little pubs to enjoy a well-earned supper. Walking along and chatting with Dad reminded us both of those family holidays spent in Cornwall, Devon and Kent when our younger selves were not shy about setting off on several-mile hikes.

Basingstoke, Camberley and Staines fell in quick succession until Dad and I found ourselves in a small bed and breakfast just outside the Greater London suburb of Staines. There was just 48 hours to go, with a stop off at Hammersmith and then a leisurely stroll to Buckingham Palace to finish the next day. Mum and Margaret left us in order to rally the troops back in Southend for the grand finale on Saturday 17th December.

A cavalcade of emotions ran through me as we stepped out on that penultimate day. Walking alongside Heathrow Airport gave a really poignant reminder of the scale of the adventure that was rapidly coming to an end. I was in many ways sad that it was almost over. Every nuance of frustration and every huge impediment en route had been swatted away by the dream of these final days bringing the ultimate reward. Now I was here, I wanted to eke out the prevailing triumph in each moment, each step that I took towards completing this masterpiece. As always, the practicalities won out and I steered Dad and I through the London suburbs of Hounslow, Isleworth and Brentford, along Chiswick High Road and into Hammersmith.

At 3:30 I walked past St Martin's House, just off King Street, where I had spent four years working for Citibank over 15 years earlier. The area was barely recognisable, save for one or two indisputable buildings surrounding the tube stations. We walked down Shepherd's Bush Road as the daylight began fading fast, dodging the early office absconders dashing for home on that cold December Friday night.

I finished as I had started - in a £30 hotel room in London, although this time everything was behind me rather than ahead of me. Dad lost the toss and picked up the bill for supper and we settled in for the night ahead of the last day of walking.

~ 39 ~
The Last Day

I woke up. Looking around the hotel room (it didn't take long), I reflected that this was the last time I would need to stir myself ahead of a long day's walk. Christmas was eight short days away and I fully intended to make up for the previous year's missed festivities. The rapid hot blast of shower jets gradually roused my yet slumbering senses and I emerged to face the day.

My first task was to do an interview 'live' on the BBC's national *TV News* breakfast show. Hammersmith had turned out to be an inspired choice for the penultimate stop as an official car appeared just after 7:00 to whisk me down to the studios at Shepherd's Bush. Sitting next to Bill Turnbull on the studio set was quite thrilling and we conducted the interview as if having a nice chat over a cup of tea. That concluded, I returned to the hotel and went on to do interviews for BBC London Radio, Five Live, LBC Radio and ITV's *London Tonight*. Things had certainly picked up on the last day in terms of media coverage.

We were once again blessed with fine weather as we made our way out of Hammersmith and along Kensington High Street. The day had a surreal quality to it, with the sands fast running out on the most exciting period of my life. The London streets, so familiar to me, appeared as pages out of a long-forgotten childhood book and I felt keenly those sensations that had beguiled me as a young man exploring the capital many years ago. Following the TV appearance, people called out to me, stopped for a chat, shook my hand and asked me, "How did you do it?" "How many pairs of shoes did you use?" "What are you going to do next?" The only one I felt confident about answering was the number of shoes!

Knightsbridge came and went before we swung around Hyde Park Corner and into Piccadilly. The sun beamed down on our progress and, try as I might to focus on the present scenes, my mind kept wandering back over the year's events …

The hike along the A2 in Kent ... the flatlands of the Low Countries and the monks ... the panic of turning up in German and Polish towns with nowhere to stay ... the Russian interrogations at both ends of the country ... the Aussie wilderness and advent of the abscess ... the oppressive heat of the American West ... the strains of the Midwest ... the triumphant arrival in New York ... the final dash across England ... all of which brought me to here - standing a few hundred feet away from Trafalgar Square, gateway to The Mall.

I didn't want it to end. This mission had become my defining achievement in my life and if I could have headed straight through London and back out onto the open road I'd have probably done it. The idea ran through my mind briefly of walking on to arrive back in Southend, but as Dad and I enjoyed a coffee opposite the Haymarket Theatre I knew that was one flight of fancy that would not get off the ground.

Ironically, the walk was extended a little, as we had arrived a good hour ahead of the target time of 1:00. Buckingham Palace had advised us that we could not arrive until then, as the Changing of the Guard would be dominating proceedings until 12:30. After weighing up our options, I decided we should cut across Leicester Square and walk along the Embankment so that I could get a photo standing alongside Big Ben. Dad was all for having another coffee until the appointed hour, but I held the casting vote ...

An hour later we rounded up and walked up Whitehall into Trafalgar Square. *ITV News* cameras were waiting for the interview, which I did as a crowd of family, friends and supporters - many of whom had been there for the start 14 months earlier - grouped around me with congratulatory hugs. The 'World Walker' banner was hoisted once again and a slow procession began down the Mall, with two metropolitan policemen once again providing an escort as the shimmering winter sun illuminated the last mile of the journey. A *Sky News* cameraman leapt nimbly around us as our entourage and I blazed my way towards the Palace once again, this time with unbridled relief replacing the previous apprehension. Curious tourists once again latched on to the group and looked suitably impressed as the story unfolded.

Buckingham Palace stood with appropriate majesty before me and the voices of my walking companions intermittently faded as I gazed up at the prize that had been waiting patiently for my return. Following the Russian visa debacle, it was now 415 days later that I approached once again the Victoria Memorial and, just beyond, the gates to one of our most iconic buildings. The massive pale walls conceded the slightest glint in the sun as my feet inched ever nearer. I felt no effort, no strain, just the bubbling thrill of anticipation ahead of completing my walking odyssey. All eyes were now upon me as we arrived at the final road crossing and I steered the stroller along its final passage. Cancer Research UK were on hand to deliver me an Outstanding Achievement Certificate, grateful for the support and coverage I had managed to drum up.

I crossed the road and strode purposefully towards the gates of the Palace, once again obscured by a gaggle of tourists. "Can you stand aside please, ladies and gentleman" came the familiar voice of authority and the path was cleared for me. Ten feet to go. I trod slowly forwards and muttered a silent thank you to the many souls who had helped me along the way. However, this was my moment and, turning to face the crowd and cameras, I placed my right hand on the right-hand gate.

The journey was complete.

~ 40 ~
Feet Up

Sitting here at home, I look back in wonder at the experience. Most days I am very much back in the swing of 'normal' life, but occasionally I will be caught unawares by a thought, some memory of the walk, and I am instantly transported back to those moments. Various feelings of fear, triumph, desperation, ennui and sheer joy jostle good-naturedly in my recollections.

This was a dream of my own creation, finally realised. We can sometimes become blinkered by circumstance when considering our future, and without applying imagination of what could be achieved our prospects can easily become our goals. Alternatively, we can occasionally be saddled with, or take on the dreams of others. Family and friends will frequently say, "We only want to you to be happy," but this often comes with a predetermined idea of what constitutes happiness according to their own definition. It takes no small degree of will to define your own realm of happiness and apply yourself to making it happen. We can't all walk around the world, just as we can't all play football for our country or be rock superstars; but we can do our best to try to meet life on our own terms.

Two questions are often asked these days: "How did you keep going?" and "What are you going to do next?"

I put my ability to keep going down to a few factors. Firstly, there was a fear of failure - even when sitting miserably on that bench in Poland having virtually given up, I was haunted by the prospect of people kindly telling me, "Never mind - you did your best." Those kinds of sympathetic statements, although well meant, are somehow more cutting than barbs of stinging criticism. Next, I felt an obligation to all those who had invested their faith in me. I doubt anyone among my family or friends would have taken me to task, but I had given them many reasons to be anxious and felt a duty to bring success home with me. Finally, there was my own need to be fulfilled by a tough job well done. Much as I delighted in the press coverage and good wishes from the thousands of people who visited my website, I wanted desperately to seal this achievement for myself, having carved it from my own efforts.

As for what I will do next - how do you follow a Tri-Continental Walk around the World? In truth I don't feel any more raging dreams inside me at this moment. This one had been years in the dreaming, planning and execution. As I prepare to say goodbye to my thirties, I have a magnificent achievement behind me and, whilst there may be other challenges ahead in my life, I can finally enjoy a period of quiet contentment. And for now, that's good enough.